SOCCER IN AMERICAN CULTURE

ALSO BY G. EDWARD WHITE

The Eastern Establishment and the Western Experience (1968)

The American Judicial Tradition (1976)

Patterns of American Legal Thought (1978)

Tort Law in America: An Intellectual History (1980)

Earl Warren: A Public Life (1982)

The Marshall Court and Cultural Change (1988)

Justice Oliver Wendell Holmes: Law and the Inner Self (1993)

Intervention and Detachment: Essays in Legal History and Jurisprudence (1994)

Creating the National Pastime: Baseball Transforms Itself, 1903–1953 (1996)

Oliver Wendell Holmes: Sage of the Supreme Court (2000)

The Constitution and the New Deal (2000)

Alger Hiss' Looking-Glass Wars (2004)

Oliver Wendell Holmes, Jr. (2006)

History and the Constitution: Collected Essays (2007)

Law in American History: Volume 1,
From the Colonial Years through the Civil War (2012)

American Legal History: A Very Short Introduction (2014)

Law in American History: Volume 2,
From Reconstruction through the 1920s (2016)

Law in American History: Volume 3, 1930–2000 (2019)

(with Kenneth S. Abraham) *Tort Law and the Construction of Change: Studies in the Inevitability of History* (2022)

SOCCER IN AMERICAN CULTURE

The Beautiful Game's Struggle for Status

G. Edward White

UNIVERSITY OF MISSOURI PRESS
COLUMBIA

University of Missouri Press, Columbia, Missouri 65211
Printed and bound in the United States of America
 First printing, 2022.

Library of Congress Cataloging-in-Publication Data

Names: White, G. Edward, author.
Title: Soccer in American culture : the beautiful game's struggle for status / G. Edward White.
Description: Columbia : University of Missouri Press, 2022. | Series: Sports and American culture | Includes bibliographical references and index.
Identifiers: LCCN 2021048528 (print) | LCCN 2021048529 (ebook) | ISBN 9780826222534 (hardcover) | ISBN 9780826222930 (paperback) | ISBN 9780826274700 (ebook)
Subjects: LCSH: Soccer--United States--History. | Soccer--Social aspects--United States
Classification: LCC GV944.U5 W55 2022 (print) | LCC GV944.U5 (ebook) | DDC 796.3340973--dc23/eng/20211020
LC record available at https://lccn.loc.gov/2021048528
LC ebook record available at https://lccn.loc.gov/2021048529

∞™ This paper meets the requirements of the American National Standard for Permanence of Paper for Printed Library Materials, Z39.48, 1984.

Typefaces: Adobe Garamond Pro and Aktiv Grotesque

Sports and American Culture

Adam Criblez, Series Editor

This series explores the cultural dynamic between competitive athletics and society, the many ways in which sports shape the lives of Americans in the United States and Latin America, from a historical and contemporary perspective. While international in scope, the series includes titles of regional interest to Missouri and the Midwest. Topics in the series range from studies of a single game, event, or season to histories of teams and programs, as well as biographical narratives of athletes, coaches, owners, journalists, and broadcasters.

For Elisabeth White Varadhachary

Contents

Illustrations

Preface

THIS VOLUME IS analogous to my 1996 book *Creating the National Pastime*, a study of the history of major-league baseball, in three respects. First, it is a venture in sports history, containing comparatively little coverage of legal issues, and in that respect is a departure from my usual scholarly concerns. Second, it focuses on a sport in which I have spent a fair amount of my life as a player and coach. And third, it represents something of a break, or perhaps a treat, after a long interval of scholarship on legal and constitutional history. I began work on *Creating the National Pastime* after one such interval, which took place from around 1983 to 1993; and turned to this book after another, from around 2009 to 2019. I am of the view that one of the ways to stimulate the consistent production of scholarship over time is to change topics, time frames, and methodological approaches as one sequences scholarly projects. As my colleagues have often noted, I like to learn through researching and writing, and one way I do that is by identifying topics and approaches with which I am generally unfamiliar and seeking to say something distinctive about them. I have learned a lot in writing this book, and I hope I have been able to make a contribution to the understanding of its subjects.

Because the history of American soccer has been a generally underresearched topic, especially by scholars, and because many of the secondary works in the area lack scholarly documentation, this book has been something of a research challenge, and I have had to rely even more heavily than usual on the help of the reference librarians at the University of Virginia School of Law. Thanks to Amy Wharton, Kent Olson, Leslie Ashbrook, Randi Flaherty, Ben Doherty, and Kristin Glover for tracking down sources, a task made more complicated by the pandemic and its effect on interlibrary loans. Thanks as well to Loren Moulds for his assistance in identifying illustrations and facilitating permissions for images. And a special thanks to the LawIT department for their multiple Team Viewer sessions, in which I received various sorts of technical help. I am one of their least competent clients, and I appreciate their patience.

Kenneth S. Abraham and Neil Duxbury each read an early draft of the book manuscript and gave me helpful comments. Persons familiar with their scholarship might initially wonder what qualified them to opine on the subjects covered in the book, but they each bear a connection to the history of soccer in England and America. Ken grew up in one of the communities where soccer was first played in the United States, and Neil is a resident of a UK city hosting two of the world's best-known soccer clubs (and a far less celebrated club of which he is unfortunately enamored). I leave it to readers to attempt to guess the respective locations, if they feel the need for a break from the book's text.

The book has been immeasurably improved by the efforts of Adam Criblez, the editor of the University of Missouri Press series Sports and American Culture in which it appears, and Andrew Davidson, editor in chief of the press. Both Adam and Andrew read successive drafts of the book manuscript and gave me line-by-line comments, as well as made suggestions about the overall scope and content of the work. I also profited from the comments of Steven Reiss on an earlier draft and two anonymous readers of the penultimate draft. I want to emphasize the contributions of Adam and Andrew, however, because it has been a very long time in my publishing history since someone associated with a university press has engaged in the close reading and editing of one of my manuscript drafts. When I first submitted book manuscripts to university presses, in the late 1960s, such reading and editing was the norm, but with the dramatic changes in book publishing that have taken place since that decade, it is now quite rare. I lament its loss—there is nothing more helpful to an author than to have engaged, critical readings of manuscript drafts—and have welcomed Adam's and Andrew's interventions.

This book is dedicated to my younger daughter Elisabeth, once a soccer player who had to endure her father as her high school coach for three years. Perhaps Elisabeth's daughters will become attracted to the sport and Elisabeth will end up coaching them. And my love to Susan Davis White, Alexandra White, and the other members of the Whites' extended family, who hopefully will be safe, healthy, and able to see one another in person by the time this book appears.

G.E.W.
Charlottesville, Virginia
March 2021

SOCCER IN AMERICAN CULTURE

Introduction

SOCCER IS THE world's most popular sport, both in terms of participation and spectator appeal.[1] The men's and women's World Cup tournaments have, since the 1990s, attracted huge numbers of fans and television viewers across the globe and made large amounts of money for their host countries and FIFA (the Federation Internationale de Football Association), the organization that stages the tournaments. The Union of European Football Association (UEFA)'s annual Challenge Cup, a round-robin competition of teams from the top-division soccer leagues in European nations, has recently garnered the world's largest television audiences for its final matches.[2] And more people around the world play soccer, as a recreational activity, than any other team sport—except in the United States.

It is conventional wisdom among those who have written on the history of international sports that during the period of soccer's late nineteenth- and early twentieth-century growth,[3] and for most of the remaining years of the twentieth century, men's soccer never became established as a major sport in the United States, either in professional leagues or in colleges and universities.[4] Soccer was played only sparingly in American colleges during the first five decades of the twentieth century, and rarely in American public high schools. Women's soccer, although seldom played elsewhere in the world, was virtually not played at all in the United States until the late 1960s. For most of the twentieth century the United States was the only large national sports market in which soccer did not take root in any substantial fashion.

Several explanations have been advanced for the seemingly anomalous twentieth-century history of soccer in the United States. One is that there was a critical period in world history in which a sport might have grown sufficiently popular, in any given nation, to achieve major status. That period, roughly from 1880 to 1930, was the one in which the growth of international sport mirrored the growth of a global industrial economy.

And since soccer failed to achieve major status in the United States during that period, the argument runs, nothing short of massive cultural change could reverse the situation.[5]

Another, partly complementary, explanation is that there is a finite space in which sports can successfully operate in any given nation, so that already established sports tend to crowd out others. In the United States, then, soccer was crowded out by the indigenous "American" sports: baseball; gridiron football (a version of rugby that came to be played in certain American colleges in the late nineteenth century); and basketball. As those three sports flourished during the critical period, there was no space for soccer to gain a foothold.[6]

A third explanation is based on the economics of professional sports generally. To thrive, a professional sport requires competitive balance among its teams: if that balance is lost, the stronger teams tend to overwhelm the weaker ones, making a great many matches less attractive to spectators and eventually having adverse effects on players' interest in competing. Most professional soccer leagues around the globe seek to achieve competitive balance by imposing constraints on the ability of clubs to bid with one another for players, and by creating tiers or divisions of leagues. At the conclusion of a league's season, some clubs, typically the top three or bottom three in the standings, are promoted to higher-tier leagues or relegated to lower-tier ones. Constraints on bidding for players serve to prevent wealthier clubs from acquiring talented players at the expense of less wealthy clubs, and promotion and relegation serve to create incentives for clubs to compete fully throughout a season regardless of their place in the standings. Promotion and relegation also tend to ensure that a given club, whatever its performance in a particular season, will remain extant during the next season, even if it finds itself in a lower-tier league, and that some clubs will be able to move up to higher-tiered leagues. Over time, promotion and relegation promote the stability of club franchises by creating constant incentives for clubs to improve their league affiliations in the hopes of garnering the financial rewards associated with play in higher leagues. As such they reinforce loyalty among the fans and supporters of the individual clubs, which are typically identified with cities or certain districts therein.

One might call this organizational structure quasi-socialistic, in that it requires the owners and operators of individual soccer clubs to think first about the collective success of the league to which a club belongs and less about their individual fortunes. I will hereafter refer to this organizational structure as "command-and-control," borrowing the term from the regulation of certain industries by governmental agencies in the United States. Even so, the analogy is not a perfect one. In American regulated industries, command-and-control regulation has a particular meaning,[7] specifically that an agency given oversight over an industry specifies the behavior that it will and will not permit on the part of individual corporations within the industry, such as when the Environmental Protection Agency specifies the number of particulate emissions a chemical plant may release into the atmosphere in the course of its daily operations, and imposes sanctions on plants that violate the agency's prescribed guidelines.

Command-and-control regulation, understood in that technical sense, does not quite capture the model of organization adopted by the English Football Association, the English Football League, and their affiliated clubs as soccer spread throughout the UK and eventually across the rest of Europe and much of the rest of the world in the late nineteenth and early twentieth centuries. Although UK and European soccer associations and leagues established rules of conduct for their affiliated clubs and occasionally penalized violators, their regulatory activity was primarily organizational. In each nation a central body, operating through some executive council or committee, required clubs seeking to play soccer and participate in matches intended to attract admission-paying spectators to join it (typically for a nominal fee) and abide by a set of uniform rules regarding play. The central body also controlled the recruitment of players, the staffing of clubs, and the playing of matches against other clubs. Over time, those rules extended to the oversight of players' wages and salaries, retaining and transferring players at season's end, and the division of the profits of tournament matches. Instead of the operators of clubs having the autonomy to make their own decisions about how to run their respective franchises, the central body made most of the decisions for all its member clubs. That organizational structure amounted to the UK, European, Latin American, Asian, African, and Oceanian football associations' version of command-and-control.

In the United States, no sort of command-and-control organizational structure came to oversee professional soccer leagues when those leagues began to form in the late nineteenth and early twentieth centuries. The leagues that did form were simply entities composed of individual clubs whose owners and operators controlled their expenses and sought to run them for profit. As we will see in subsequent chapters, many of the clubs in American leagues that performed poorly were either moved to other cities or simply disbanded by their owners. Promotion and relegation among tiers of leagues never materialized, making competitive imbalance among clubs harder to forestall. Finally, club owners were not constrained in bidding for players. The first American professional soccer league with major ambitions, the North American Soccer League, which commenced play in 1968 with strong expectations of success, including television contracts, eventually collapsed in 1984 due to the lack of restraints on owners' bidding for players' salaries, which produced competitive imbalance and uneven attendance at league matches, and the absence of promotion and relegation, which created incentives for disappointed owners to relocate or disband their clubs rather than continue to operate them in a lower-tiered league.

But the absence of command-and-control regulation of professional soccer leagues in the United States cannot fully explain the sport's failure to acquire major sport status. Commentators have pointed out that American professional leagues in sports such as hockey, gridiron football, basketball, and ice hockey have succeeded without ever having adopted a quasi-socialistic organizational structure.[8]

A final explanation emphasizes when and where, and by whom, soccer was first played in the United States. In the late nineteenth century, soccer in America was mostly played in a handful of communities distinctive for their large immigrant populations, people who had migrated from countries in which soccer was well established as a recreational activity and spectator sport. Those communities included a cluster of towns in northwestern New Jersey, another cluster in southeastern Massachusetts and Rhode Island, and ethnic enclaves in the inner cities of St. Louis, Detroit, and Chicago, each of which was home to large and concentrated immigrant populations. The European nations from which the residents of these ethnic enclaves (or their parents) had come to America included England, Scotland, and Ireland, as well as in some cases Portugal and Italy. Unsurprisingly, the first semiprofessional and professional soccer leagues in the United States sprang up in those communities, their teams composed overwhelmingly of immigrants, occasionally former residents of European nations who were recruited to play soccer in the United States, and the first-generation offspring of immigrant families. The leagues were formed to allow "company teams"—those composed of workers in textile factories and other businesses heavily dependent on inexpensive immigrant labor—to play matches against one another. Those matches were attended almost exclusively by male members of the immigrant communities in which the companies, or their factories, operated.

The ethnic emphasis of early twentieth-century soccer, according to this explanation, served to diminish the sport's appeal across the broader spectrum of the US population, which included some nativist groups who were generally apprehensive about the growing numbers of residents of foreign nations emigrating to America.[9] The perception that soccer was a game primarily played by immigrants became particularly damaging to the sport's growth after the National Collegiate Athletic Association (NCAA) began to organize college sports in 1906, and "comprehensive" public high schools took over the administration of athletics programs in the first two decades of the twentieth century. At that time few members of immigrant communities attended college, so the number of male college students interested in playing soccer never grew large. Indeed, the NCAA did not even assume regulatory control over the sport until 1959. Prior to that date it had allowed an independent association of a few northeastern colleges to control the administration of college soccer, including designating a "national" champion by the vote of a committee rather than as the outcome of any sort of tournament. And in high schools soccer was played even less frequently: when high schools did begin to fold athletics into their in-school activities and offer varsity sports, they offered only the indigenous sports of baseball, gridiron football, and basketball. This was, in part, the explanation suggests, because of the perception of soccer in the eyes of most Americans as an ethnic sport played largely by members of immigrant communities.

Each of those explanations contains a kernel of truth, but each also has its limitations. The "critical period" explanation for the emergence of a sport to major status fails to account for the emergence of professional basketball in that capacity only after the 1940s, and that of professional football only after the 1950s. The "sports space" explanation does not account for the fact that although baseball, gridiron football, and basketball have continued to thrive in the United States in the first two decades of the twenty-first century, in that same time soccer has not only become the fourth-most-popular participatory sport in the nation[10] but continues to grow in popularity as a high school, college, and professional spectator sport. The "competitive balance" explanation fails to explain why the other major American professional sports leagues—Major League Baseball, the National Football League, the National Basketball Association, and the National Hockey League—achieved growth and financial stability in the late twentieth and early twenty-first centuries despite imposing few constraints on the ability of owners to compete (sometimes in a blatantly unfair manner) to sign the best players or move franchises, and despite the absence of promotion and relegation. Finally, the "immigrant sport" explanation fails to account for the fact that even though baseball, basketball, and ice hockey are played in numerous countries other than the United States, and the number of foreign-born players in professional leagues in those sports has dramatically increased in the late twentieth and twenty-first centuries, all of those sports have retained major status in the United States.

So, in a sense, one needs to start afresh in seeking an explanation for the distinctly marginal status of soccer in the United States for most of the twentieth century. At the same time, one also needs to start over in trying to solve the second puzzle with which this book is concerned: What has caused the dynamic renaissance of soccer in America in the twenty-first century? To get a sense of the magnitude of that development, one need only look at the international and domestic state of American soccer as the 1990s dawned. Although the US national soccer team had participated in the World Cup as early as the 1930s, the United States had never hosted a World Cup tournament before 1994. No American men's professional soccer league, including the ambitious North American Soccer League (NASL) launched in 1968, had ever become a success, either in terms of financial solvency or in its capacity to attract gifted players. Only a handful of male soccer players from American colleges and universities were given opportunities to play professionally, either in the NASL or in overseas leagues.

Although the participation of both men and women in soccer had grown exponentially in both colleges and high schools in the 1970s and 1980s, no US national women's team existed until 1988, by which time FIFA (the Federation Internationale de Football), which organizes World Cup competitions, had not definitively committed itself to staging a women's

World Cup. Most significantly, perhaps, soccer in the United States, unlike the "major" sports, had not profited from the ubiquity of television and the advent of the televising of live sporting events across the nation. Whereas by the 1960s the televising of soccer matches in the first-division European leagues and the English Premier League was to dramatically increase the wealth of franchises in those leagues, no American first-division soccer league even existed to potentially capitalize on that development. American television networks found it difficult to adapt soccer broadcasts to their commercial advertising, and the NASL failed to secure a renewal of its initial television contract. Moreover, the US sports media generally devoted very little coverage to high school, college, or professional soccer, especially after it became clear, after 1978, that the NASL was very far from becoming profitable.

Finally, despite the sharp increase in soccer as a participatory youth sport for girls as well as boys, still relatively few Americans understood the sport well enough to become strong supporters of soccer teams. Few adult Americans had seriously played or followed the sport in their youth. Few had any familiarity with the professional soccer then being played in Europe, the UK, or Latin America. A stereotyped impression, held by members of the sports media as well as general audiences, was that soccer was boring: there were too many intervals of seemingly purposeless activity, during which players passed the ball back and forth but took few shots on goal; not enough goals were scored; and players' movements to spaces on the field seemed inexplicable.

And yet within four years of the start of the 1990s, the United States hosted a financially and athletically successful men's World Cup; the women's soccer final at the 1996 Olympics in Atlanta, featuring the US national team, drew the largest crowd in American soccer history; the United States was tapped to host the 1999 women's World Cup, in which attendance records were further shattered; and US women's team players gained national fame and became cultural icons. In 1996, in the midst of those events, Major League Soccer, the latest US men's professional soccer league, was launched; twenty-five years later MLS is not only extant but expanding—and well on its way to profitability. Meanwhile, an American women's professional league, the National Women's Soccer League, has been in existence since 2013 and has secured a contract with CBS Sports to televise some of its games; two major cable networks are televising MLS games; and two others are broadcasting matches from the English Premier League and Germany's Bundesliga. Even before the start, then, of the twenty-first century, a generation of Americans has grown up playing and watching soccer—and can appreciate the game. Meanwhile, as noted, soccer has become the fourth-most-popular sport in the United States in terms of participation.

How, then, can one explain these two seemingly contradictory aspects of the history of soccer in America? In other words, how does one account for the singular marginality of the sport in the United States for most of the twentieth century, even as it was thriving across the rest of the globe, and at the same time make sense of the equally singular emergence of soccer as a recreational and spectator sport in the United States since 1990? This book seeks to explore and ultimately to answer those questions.

Chapter One

English Origins

A SCHOOLBOY'S GAME

THIS CHAPTER, WHICH considers the birth of soccer and its early evolution, centers on England, the sport's nation of origin. It emphasizes four themes that would define what would be called association football as it grew and spread within the UK and subsequently around the world, including the United States, in the late nineteenth and early twentieth centuries. The first of those themes is the standardizing of the rules of play, which served to distinguish soccer from rugby, a sport also being played in mid-nineteenth-century England. The second is the struggle within soccer, throughout the latter decades of the nineteenth century, over whether to include professional players—that is, ones paid for their services[1]—or to maintain an amateur ethos under which players participated solely for the "joy of competition."[2] The third theme, related to the second, is the struggle, as soccer clubs multiplied and began organized competitions in nationwide tournaments and leagues, to determine whether they should operate as the equivalent of profit-making businesses or as civic enterprises, focusing on the development of their facilities and their integration with the communities they represented. The fourth and final theme is the spread of English soccer abroad in the late nineteenth and early twentieth centuries, as it became established in other nations with resident British populations whose presence was connected to the growing political and commercial reach of the British Empire.

Each of these four themes stems from the public-school origins of soccer in England. Versions of the game were first played as early as the 1830s, with the rules of play varying considerably from school to school, constraints imposed by the physical spaces in which matches took place. Notwithstanding these variations, the game before the 1860s invariably featured running with the ball as well as kicking it, catching it in the air, tackling other players, and "hacking"—that is, kicking other players in an attempt to take possession of the ball as those in possession ran with it or tried to kick it forward. At this point the game more resembled the current sport of rugby than that of soccer. Rugby was to receive its name, and be distinguished from association football, after the 1863 rules of the Football Association openly rejected some of the features of the mid-century public-school game, and some of the men involved in the creation of those rules signified their wish to retain the running with the ball, tackling, and hacking in the game as played at Rugby School.

Over time soccer began to have less and less in common with rugby.[3] The impetus for rule standardization came from those who had played in public schools and wished to continue playing at English universities or in clubs. Increased pressure for standardization came about when graduates of public schools who congregated to play the game later in their lives discovered that their understanding of the sport's rules varied considerably from that of others because, as mentioned, its rules varied from school to school. At the same time, some persons interested in continuing to play soccer resolved to eliminate some features that they thought dangerous or otherwise unattractive, notably catching the ball in one's arms, running with it, and hacking other players. Those persons were determined to make soccer a game played primarily "below the waist," that is, with feet and legs rather than arms, and to minimize the scrimmages and collisions on the field that resulted from running with the ball and hacking. Thus the identity of soccer as a sport would become connected to its adoption of particular standardized rules.

The second theme, also connected to soccer's public-school origins, involved professionalism. Initially the persons who formed clubs to play the sport in mid-nineteenth-century England were overwhelmingly graduates of public schools, many of them wealthy individuals from upper-class backgrounds who conceived of participation in sports as recreational and social activities pursued by gentlemen with ample leisure time. As soccer grew and spread from London to other regions in the UK, notably Yorkshire, Lancashire, Warwickshire, and Scotland, many more individuals who had not attended public schools began participating in the sport, and some soccer clubs were formed in connection with local businesses. The Football Association, initially founded in 1863 as an organization concerned with standardizing rules, became involved with the administration of soccer throughout the UK. It created a tournament known as the FA Cup, in which clubs competed with one another on a yearly basis for possession of a chalice cup. With the growth of soccer as not only a participatory but also a spectator sport later in the century, club owners began to charge admission for matches between certain highly popular clubs, as well as the latter-stage matches of the FA Cup competition, which began to attract a good number of spectators. Indeed, clubs that reached late-stage rounds could often amass revenue from gate receipts.

As participation and spectator interest in the FA Cup grew, some clubs in cup competition, particularly those with direct ties to businesses, desired to field more highly competitive teams in order to make money. The competitions were organized on a "one and done" basis, with the winner of each match proceeding to the next round and the loser eliminated for the year. Naturally, the longer a club survived in the tournament, the more revenue it stood to garner, money that could offset team travel expenses. In this context some clubs, initially from Yorkshire and Lancashire, bucked tradition by beginning to recruit players who were not already residents of the club's locality, furnishing them with jobs in the area or paying them directly. Paying players to perform for soccer clubs presupposed a coterie of professional soccer players, men engaged in the sport as a livelihood rather than as an amateur pursuit. Professionalism was initially regarded as antithetical to the ethos of the Football Association, and the resultant controversy and debates, which stretched over two decades in the late nineteenth century, would have distinct class overtones, as well as have significant implications for the growth of soccer around the world as well as in the United Sates.[4]

The realization that the FA Cup tournament could serve as not only an enjoyable competition but a source of revenue for clubs who fared well in it highlighted another fundamental issue as soccer grew and expanded in the UK: What did soccer clubs represent? Initially such clubs had only been organizations of persons desirous of playing the sport recreationally, and they served to provide a base for forming teams who wanted to play matches against other teams. The early clubs tended to be organized geographically, typically in city neighborhoods, with some field or building serving as the source of their team's name. The initial organization of soccer clubs again reflected the sport's public-school origins, as clubs tended to form among groups of friends and associates who came from the same neighborhood or who at least had similar backgrounds, which, of course, included exposure to soccer in a public school.[5]

Association football was initially a distinctly minority sport, there being only twenty clubs in the Football Association in 1868. But as the sport spread from London to other regions of the UK, the number of clubs expanded, and clubs began to play regularly scheduled matches, culminating in the creation of the English Football League in 1888. Club teams began to garner fan support, thereby identifying themselves with particular communities. In that capacity the clubs came to represent more than collections of individuals who wanted to play soccer together. Sometimes they were associated with particular businesses, sometimes with educational institutions, and sometimes with city neighborhoods. In this way clubs with close affiliations began a transition into teams, garnering even stronger fan support and becoming increasingly attractive to prospective players. Indeed, a team's prospective success came to be regarded as important to a variety of persons, not only players but persons ranging from shareholders of the clubs to residents of the communities in which the teams were based.[6]

As the operations of some clubs became more lucrative with the expansion of cup competitions and Football League matches, their function came to a significant crossroads. Were they to continue to reflect the amateur ethos of their origins, as entities organized simply to facilitate the playing of soccer for "the joy of competition," or were they to take on the character of business operations, even to the point of emphasizing profits and losses? On this issue the Football Association remained quite firm throughout the nineteenth century: clubs were not for-profit enterprises designed to make money for their organizers and shareholders but should serve as the equivalent of civic organizations, plowing any profits into developing their facilities and strengthening their ties to the communities they represented.[7] Moreover, business aspects such as player salaries, competition to recruit players, and the garnering of revenues from matches were to be expressly controlled by the Football Association or the affiliated Football League. After 1904 the FA relinquished control over financial dealings between the league and its clubs to the league's management committee, although it continued to attempt to oversee the league with its policies on the retain-and-transfer system—a practice designed to avoid clubs from entering into bidding wars for players—and the general remuneration of players. After 1910 the FA essentially delegated all of those matters to the league,[8] and by 1930 the league had eight members on the FA's Management Council, the official name for its management committee.[9] Administrative issues had evolved from ones centering on the relationship between the FA and the league to ones affecting the relationship between the league and its clubs.

Nonetheless the administration of English soccer continued to employ a command-and-control model. A central body restricted clubs' salary structure, the use of their profits, and, over time, the scheduling of their games and the size of their club rosters. This command-and-control business model was to characterize English association football as it spread throughout the UK and subsequently around the world.

The fourth and final theme has less to do with the origins of soccer as a game played by boys in public schools, but nonetheless bears an indirect connection to those origins. In the same years during which soccer began to evolve and to enjoy greater and greater popularity, the British Empire continued to expand across the globe, resulting in, among other things, clusters of British residents in overseas nations. These expatriates—military personnel and others in the service of commercial enterprises or religious organizations—tended to form communities comprised of familiar British-style institutions, social clubs, and schools, and often emphasizing sporting pursuits including, in many cases, soccer.[10] As national soccer associations were founded in European nations in the late nineteenth century, in part because of the influence of British residents, those associations sought contact with the English Football Association, and even invited English soccer clubs to engage in overseas tours.

The first English clubs to embark on such tours were amateur ones that after the 1880s, as English football became more professionalized, had disengaged themselves from Football Association–sponsored competitions to underscore their commitment to an amateur ethos. Those clubs were overwhelmingly made up of graduates of public schools and universities, many of whom were independently wealthy and engaged in sports because they had the leisure time and inclination to do so. The English amateur soccer clubs in the late nineteenth century were strongly dedicated to the pursuit of what one writer referred to in 1906 as the "British idea of true sportsmanship," with an emphasis on fair play, which included avoiding violent encounters on the soccer field, respect for one's opponents, and losing with grace.[11] Spreading "true sportsmanship" around the globe was a distinct mission of the early English traveling clubs, the concept having originated in English public schools. But when association football began to spread internationally in the late nineteenth and early twentieth centuries, efforts to resist professionalism in the sport had largely been overcome in England, and the global version of soccer would at its highest levels be played primarily by professional players, most of them with working-class backgrounds.

The remainder of this chapter pursues those themes in more detail.

REGULATION: THE RULES OF THE GAME

In the fall of 1863, representatives of eleven "metropolitan and suburban football clubs" in the London area held a series of six meetings, beginning on October 26 and culminating on December 8, in which they formed an organization named the Football Association, intended to standardize the rules for "regulation of the game of football" and to encourage the game's growth in England.[12] Despite abundant evidence that the initial meeting took place on October 26 and that six meetings were required to secure agreement on the rules,[13] some histories of soccer have concluded that only one meeting took place, and that it did so on a different date in October.[14] They also intimate that after that meeting, the rules were universally adopted throughout England, whereas they were actually adopted only by clubs that had gathered for the meeting, and not by all of those.

The fact that eleven clubs playing what came to be called soccer in the London area resolved to meet in an effort to standardize the game's rules illustrates its state in mid-1860s England. Several groups of persons had formed soccer clubs: there were at least eleven in the greater London area and others throughout England. In addition, most of the English public schools—including Charterhouse, Cheltenham, Eton, Harrow, Marlborough, Rugby, Westminster, and Winchester—played the game. After the first meeting, the Football Association wrote letters to those public schools to solicit their participation in the league, but Charterhouse, Harrow, and Westminster declined, and the others did not respond.[15]

The surfacing of an issue about public-school participation in the league when that body first convened also provided a clue about the genesis of the league itself. Not only was there a critical mass of persons playing soccer in England in the 1860s, but many of them had learned to play the game under different rules. This was because soccer, although an ancient activity in the sense of players chasing an animal bladder around a field and often colliding with one another in the process, had come of age as an organized sport in the English public schools.

In the 1830s Thomas Arnold, the headmaster of Rugby School, initiated a reformist program of education that stressed discipline, religious training, organized athletic activities, and the suppression of bullying and gambling. Arnold's emphasis on what others called "muscular Christianity"[16] became a blueprint for other public schools, and several of those introduced into their curricula mandatory organized sports, which were thought to "build character" and provide ways of releasing energy.[17] Soccer, requiring only a ball and a field with some boundaries to play, was an obvious choice for an organized athletic activity at Rugby and its peers.

As mentioned, the rules for playing the predecessor of soccer in public schools varied according to where the game was played. At some schools, such as Charterhouse and Westminster, whose designs were medieval, play took place in courtyards surrounded by cloisters, making it difficult to transmit a ball long distances, so an emphasis on dribbling and passing skills emerged. At others, such as Eton and Harrow, the fields of play were larger and more regular, facilitating more kicking as well as some "free catching," a tactic that permitted a player to catch the ball with his hands and then kick it, although not advance it by running. At Rugby, for example, free catching was an integral part of the game.[18]

In 1848 a group of undergraduates at Trinity College, Cambridge, resolved to "get up some football in preference to the hockey then in vogue." But the result, one member of that group recalled,

> was dire confusion, as every man played the rules he had been accustomed to at his public school. I remember how the Eton men howled at the Rugby men for handling the ball. So it was agreed that two men should be chosen to represent each of the public schools, and two, who were not public school men, [were added as] being unprejudiced [to arbitrate rule disputes]. . . . Well, sir, years afterwards someone took those rules, still in force in Cambridge, and with very few alternations they became the league rules. A fair catch, free kick . . . was struck out. The offside rule was made less stringent. "Hands" was made more so.[19]

FIGURE 1. Representation of "football" at Rugby School in England, published in *The Graphic* magazine, January 8, 1870. Courtesy Zentralbibliothek Zürich.

The "Cambridge rules" entirely prevented handling or running with the ball, even when it had been caught in the air. They also prevented players from "loiter[ing] between the ball and the adversaries' goal" (the offside rule). And they prevented "holding a player, pushing with the hands, or tripping up" a player, or allowing any other means of "prevent[ing] another from getting to the ball."[20] In short, they represented a determined effort to eliminate the use of hands, or the ability to move the ball by carrying it on one's person, from the game that had been played in multiple versions in public schools. That development, which transformed soccer from a sport played both above and below the waist to one primarily emphasizing the players' legs and feet and thereby detached the sport from what became rugby, would be crucial to the identity of association football.

By their fourth meeting, on November 24, the group of persons who had formed the Football Association turned directly to the content of rules, and a central issue: whether to eliminate from the game running with the ball and the holding, tripping, or hacking of other players (the so-called Rugby rules).[21]

The draft rules introduced at the November 24 meeting differed from the Cambridge rules in two important respects. Rule IX of the league draft stated that "A player shall be entitled to run with the ball toward his adversaries' goal if he makes a fair catch, or catches the ball on the first bound; but in the case of a fair catch, if he makes his mark, he shall not run."[22] A fair-catch rule had not been included in the Cambridge rules.[23] And Rule X provided that "if any player shall run with the ball toward his adversaries' goal, any player on the opposite side shall be at liberty to charge, hold, trip or hack him, or wrest the ball from him; but no player shall be held and hacked at the same time."[24] Not only did this rule retain running with the ball and laying hands on opposing players in the game, it ran directly counter to the Cambridge rules, which provided that "the ball . . . may NOT be held or hit with the hands, arms or shoulders," and that "holding, pushing with the hands, tripping up and shinning is forbidden."[25] The meeting adjourned without any action being taken on Rules IX and X.

The introduction of the proposed Rules IX and X was a clear signal that at least some members of the league did not favor adoption of the Cambridge rules. At the fifth meeting of the league, on December 1, 1863, F. W. Campbell, the representative from Blackheath, expressed strong opposition to the Cambridge rules' elimination of running with the ball and hacking. After Campbell unsuccessfully made a motion to, in effect, substitute Rules IX and X for the Cambridge rules, three other representatives spoke in favor of those rules.[26]

At that point Arthur Pember asked for consideration of the motion to expunge Rules IX and X, and Campbell moved an amendment, that the meeting adjourn "until the vacations so that the representatives of the schools who are members of the Association may be enabled to attend." That amendment was voted down, 13 to 4, and the original motion then carried.[27] The meeting adjourned, with the Cambridge rules apparently having been adopted.

One last meeting took place on December 8. It was about to adjourn when Campbell rose to say that although he and his club, Blackheath, "entirely approved of the objects of the Association," the laws just adopted "entirely destroyed the game and took away all interest in it." Consequently, Blackheath wished "to be withdrawn from the list of the Association's members."[28] Efforts were made to persuade Campbell to encourage Blackheath to try the new rules for one season, but they failed, and eight years later, in 1871, a group of clubs formed the Rugby Union to play a game that included running with the ball, tripping, pushing with the hands, and hacking.

With the formation of the Rugby Union, the league version of football—which for the next ninety-odd years would be called soccer—was definitively separated from the Rugby version. In the 1863 version of the league rules, the free-kick rule was retained, but eventually it would be modified so that no player save the goalkeeper could touch the ball with his hands. Running with the ball and all forms of hacking were permanently abolished from the game of association football. The 1863 association rules made that emphasis abundantly clear, providing that "no player shall carry the ball," "no player shall take the ball from the ground with his hands while it is in play under any pretence whatever," and "neither tripping nor hacking shall be allowed and no player shall use his hands to push an adversary."[29] Association football was to be a sport emphasizing dribbling, passing, and shooting the ball with one's feet.

SOCCER'S EXPANSION IN ENGLAND

In the two decades after association football was established as a discrete sport and its rules standardized, the Football Association's membership grew and expanded. Initially the progress was slow. One of the centers of soccer outside the London area, Sheffield in Yorkshire, had originally sent a representative to the 1863 London meetings but had resolved to establish its own association and play by slightly different rules.[30] In 1866 the Sheffield Association proposed a match between London and Sheffield, to take place in March of that year at Battersea Park in London, with eleven players on each side. The Football Association accepted the proposal, and a match was held on March 31, played under London rules, with the team made up of London clubs winning, two goals and "four touchdowns" to nothing.[31]

By 1869 the number of clubs in the league had grown to twenty-nine, and Sheffield had agreed to join, on the condition that its clubs be permitted to play by their own rules. And as further expansion of both the league's membership and the number of intracounty matches seemed imminent, two additional issues surfaced.

The first issue, which the members of the league would continue to debate into the 1920s, stemmed from the class dimensions of English soccer at the time of the league's founding. The question at hand was whether clubs affiliated with the Football Association should be permitted to hire professional players. The other, which was less divisive but arguably more fundamental, was whether the league should consider itself a business entity, with regular expenses and a profit-and-loss ledger, as opposed to a group of gentlemen amateurs promoting the sport of soccer for the sheer joy of engaging in physical activity and recreation.

The issue first arose when the Football Association, largely at the direction of its secretary, Charles W. Alcock, began organizing international matches, first making overtures to a Scottish club, Queen's Park, for an informal match involving English and Scottish players in London.[32] As international matches involving those players materialized, culminating in a November 1872 match between England and Scotland in Glasgow, Alcock conceived another initiative, this one designed to further intracounty and intraclub competition within the Football Association.

That initiative was the creation of a "Challenge Cup Competition," a tournament to which all clubs belonging to the league were invited, with the winner to receive an eighteen-inch-tall silver cup with two handles. Competition for the Football Association's FA Cup was first launched in 1871–72, with fifteen teams in contention;[33] by 1876 that number had grown to thirty-seven.[34]

One of the prominent features of the FA Cup at its creation was the apparent absence of any interest on the league's part in charging spectators admission to cup matches. The historian of the league described the prevailing attitude toward finances at the time of cup competition's creation:

> Football at this period, and indeed for some years yet to follow, in the main was a happy-go-lucky affair. It was a game for pure enjoyment, played in that spirit, with no especial point to it beyond being an enjoyable method of exercise. Matches were arranged in a haphazard fashion, and teams turned up to honour their engagements, or they did not turn up. . . . It was largely a matter of mood, inclination or convenience. . . . It was just an afternoon's good fun.[35]

Charles Alcock's idea of a cup competition, in this context, was not connected to finances; he simply wanted to create "something really to play for." It was "an adaptation on a larger scale of what [Alcock] had known at Harrow in his youth," the "Cock House" competitions engaged in by schoolboys who were assigned to different "houses" on first matriculating at the school.[36] Competitions among houses included not only athletics but academics and deportment, and at the end of a school year one house was declared the winner of that year's competition. Victory in an athletic contest "led to an extension of life in the competition; defeat meant death." The idea of FA Cup competition was thus a romantic conception, anticipating "a thousand heroic battles." It was apparently designed only to encourage clubs to take their matches seriously.[37]

But as the number of clubs the association comprised continued to rise throughout the 1870s and 1880s,[38] and more and more teams vied for the FA Cup, the possibility that cup competitions could become a mechanism in which clubs could garner revenues for themselves emerged. In particular, clubs, FA Cup officials, and the association itself became aware that clubs which survived deep into the FA Cup competition could make some money from their participation.

A look at the association's statement of accounts for that period reveals that it had begun to charge admission for some of its international and cup matches.[39] In some cases the difference between expenses and receipts for a match showed that the association had made a profit; in others, such as the London-Birmingham match, expenses exceeded gate receipts by a fairly substantial margin.[40] By 1883 the association had instituted a rule that in FA Challenge Cup matches, proceeds from gate receipts would be equally divided among the participating clubs until the semifinal and final tiers, "when the whole of the proceeds shall be taken by the Association."[41] That practice allowed the association to build up "a substantial reserve fund" from holding cup and international matches.[42]

After 1883 the association's annual account came under official audit.[43] The 1885 statement revealed a substantial growth in receipts and a somewhat less substantial growth in expenditures. It also demonstrated that for the first time, FA Cup semifinal and final matches were beginning to outdraw even the annual England-Scotland international match. Four international matches were held in the fiscal year beginning in August 1884 and ending in August 1885: North versus South, held at Derby; England versus Ireland, held at Manchester; England versus Wales, held at Blackburn near London;

and England versus Scotland, held at London. Of those, only the England-Ireland and England-Scotland matches generated more receipts than the least-well-attended FA Cup match, a semifinal between the Blackburn Rovers, from Lancashire, and the Old Corinthians, a London-based club. All the other cup matches had larger gates than the international ones. Further, the association lost money on only two matches, the North-South match (on which it virtually broke even) and the Blackburn Rovers–Old Corinthians semifinal. As the official history of the association put it, its "assets . . . had increased appreciably."[44] Association football had become a potentially profitable business.

THE RISE OF PROFESSIONALISM

The proliferation of the FA Challenge Cup, the steady diet of international matches, and the expansion of association football to include many clubs affiliated with district and county associations, and eventually with associations that had come into being in Scotland, Wales, and Ireland, was by the 1880s to have an additional effect on soccer in England. The period between the 1870s and mid-1880s, Geoffrey Green's *History of the Football Association* recalls, was a golden age of amateurism, dominated by "the amateurs of the south," in which clubs "composed of men from the great public schools of England had held sway in friendly and competitive play," winning the FA Cup consecutively from 1872 through 1880. Those, Green concludes, were the "years of glory" for clubs such as "the Wanderers, Old Etonians, Royal Engineers, Clapham Rovers, Old Carthusians [and] Oxford University." But by 1882, according to Green, "a new force was beginning to grow in the north and midlands," and the rapid spread of the game to the masses combined with fierce rivalry among the provincial clubs to produce "practices that shocked the sensibilities of the purest amateur and caused the gravest concern to the rulers of the game."[45]

Those practices involved "importation, deceit and veiled professionalism." By the early 1880s they had allegedly "begun to advance like a silent tide, creeping in by a hundred creeks and inlets."[46] As the provinces outside London entered "the first stages of Cup fever," a "moral decline" set in.[47] As Green put it, "The northern clubs, in a state of high competition, embarked on a policy of importing players from Scotland, poaching from one another, of underhand payments, all with the single object of building up their several strengths. . . . The age of deep problems in the government of affairs had begun."[48] All of those practices were inconsistent with the amateur ethos that had marked English soccer's early development. As was mentioned, at first clubs were typically fielded of players who were residents of a particular community or its environs, the local composition of clubs remained relatively constant, and, above all, players participated for the fun of the sport, which could include keen competition and a desire to win but certainly not remuneration. Indeed, no soccer players, even those whose independent wealth meant that they did not need to work for a living, devoted most of their time to the game. It was a recreational pursuit, a way of getting exercise through playing a sport. The vast percentage of soccer matches were "friendlies," games arranged spontaneously between club teams that might or might not come off, depending on the number of players who showed up at a field on a given date and time, were not typically attended by spectators, and certainly did not charge admission.

Importation, the poaching of players from other clubs, and concealed payments to players were antithetical to the idea of soccer as a sport played by amateurs for the joy of competition. Importation, the practice in which clubs located in the north of England enticed Scottish players to join them, was technically not illegal—the only rule regarding participation imposed by the league was that association clubs play only against other association clubs—but it was clearly inconsistent with the expectation that clubs would be formed from local players.[49] Poaching was also inconsistent with that expectation, presupposing as it did that a player could move from a club near his residence to some other club with which he had no geographic affiliation. And paying players, and concealing that fact, was the worst of all: the ethos of amateurism conceived of soccer as a sport, not a profession. When in the early 1880s the association realized that it was making a profit through staging the FA Cup and international matches, it began giving some of the proceeds that its committee members regarded as "excessive," after particular matches, to charities in the areas where the matches had been played.[50]

As soccer, fueled by the expansion of association clubs and the FA Cup, "asserted itself firmly in the public imagination,"[51] the class dimensions of the English game began to recede. When Blackburn Olympic, "a team composed of simple tradesmen and fashioned in the mould of approaching professionalism,"[52] defeated the Old Etonians in the cup final in 1883, they did so with "new ideas" of how to play soccer, featuring "more general and expert . . . passing" and less emphasis on individual dribbling.[53] And over time new ideas became associated with new men, those who played soccer for a living, the "professional footballers" who became "respected member[s] of the community" and ambassadors for the game, living lives of "disciplined skill and fitness" and promoting "international goodwill."[54]

THE STRUCTURE OF ASSOCIATION FOOTBALL IN THE UK

By 1883 the English, Scottish, Welsh, and Irish associations had agreed upon a standardized set of rules,[55] and the structure of association football was firmly in place. It had three dimensions. At its core was the playing of matches between clubs affiliated with county or district associations, culminating in the annual Challenge Cup, with a sprinkling of international matches. The Football Association had become a financially solvent entity, and all of its affiliated member associations had agreed that games would be played with a uniform set of rules. In 1881 the Football Association had moved from its informal headquarters at the Freemason's Tavern to Paternoster Row in London, and hired a permanent clerk.[56] It continued to be controlled by a committee of sixteen members, most of whom, by 1885, still represented the public-school-oriented clubs that had figured prominently in the association's initial formation.[57] But it also included representatives of a large number of affiliated associations, numbering twenty-six in that year.[58] The committee was the controlling force of English soccer, not only setting the game's rules and mandating their uniform application but literally determining who could play soccer in England. Any group of friends or associates that wanted to start a club and compete in association matches had to not only join the Football Association but also agree to limit its play to matches against other association clubs.

The second identifying dimension of association football's structure, by the 1880s, was its command-and-control model of administration. In addition to needing to join the Football Association and to play matches only against other association clubs, new clubs had to agree to play by the rules of the game as dictated by a committee of largely London-based members. The individual clubs were not financial enterprises in the usual sense, although they could retain half of the receipts they amassed for FA Cup matches. The Football Association itself was not a registered corporation, had no shareholders, and was not required to disperse any of its profits to its affiliated clubs. When a club sought to join the Football Association, then, it did not do so to participate in a financial venture. In sum, clubs affiliated with the association joined to gain the benefit of an organized structure of matches and a common set of rules. This mode of organization would be followed by the Football League after its inception in 1888. The command-and-control organization of English football would become, as the sport expanded and spread in the late nineteenth and early twentieth centuries, the model for soccer across most of the globe—but not, as we will see, in the United States.

Finally, the structure of English soccer at the period of its origins was, as mentioned, overwhelming local in its emphasis. The initial clubs that joined the association did not so much represent cities as neighborhoods within cities. The first set of member clubs largely hailed from London, and new member clubs represented districts, counties, or even educational institutions such as Eton ("Old Etonians"), Carthouse ("Old Carthusians"), or Oxford University.[59]

As English soccer expanded outward from London, and the number of clubs that belonged to the Football Association grew, new clubs tended to spring from three bases: churches and chapels; public houses or taverns; and places of employment. Early examples of the first group were Aston Villa in Birmingham, initially affiliated with the Aston Villa Wesleyan Chapel, and the Bolton Wanderers from Lancashire, initially affiliated with Christ Church Schools in Bolton. Over time such clubs, which included Birmingham City, Everton, and Fulham, tended to shed their religious affiliations. A study of physical recreation in the city of Birmingham between 1871 and 1892 concluded that 25 percent of association football clubs in that city were connected to religious organizations.[60]

Taverns, typically called public houses, or pubs, were another base for soccer clubs. The connection between football clubs and pubs was an outgrowth of the functions the latter enterprises served in the nineteenth century. A study of public houses in the Victorian era has demonstrated that they served three principal functions: as transport centers, particularly before the advent of widespread rail travel, where carriages would stop on their routes; as social centers, where persons would meet after work; and as recreational centers, featuring games such as darts and snooker and sometimes serving as venues for prize fights.[61] When public houses owned adjoining paddocks or pieces of grassland, they could host recreational activities such as cricket or football, with the pubs providing facilities for changing before matches and dining afterward. When clubs associated with a public house began to include "imported" players on their rosters, those out-of-towners would often be offered employment at the pub. A comparatively large number of the shareholders and directors of clubs affiliated with the Football Association had connections to the liquor trade.

The third, and what would come to be the largest, base for the formation of football clubs in late nineteenth-century England was the workplace. Some of those clubs came into being simply because of the presence of a critical mass of employees who wanted to play football in their leisure time, which was significantly limited for most of the century, Saturday being regarded by most industries as a full working day, and the clergy discouraging recreational activities on Sunday. Most clubs affiliated with workplaces, however, received active support from the enterprise because a particular owner or executive was either eager to play football or a keen supporter of the game. Some clubs affiliated with workplaces emerged because enterprises regarded the success of their soccer club as good publicity and a source of goodwill for their business. Prominent examples of clubs formed from workplaces were Arsenal and West Ham United in the London area, the former created by a group of workers at the Woolwich Arsenal in 1886 and the latter established by the Thames Ironworks shipyard in 1895.[62] That emphasis would continue in the future: clubs that joined the association or, after 1888, the Football League, tended to represent workplaces. As English soccer came to be played professionally, with clubs organizing themselves in a league in order to have a regular schedule of interclub matches to which they could charge admission, clubs tended to attract increasing numbers of local followers. When the Football League came into being in 1888, it took pains to foster club loyalties, which manifested themselves in regular attendance at matches and visceral attachments and loyalties.[63]

In 1892 officials of the Football League, whose clubs had profited in its first four years, resolved to expand and created a second division. The theory of multiple divisions in the league—there would be four by the 1920s—was to encourage new clubs, which might not have achieved the quality of play of existing members, to join and participate in competition with clubs that might approximate their level of competence. To create incentives for lower-division clubs to improve, the league instituted a system known as promotion and relegation, under which, at the end of a division league's season, the bottom three clubs in the league standings would be relegated to a lower division, and the top three clubs in that lower division would be promoted to replace them. Prior to 1892 the league had introduced a system designed to encourage clubs with poor records to maintain their interest and competitive level throughout a season: the bottom three clubs in the league were excluded for the next season. Once a second division was created, league officials considered promotion and relegation to be a superior alternative to elimination, since it allowed less competitive clubs to continue to play and gave them an incentive to attempt to get back into a higher division.[64]

Promotion and relegation had another effect, one perhaps unanticipated when it was introduced: it ensured the stability of club franchises. Even if for some reason a club was unsuccessful in a division, and relegated, it still had the opportunity to play. Hence there was rarely a question of a club being disbanded, or moved from one locality to another, if it fared poorly in a given league season. The Football League's command-and-control mode of organization thus served to cement relationships between clubs and the communities they represented. Nonetheless , both the FA and the Football League would have to devise other methods of oversight to deal with the issue of uneven performance among competitive clubs, an issue that surfaced as association football expanded.

SOCCER CROSSES THE POND

One of the obvious venues for the international spread of association football in the early twentieth century was the United States. As mentioned, soccer first began to develop in America in the late nineteenth century, with clubs becoming established in New Jersey and southern New England, Chicago, Detroit, St. Louis, Omaha, and Salt Lake City.[65] The sport mainly surfaced in communities that had a critical mass of recently arrived immigrants from the UK or Europe, and, as in England, centered on voluntary clubs and associations whose members played the sport recreationally. By the opening of the twentieth century, some businesses had begun to form company teams, and amateur and semiprofessional leagues had sprung up in New York, Philadelphia, Pittsburgh, Cincinnati, Cleveland, and Denver.[66] A US soccer league, the American Football Association (AFA), came into being in 1884 and lasted until 1899.[67] It was a distinctly regional and amateur organization, centered in New Jersey, where association football had emerged in towns with textile factories and large immigrant populations from the United Kingdom. Following the model of the English Football Association, the AFA organized an American Cup tournament, which was played from 1885 to 1898, principally featuring clubs from Pennsylvania, New Jersey, and Massachusetts.[68] The AFA established some connections with the Football Association, and when English clubs began international touring in the last years of the nineteenth century, America seemed to be a promising location.

The first English club to make a tour of the United States was the Pilgrims, a London-based amateur team that, as early as the 1870s, had a representative on the league's committee.[69] In September and October 1905, the Pilgrims embarked on a tour of North America, beginning in Canada, traveling south to Detroit and St. Louis, then going east to Chicago, Philadelphia, Fall River, Massachusetts, Boston, and New York City, with one final match in Philadelphia before departing for England.[70] Newspaper reports of the Pilgrims tour are sketchy, but Fred Milnes, who played for several English amateur clubs, wrote an account of the trip, *A Football Tour with the Pilgrims in America*, that appeared late in 1905.[71] Attendance at the Pilgrims' matches against local North American clubs seems to have been significant, with many such contests allegedly drawing as many as 5,000 spectators, and those in St. Louis and Philadelphia more than 10,000.[72] During their tour across the pond, the Pilgrims won all but a few of their matches. American observers of the games regularly ascribed to the English players, with their controlled passing, a superior style of play to that of their hosts.[73]

In August 1906 the Corinthians made their first tour of Canada and the United States, playing five matches in Canada before moving on to Chicago, Cincinnati, Philadelphia, New York, and Fall River, and concluding in Boston.[74] They occasionally lost matches, one to the experienced Boston club, but those matches were played on small, narrow fields that limited the Corinthians' ability to control the game with their passing.[75]

Attendance for the Corinthians tour was lower than for that of the Pilgrims, and the trip was not a financial success. Nonetheless, both clubs subsequently returned to North America, the Pilgrims accepting a $10,000 offer from a consortium in St. Louis to play twenty-two matches in forty-five days, beginning in August 1909, and the Corinthians making additional tours in 1911 and 1924.[76] Even though both clubs were given guarantees before their tours and, despite their amateur status, permitted to take 25 percent of the gate receipts of their matches,[77] there is no evidence that either made a profit from the North American tours.

The symbolic significance of the tours was more difficult to gauge. Each time an English club launched a tour, it raised expectations that its visit would go far toward enhancing interest in the game of soccer in the United States. Particularly in the first decade of the twentieth century, some persons who had witnessed the spread of the American version of football at colleges expressed hope that soccer would supplant football as a fall sport at those institutions, principally because soccer struck them as a vastly safer game.[78]

American football, which had developed at colleges in the 1890s, was an even rougher version of rugby. It featured headlong assaults by players on their opponents, and the absence of protective helmets or pads.[79] In 1905, around the time the Pilgrims were about to play a match in New York on their first North American tour, an article in the *Harvard Bulletin* likened the play of football to "a hospital clinic which injures men so that they are crippled for weeks and in some cases permanently unfit for athletic exercise." The article noted that "association football" was among the sports that were "strenuous enough, and have a moderate risk of injury," but were not "so dangerous that several players are sure to be hurt in every contest."[80] Eventually, late in the 1905 football season, a Yale player punched a Harvard opponent in the face when the latter sought to fair-catch a punt, drawing blood, but was not penalized, and a player from Union College, attempting a tackle, struck his head and shortly thereafter died from a brain hemorrhage. Between 1906 and 1910 Columbia, Arizona, Baylor, Nevada, Northwestern, South Carolina, and Temple dropped intercollegiate football, with the University of California and Stanford replacing it with rugby.[81] Harvard's president, Charles Eliot, was said to be campaigning for the abolishment of football at his university. And in 1909 two more players, one at Army and the other at the University of Virginia, died of football injuries.[82] One journalist speculated that "so-called 'intercollegiate football' has been killed beyond the possibility of recognition by its own most ardent votaries," and that soccer would "undoubtedly be the football sport of the future all over the country."[83]

But that did not happen. The failure of soccer to displace football as the predominant fall sport at colleges and universities in early twentieth-century America was not simply a function of some adjustments made in football rules, such as introducing the forward pass and banning plays during which mass numbers of one team attacked those of the other. It was for more numerous and complex reasons that soccer failed to gain a foothold in American colleges and universities and the nation writ large as a major sport, reasons that are the subject of the next several chapters.

Chapter Two

Association Football Comes to America I

Early Impressions

THIS CHAPTER BEGINS by pondering one of the principal puzzles around which this book is organized: Why, in the years when association football spread around much of the world, taking decisive root in western Europe, Latin America, and British colonies in Asia, Oceania, and Africa under the auspices of FIFA, did it fail to become established in a like fashion in the United States?[1] There was, of course, some soccer being played in America in the early twentieth century: as we will see, the game had taken root in certain communities, and there were regular efforts to establish soccer leagues along the lines of the English Football League. A brief recapitulation of the state of association football in the UK at the time British clubs first began touring the United States, however, reveals that in two respects soccer in America, in the period when association football dramatically spread around the world, was distinctive.

THE CHALLENGE OF GRIDIRON FOOTBALL

Between 1905 and 1924 the English amateur clubs the Pilgrims and the Corinthians made tours of North America, including the United States. As noted, those tours were not, on the whole, financially successful, and they do not appear to have stimulated sufficient interest to firmly establish association football in America. Based on the scattered sources, there seem to have been two divergent reactions to the arrival of amateur English soccer clubs in early twentieth-century America. One was to precipitate a comparison of association football with what was then called the gridiron version of the game,[2] which initially featured mass scrimmages between teams in which one sought to bludgeon the ball down the field in running plays and the other sought to resist that advance, often by violent physical collisions.[3] As we have seen, gridiron football matches in American colleges often resulted in injuries and sometimes in deaths, and some colleges abolished the sport in the first two decades of the twentieth century.

The obvious roughness of American gridiron football, when compared with the UK version, prompted two quite different sorts of comments. One was illustrated by the *Harvard Bulletin*'s 1905 observation, previously quoted, that unlike the gridiron game, which "becomes so dangerous that several players are sure to be hurt in every contest," association football was "strenuous enough" and had only "a moderate risk of injury."[4] Other commentators went further, one praising a victory of the Pilgrims over a New York club in 1905 as "bristling with clever passing, intricate dribbling, capital dodging, and exceptionally hard kicking," but, "unlike the American college game," resulting in "no time . . . lost in tending the injured." The correspondent felt that "the English game . . . is destined to occupy a high place in American sports."[5] That view was echoed in 1907 by the secretary-treasurer of the Amateur Athletic Union (an organization founded in 1887 to establish standards and uniformity in amateur sports), who predicted that "in the course of a few years there would be more soccer than intercollegiate football teams in this country,"[6] and in 1900 by a journalist who claimed that soccer would "undoubtedly be the football sport of the future all over the country as soon as the people have passed through a term of education and understand it."[7] By 1913 the *New York Sun* found it "a rather strange condition that this country, excelling in almost every other branch of sport . . . has never been much interested in soccer," which as a game "is acknowledged to be on a par with the best of American sports."[8]

But there were others who found the comparison between the UK and gridiron versions of football not to the former's advantage. Julian Curtiss, an official of the A. G. Spalding Company who managed the Yale-Princeton and Yale-Harvard gridiron football games in 1903, said that "if an Association game were played on one field and a game under the college rules were played next door, the latter would so far outdraw the former that there would be no comparison."[9] He added that association football had a " 'tag, you're it' style of play" that "would not draw a corporal's guard when there was a game of the other sort going on."[10] After having watched the Pilgrims in their first tour in 1905, Bozeman Bulger, a writer for the *New York World*, was quoted as saying, " 'Socker' football affords a very quiet afternoon's entertainment," but "you can't fool the American sports lover, who likes science and excitement," and that of twelve American spectators that he interviewed at the Pilgrims game at the Polo Grounds, "eleven of that number said they would take a game of . . . college football" instead.[11]

Other commentators expressed similar sentiments after viewing the Pilgrims. "Captain [Fred] Milne[s] has another think coming," one maintained, "when he says that socker will entirely supersede the game as now played. Football has received some pretty hard knocks the present year . . . but it is a certainty that the dull and uninteresting socker will never take its place."[12] Amos Alonzo Stagg, the gridiron football coach at the University of Chicago—admittedly not an unbiased source—suggested that "the English association football game cannot be used in this country to displace the present game because American colleges have chosen the style of play that is in vogue here."[13] A caricature of that perspective was advanced in 1910 by a reporter who allegedly interviewed a "dashing girl with good American blood coursing through her heart" at a soccer match at the University of Pennsylvania. "It is so idiotic," the girl reportedly said.

> Now, they just kick the ball right up to the point of doing something, along comes a fellow and with one boot he undoes all their labor or the fellow that stands in that hoopskirt net kicks it, and someone bawls, "Well played, sir." Permit me to remark that in football it's different. Let Billy Hollenback or Danny Hutchinson get the ball on the one-yard line, third down and a yard to go, and if they don't take it across there will be half a dozen hurt. Let's go home.[14]

Interestingly, none of the American commentators seemed to assume that soccer could coexist with gridiron football, a game at the time exclusively played in colleges. They viewed the two games as competitors, as if the prospective arrival of soccer in America might or might not displace gridiron football. This notion is puzzling. When soccer was played at all in the United States in the late nineteenth and early twentieth centuries, it was mainly outside of colleges, and not exclusively in the fall, as was the gridiron game. There was no particular reason why gridiron football and soccer should have been viewed as natural competitors: perhaps the coincident arrival of the Pilgrims and Corinthians just when gridiron football was coming under heavy criticism for being too dangerous made certain commentators feel a need to describe the sports as adversaries.

As the Pilgrims and Corinthians continued to make tours in North America after their initial visits, in a period in which gridiron football continued to be marred by injuries and occasional deaths, the view that soccer was a competitor of gridiron football persisted. In 1909 the *New York Times* quoted comments from Harvard students and a Yale faculty member about the ability of persons of all sizes and weights to play soccer, as distinguished from football. A Harvard senior reportedly said that "the gravest defect of modern college athletics is that they are not playable by a properly representative portion of the university," and that soccer was a game that, while featuring "initiative, courage, agility, and speed," could be played by "the man of slender means . . . who is not a member of a Varsity squad." Another Harvard student noted that soccer was "a safe and sane sport that every one of us can play and enjoy . . . without fear of serious injury," and that "speed and courage" were more important "than mere brute strength." A Yale faculty member added that soccer was a game equally well suited to participants as well as spectators. Unlike gridiron football, it could be "universally played."[15]

The same comparisons with gridiron football with respect to safety and opportunities for more people—of any build—to play soccer appeared in other newspapers. The *Washington Post*, in a 1907 article entitled "Association Football is Getting a Tighter Hold on American Public," suggested that "soccer football took its first great start during the year 1905, . . . following the fatality rank season so staggering to [gridiron football]," as "soccer enthusiasts, seizing the chance, came forward with the great claims of the pure kicking sport."[16] The *Chicago Tribune* noted two years later that soccer was "a sport at which the 130 pounder can shine as brightly as the man of much heavier weight."[17] In 1912 the *Kansas City Star* pointed out that in soccer "the liability of injury is agreed to be about the same as in baseball," making it "a new brand of football in this country."[18] As early as 1907 the *Portland Oregonian* had argued that soccer was not in fact competitive with gridiron football because the latter game was essentially "for students to play and for students' friends to watch," a "game for a class," whereas soccer could be expected to attract baseball fans, who were devotees of professional clubs rather than college teams. Baseball fans went to "Winter's sleep" after the baseball season ended, but might be expected to watch soccer games played in the winter.[19]

The prospect of soccer becoming a winter sport in America was picked up by several other newspapers in the second decade of the twentieth century. The *Lexington (MA) Herald*, while emphasizing in a 1912 article that interest in soccer began to develop only "when more or less dissatisfaction was expressed with [gridiron football]" on safety grounds, also noted that soccer had the potential to "dominate as a winter sport" in the United States because it could be played over "a long season."[20] The next year the *Seattle Morning Olympian* quoted a resident as saying that he thought that soccer would become established in the community because "the public desires some universal game for the winter months."[21] A 1914 *Wilkes-Barre (PA) Times* article entitled "It's Time for Winter Sports. Why Not Soccer?" argued that "the game can be played under weather conditions which would make any other outdoor sport of its kind impossible."[22]

THE SETTINGS OF AMERICAN SOCCER

Something else informed the perceptions of soccer formed during the first American tours of the English clubs. English association football, at the same time, had just migrated from London to the provinces, and had come to include professional as well as amateur players, typically from working-class backgrounds, who played football in addition to holding day jobs. But as we have seen, soccer had begun as, and to an important extent remained, a sport linked to British public schools, gentleman amateurs, and an ethos of playing the game not for money but for the joy of exercise and competition. The gridiron footballers in American colleges at the time were also playing for "fun" rather than pay, and were overwhelmingly from families that had accumulated wealth and high social status—families that, had they lived in England, likely would have sent their sons to public schools and sometimes to Oxford or Cambridge.

Association football in the United States, by contrast, was not primarily played by college amateurs when the first English touring clubs arrived. Some colleges, such as Penn, Harvard, and Yale, did have soccer clubs, although even at those schools the gridiron game was played more. As mentioned, in the late nineteenth and early twentieth centuries, association football tended to cluster in a few isolated communities distinguished by enclaves of immigrants from England, Scotland, Ireland, and Italy. The formation of soccer clubs in those communities began in the 1880s, and was directly connected to the presence of those immigrants. These clubs, which bore names such as the Kearny Rangers, the Fall River Rovers and East Ends, the Pawtucket Free Wanderers and Rangers, the St. Louis Thistle and Mound City Club, and the Chicago Thistles and Wanderers, were mainly composed of men who had migrated to the United States from Scotland or the Lancashire region in England, two early centers of association football in the UK. In many instances, the men who played on those teams made their livelihoods in textile factories.[23]

The cotton industry had developed in England in the late eighteenth century and was first brought to the United States by Samuel Slater, a native of Derbyshire in England who in 1797 built a spinning mill in Pawtucket. While in England, Slater made connections with Moses Brown, a native of Pawtucket who had been attempting to construct a spinning machine. Brown was seeking to apply the expertise he had gained as an apprentice to Richard Arkwright and Jedediah Strutt, who had constructed the world's first successful cotton mill in Derbyshire in the 1770s. When Slater left England for America in 1789, he did so with the knowledge that Arkwright's patents on textile machinery had been overturned, opening the cotton industry to anyone with sufficient capital and expertise to start a mill. Slater turned out to be that person in Pawtucket, whose moist climate and proximity to the ocean made it an ideal location to weave yarn into cloth.[24]

As Slater's mill was expanding, in 1825, England dropped its restrictions on the emigration of textile workers. During the Civil War, a Union blockade of cotton-producing Confederate states brought about a temporary collapse of cotton markets, but after the war's end the market for cotton and silk fabrics dramatically expanded. Pawtucket, as well as Fall River and New Bedford, where other mills had been established, were poised to capitalize on that growth. But Slater's emphasis on his mill operating at full capacity, in order to produce as much yarn as possible, made large numbers of factory workers necessary. In response to depressed economic conditions in the UK in the 1870s and the absence of restrictions on emigration to the United States, cotton-mill workers from Lancashire flocked to America in large numbers, many of them emigrating to Fall River, whose population increased from 17,841 to 56,870 between 1865 and 1885. Seven-eighths of Fall River's labor force worked in the textile industry.[25]

Meanwhile connections comparable to that between the textile workers in Lancashire and southern New England were established in the New Jersey cities of Newark and Paterson after the Civil War. Whereas the development of American cotton mills had featured the emigration of individuals with expertise in the cotton industry to the United States and their subsequent establishment of mills, the pattern in the nascent American silk industry was different. English proprietors, facing a downturn in profits after England abandoned tariffs on silk products for free trade, simply moved their operations to America, whose government continued to favor protective tariffs for the silk industry. Two competing silk thread companies in Paisley, one owned by Patrick Clark and the other by James Coats, chose, respectively, the Newark/Paterson and Pawtucket areas to establish silk mills, bought additional mills, and centered their businesses on their American operations. One of the new mills established by Clark was in Kearny, east of Newark. That mill was staffed by a large number of Scottish immigrants, who brought with them not only expertise in manufacturing silk thread but an interest in association football.[26] Meanwhile, as the Coats mill was established in Pawtucket, the town of New Bedford, known as an early nineteenth-century center of the whaling industry, coped with that industry's collapse after the Civil War by turning to textiles. The result was that another group of Scottish immigrants found its way across the Atlantic to New Bedford.[27]

Soon after those mass migrations of English, Scottish, and subsequently Irish immigrants to America as textile workers, association football clubs began to form in Pawtucket, Kearny, Fall River, and New Bedford, with virtually none of the players who joined the clubs being gentleman amateurs.[28] As in their home countries, these men made their way in the United States as industrial workers. They likely lived in unventilated tenement apartments and drank polluted water, and their working conditions were little better; most mills were poorly ventilated, the air thick with breathable fibers and the constant activity of the machinery at times creating stiflingly hot conditions. Mill workers worked very long hours to meet the demands caused by the industries' ethos of constant production.[29] It is hard to imagine soccer clubs emerging from a population of players living in those conditions, but by the 1880s all of the communities that had seen influxes of English and Scottish textile workers had them.

The clustering of association football in discrete communities in late nineteenth-century America, and the backgrounds of those who joined clubs at that time were to have significant ramifications in the next decades, not only for the growth of the game but for the perception of it formed by most Americans. From its outset, association football in the UK had a class dimension, one reflected in the persistent interest of those promoting the game, whether within the UK or internationally, as a "pure" sport that, despite its increased recruitment of professional players, continued to have overtones of amateurism.

The late nineteenth-century history of association football in America was quite different. The leading American universities, natural candidates as environments that might have embraced an amateur version of soccer, never did so to any great extent, largely because of the established presence of gridiron football and the notion that the two sports could not coexist on college campuses. Instead, in America soccer flourished in communities with a distinctive combination of working-class immigrants from the British Isles, particularly those in the textile industries.

Those who labored in American textile factories in the late nineteenth century hailed from the working class, so when they formed soccer clubs, they did so for recreation, not for profit. Given their jobs, they had limited time for playing soccer, and even less time to travel outside their communities in search of matches. What Fall River, Massachusetts, and Kearny, New Jersey, principally had in common at the time were textile factories, a large number of residents who were immigrant textile workers, and nascent football clubs founded by those workers. Unlike those who formed the Football Association, a group of men in London-based clubs who proceeded to promote the sport after having standardized its rules of play throughout England, those who founded clubs in hardscrabble American communities had no common organizational purpose. They just happened to live where people started playing association football.

Soccer might have developed an organizational structure on American college campuses, places where gifted soccer players could have emerged. By the late nineteenth century some colleges had begun to play gridiron football against one another on a regular basis, and this would eventually lead to the formation of college "leagues," such as the Ivy League, that were somewhat analogous to the English Football League in that they included particular colleges within their organizations and arranged matches between their teams, eventually charging admission for such matches. In 1906 Columbia, Cornell, Harvard, Haverford, the University of Pennsylvania, and Yale formed the Intercollegiate Soccer League, and by 1926 there were two college conferences comprised of teams that played matches against one another. But, as we will see in subsequent chapters, men's college soccer in the United States was slow to attract players or spectators. As a men's sport, it did not attract the best athletes and its matches were little more than recreational pursuits, and as a women's college sport, it was rarely played at all until the 1960s. When American entrepreneurs made a serious effort to create a professional soccer league in the 1920s, there was no critical mass of American college players for the league to draw upon, and it turned almost exclusively to foreign players. In the place of any college-based organization of American soccer, a quite limited organizational model for the sport in the United States would surface.

THE FORMATION OF THE EARLY AMERICAN FOOTBALL LEAGUES

In 1884, in a meeting held at the Clark Thread Company's offices in Newark, the American Football Association was formed. A group of businessmen in the Newark and Paterson areas, most of them British expatriates, raised $500 to establish the AFA and to launch the American Football Association Challenge Cup, modeled on the FA Cup. The group also sought to standardize rules for an American version of association football, adding penalty kicks and nets on goals, and in 1895 connected itself with the National Association Football League, a group of affiliated clubs, modeled on the English Football League and centered in New Jersey, that had been established that same year. On its formation the AFA regarded itself as the equivalent of a subsidiary of the Football Association, paying an annual subscription fee to that organization and following its advice on such matters as whether its clubs could play matches against touring clubs from England. Its founders seemed mainly interested in the cup tournaments, which they hoped would be a profitable venture. Thirteen clubs entered the first cup competition in 1885, all but three from the Newark, Kearny, and New York areas and two of the remainder from Fall River.[30] That competition was won by the ONT (Our New Thread) club of Kearny, initially composed exclusively of workers at the Clark Thread Mills. ONT would go on to win the AFA Cup the next two years, but by 1888 the Fall River Rovers had emerged as cup champions, winning for the next two years, and two other Fall River clubs won the cup from 1890 to 1892.[31] The profitability of cup matches was adversely affected by an economic depression in 1893, and after 1898, when the competition was won by a Kearny club, cup tournaments ceased.[32]

Ten years after the AFA's founding, a group of six owners of baseball franchises in the eastern division of the National League, which had been established in 1876 as a for-profit enterprise of professional baseball clubs, started the American League of Professional Football Clubs, the first soccer organization in the United States to feature teams made up wholly of professional players.[33] The aspirations of the owners in starting a professional soccer league provide evidence of the rudimentary state of organized American soccer at the time. None of the owners of franchises in the league, which consisted of Baltimore, Boston, Brooklyn, New York, Philadelphia, and Washington, had any experience running soccer clubs: they simply wanted a way to attract crowds to their baseball stadiums after the baseball season had ended. They gave the soccer clubs they created the same names as their baseball clubs and recruited players from immigrant communities in the Northeast, where soccer had begun to be played. One team in the league, the Baltimore franchise, hired a coach and eight professional soccer players from Manchester, England, and quickly emerged as the league's most successful team, in terms of both performance and gate receipts. But outside Baltimore the league never got off the ground. Even though their principal audiences for soccer matches came from working-class immigrants, the teams scheduled games on workday afternoons, when most members of those audiences were unable to attend.[34]

In addition, the Baltimore club's importation of English players was challenged when the *Washington Post* reported, after a match in Washington in which Baltimore defeated the hometown club 10–1, that "Little, Calvey, Ferguson and Wallace of the Manchester, England team, champions of Great Britain and home of the Association game," were among the Baltimore players.[35] That report allegedly prompted officials of the US Treasury Department, then charged with enforcing immigration restrictions, to investigate whether the players were foreign "artists," who were permitted to enter the United States without restriction. The *Boston Herald*, in following up on the matter, reported on October 18, 1894, that Baltimore had applied to the US secretary of the treasury in August to ascertain whether professional football players from England could be considered artists and had received a negative response.[36] Contacted in connection with the story, officials of the Baltimore team denied that they had corresponded with the treasury secretary and asserted that "nearly all the men on the Baltimore team are residents of Detroit."[37] The Federal Immigration Service then launched an investigation into whether the Baltimore players had been issued proper work visas, which allegedly created "a cloud that hung over the league for the duration of its season."[38]

But that "season" only lasted seventeen days, in which the clubs played between six and eight games. It began on October 6 with games in Boston and New York, the *Post* reporting that "the playing of the teams was of a character to stir up lots of enthusiasm and excitement," and ended on October 23, when five hundred people in Baltimore, on a Tuesday afternoon, witnessed the Orioles defeat Philadelphia for their sixth consecutive victory.[39] Six days earlier, in a secret meeting in New York, the owners of franchises had resolved to suspend operations for the year, hoping, according to a report in the *Herald*, to "reorganize on somewhat different lines" for a spring season in 1895. The Washington owner commented that "this was intended merely as a season of education . . . the game in time will take with the masses,"[40] but other owners felt differently, very possibly for financial reasons, and the league never resumed operations.[41] In contrast to the English Football League, which had begun operations six years earlier, the American League of Professional Football Clubs was a fly-by-night operation, one designed largely as a prospective source of revenue for baseball owners who knew virtually nothing about soccer.

The American Football Association was still in existence when the American League of Professional Football Clubs disbanded. The AFA had never been more than a semiprofessional operation, and had no interest in promoting soccer throughout the United States or encouraging schools or colleges to play the game. It was not involved in the Pilgrims' or the Corinthians' early twentieth-century tours, although both clubs played against teams from Fall River. And it remained not only a subscribing member of the Football Association, but something of an appendage to that organization.

An episode in connection with the Corinthians' 1911 tour of North America illustrated the AFA's lack of independence. When the Corinthians withdrew from the Football Association in 1907 over the issue of amateurism, the FA retaliated by asking the AFA to prevent its affiliated clubs from playing games against the Corinthians on their 1911 tour. The AFA complied, spawning a series of protests against that decision. *Newark Evening Star* columnist Edward Duffy wrote that "as a free American who does not in any way depend on England for aid or advice in soccer," he "fail[ed] to see where the 'F.A.' has any strong ground to stand on in forbidding the American Football Association teams to play the Corinthians." There were "some independents among the eastern soccerites," Duffy noted, "who are independent enough to be Americans," and who will "openly defy the order from England and will pick a team from the league to play the Corinthians." That was as it should be, he concluded: "There is no reason why England should control soccer in this country now or in the future. We can take care of ourselves."[42]

Not everyone agreed. A reader of the *Association Football News*, published in Harrisburg, Pennsylvania, wrote the paper that "it is a universal admission that Great Britain is at present superior to us at soccer and why shouldn't that be? Soccer has been the national game over there for nearly half a century, whilst . . . we have yet a lot to learn about its fine points."[43] But on the whole, readers responding to the *Association Football News* endorsed Duffy's stance. One described the American Football Association as being "officered and composed . . . of men born across the water and apparently filled with the ideas that those on the other side should . . . control the destinies of the game in this country." The average American, this correspondent felt, "regards [soccer] as a foreign game played by foreigners, and the action of the AFA will tend to increase this opinion. . . . No sport will ever succeed here which is directed across the water, and until the American Association show its independence of foreign domination, Soccer will always be regarded as a sport peculiar to Britons in America."[44]

The controversy over the AFA's acquiescence in the Football Association's request that its clubs not play matches against the Corinthians during their 1911 tour prompted some participants to investigate the composition of the AFA. One found that "during the 26 years that they claim to be in existence . . . not once has an American born held the office of [AFA] President, nor is [there] any likelihood of ever doing so under the present regime." He suggested that readers ask "anyone connected with the A.F.A., What have they done to advance soccer in the United States?"[45] An even more pointed commentary on the AFA's internal operations came from the *Newark Evening News*, one of whose reporters had apparently attended the annual meeting of the organization. The *News* stated that once a report of the AFA's Auditing Committee had revealed that $689 was in the treasury, "the delegates voted unanimously" to give the AFA secretary $250 for his services, the president $100, the financial secretary $75, and the treasurer $50. The vice president was given a gold medal. "There was," the *News* added, "some disposition to 'blow in' a portion of the balance of the funds," and no action was taken when a representative of the AFA's affiliated clubs proposed that a fund be created for the purchase of "suitable grounds" on which to play soccer.[46] The clear import of the *News* article was that the officers of the AFA were primarily interested in lining their own pockets. Another writer to *Association Football News* echoed this sentiment, claiming that "the sole purpose of running this Association is not for the good of Soccer, but to furnish good times and funds for those fortunate enough to be holding office."[47]

The episode proved, over time, fatal to the continued primacy of the AFA as an institutional representative of American soccer. After the AFA's secretary wrote an ineffectual response to the report in the *News*, claiming that the organization's membership in the Football Association enabled it to be "in touch with all that is going on in the football world" and belittling the promoters of the 1911 Corinthians tour and the club itself,[48] Duffy countered that he expected the AFA to "die the slow death its antiquated methods are preparing for it."[49] When the Corinthians arrived, only one AFA-affiliated club, the Newark Football Club, agreed to play a match against them, losing to the visitors 6–2 in September. Another team that played the Corinthians, a group of "all-stars" representing New York City, included several players from AFA clubs. The AFA responded, shortly after the Corinthians-Newark match, by expelling Newark FC from the National Association Football League and suspending the "all-star" players indefinitely.

Those actions prompted the Southern New York State Association, affiliated with the AFA, to withdraw from that organization and subsequently announce that it would become an institutional competitor to the AFA, calling itself the American Amateur Football Association. "For 26 years," one of the newly christened AAFA's founders declared, the AFA had "claimed . . . control of soccer in the United States" and affiliated itself with the Football Association, but "in those 26 years it [the AFA] has done little to advance the game." During that time the members of the Southern New York State Association had "tried earnestly and consistently to broaden [the AFA's] view and to urge it to try to make its influence national in fact as well as in name." They had "pointed out that the United States, because of its size and its very proper feeling of national pride," could not "be considered as being under vassalage of an English organization." But since, to their minds, that is precisely what had happened, they were now, in the form of the AAFA, going it on their own.[50]

Immediately after breaking with the AFA, the AAFA attempted to expand its governance of American soccer by affiliating with leagues in Pittsburgh, St. Louis, Michigan, and Utah. It also launched a cup competition comparable to that of the AFA Cup, billing it as nationwide, even though in the first competition in 1912 twenty-three out of the twenty-seven clubs entered were from New York. In June of that same year, it sent a representative to the annual meeting of FIFA (the Federation Internationale de Football Associiation) in Stockholm and asked to be officially recognized by FIFA.[51] The AFA also asked to be recognized by FIFA at the meeting. It did so not through its own representative but by proxy through Frederick Wall, the current Football Association secretary.[52]

Thomas Cahill, the AAFA's representative, and Wall traveled from London together for the meeting. Cahill recalled that Wall told him that he was not prepared to support the AFA's application, and instead favored "a National body governing soccer in the United States."[53] At the meeting Cahill gave a candid review of the state of association football in America, noting that it was "badly lacking organization," and that only the AAFA stood "for honesty in sport." The AAFA, Cahill claimed, was "doing missionary work in public schools and in educational institutes," and would "lift up the game" in the United States. Cahill suggested that if FIFA did not feel in a position to recognize the AAFA fully at that point, it should give the organization provisional recognition for a year, because its members "knew what was expected of them."[54]

Notwithstanding what Wall had allegedly told Cahill on their trip from London to Stockholm, Wall then spoke "for about thirty minutes" on

FIGURE 2. Thomas Cahill, the central figure in American professional soccer in the first two decades of the twentieth century, became associated with the sport as an employee of the A. G. Spalding sporting goods firm in St. Louis, which he joined in 1902. © Southern Illinois University Edwardsville | LIS.

behalf of the AFA's application.[55] Then a delegate from Germany, Professor Robert Hefner, made a forty-minute speech on the AAFA's behalf. Austria then proposed to accept the AAFA provisionally for a year, and Germany recommended that it be accepted as a full member. Wall, now representing England, then stated that the FIFA delegates "had received two applications from America" and "had no information before it as to the constitution of either association." He maintained "that it would be a blunder to admit one of the two American associations applying for membership" at that time, though he hoped "that it might be possible to bring them together." He proposed referring the matter to an emergency committee of FIFA for further study. By a 55 to 25 vote, the FIFA delegates supported Wall's proposal.[56]

Wall subsequently told Cahill that he could not support the AAFA application "in its present form." He gave two reasons for his position. One was that the AAFA, which billed itself as an amateur organization, had not made any provision in its constitution for professional players. As noted, most of the participants in late nineteenth- and early twentieth-century American soccer were amateurs, mainly factory workers who played the game recreationally. English football had thoroughly integrated professionals into association clubs by 1913, but at the same time, in response to the Corinthians' withdrawal from the league in 1907, had launched an amateur cup competition. Wall wanted any American soccer organization affiliated with FIFA to have a clear policy signaling that it would welcome professionals to clubs. Wall's other reason, Cahill recalled, was that their "title was wrong": they needed to "select a name . . . which would indicate a National body."[57]

After the June 1912 FIFA meeting, the AAFA began negotiations with the AFA for a merger of the two organizations and the creation of a national body. The negotiations initially appeared promising, but in December the AFA backed away from the merger. Then, in early 1913, the Allied American Association of Philadelphia, which had been affiliated with the AFA, threw its support to the AAFA. The AAFA then called for a "national soccer congress" to be held in New York in April.[58] The AFA attended, its president complaining that "just at a point where great progress was being made" in the development of American soccer, "the New York State League split from [our] ranks,"[59] but most of the delegates were not inclined to be sympathetic. A resolution that a "national organization be established . . . and be given the name United States Football Association" passed, including a provision that a copy of the minutes of the congress be sent to FIFA, along with a plea for admission to that body at its 1913 meeting.[60]

FIFA subsequently notified the new United States Football Association that it was granting it provisional membership. After losing out to the

AAFA, the AFA had initially refused to join the new organization, and also refused to disband, but after the FIFA recognition of the USFA, it altered its position, and eventually a member of the AFA was elected the third vice president of the USFA. The other officers were all from the AAFA, including G. Randolph Manning, an English surgeon who had emigrated to the United States, as president and Cahill as secretary. Manning was dispatched to the 1913 FIFA meeting to request permanent recognition for the USFA.[61]

Although the USFA became a permanent member of FIFA in 1913, the issues that Frederick Wall had raised when it initially applied to FIFA for recognition were far from settled. Despite the AFA's clearly having been displaced by the USFA after the 1913 congress, it did not disband, continuing to operate independently of the USFA until the United States entered World War I. It also continued to organize the American Cup until the 1920s. Meanwhile the USFA immediately began plans to launch a cup tournament of its own, the National Challenge Cup. It was apparent that those involved in the administration of American soccer outside colleges and universities were far more interested in making profits from the gate receipts of tournaments than in creating a command-and-control structure for the game in the United States comparable to that established by the Football Association and the Football League.

Meanwhile the USFA's apparent plan to bring leagues from different sections of the country within its jurisdiction was resisted by clubs in some localities where the game had established itself in the nineteenth century. Notable were three such areas, Fall River, St. Louis, and northern New Jersey. Fall River, long a powerhouse in American Cup competition, declined to participate in the initial National Challenge Cup. St. Louis (somewhat ironically, since Thomas Cahill had long been a resident of that city) also declined, on the ground that the cup format would require its teams to travel long distances for matches, because the USFA contemplated playing most cup matches in the Northeast.[62] St. Louis clubs may also have been influenced by the brand of soccer they played, which featured long kicking and passing, in contrast to the UK style of tightly controlled dribbling and passing. They may have feared that their style of play would not be well received by referees in cup matches. When the *St. Louis Globe-Democrat* commented on local clubs having declined to participate in the National

Challenge Cup, it maintained that a more satisfactory way of "settling the soccer championship of this country" would be to have a series of local matches, progressing from "city titles and then state titles" to "interstate titles," which would not result in "forcing teams to travel inconvenient distances." Sectional titles could also be "arranged conveniently for the contending teams" to reduce travel, and they could lead to a national championship.[63]

After Fall River scheduled a number of matches against St. Louis clubs unaffiliated with the organization, the USFA responded by suspending Fall River for a year.[64] That action, however, had no effect on the most important area group of clubs that initially had declined to participate in the inaugural National Challenge Cup. This was the National Association Football League, which consisted of twelve clubs centered in northern New Jersey and was arguably the strongest center of soccer in the nation. Clubs from that league—notably Bethlehem Steel FC from Pennsylvania, which, beginning in 1915, entered both the American and National Challenge Cups, going to the finals in 1916, 1917, and 1918 and winning the competition in the first and last of those years—had regularly progressed deep into the American Cup competition in the years between 1912 and 1918.[65]

OBSTACLES TO THE GROWTH OF SOCCER IN AMERICA: FACILITIES AND WEATHER

Despite initial opposition, the USFA's National Challenge Cup was something of a financial success, especially in its late rounds,[66] and it provided a mechanism for the USFA's effort to unite clubs in leagues located in different sections of the country. In the inaugural cup competition, four clubs from Chicago and two from Detroit entered. But the presence of midwestern teams, and the USFA's interest in staging the competition in the late fall and early winter, when the professional baseball season had ended, brought to the surface two of the great obstacles the game of soccer faced in establishing itself in America: the severe winter weather over much of the country, especially in the locations in which soccer clubs were prominent, and the absence of appropriate grounds on which to play matches. Although in theory all that was needed to play soccer was a field of suitable dimensions and some adjacent place from which spectators could watch the games in relative comfort, those features did not easily come into being.

In England the close connection between soccer clubs and localities, reinforced by the introduction of promotion and relegation in 1892,[67] had combined with the prohibition against clubs taking profits beyond those necessary to maintain player and club expenses to create strong incentives for clubs to invest in the upgrading of their facilities. Better facilities for playing and watching soccer attracted more spectators at matches and hence more revenue for clubs. None of those features of English soccer were present in early professional soccer leagues in the United States. Both the AFA and the USFA had affiliated leagues, but those leagues were largely organized on a regional basis, with clubs periodically entering leagues and disbanding. None of the leagues affiliated with either organization had established rules of promotion and relegation, and sometimes clubs simply switched their allegiances from one locality to another. There was no tradition of clubs investing in spectator-friendly facilities: they simply played where fields were available. Although the National Association Football League had attempted to use vacant baseball stadiums for games, that effort had, as we saw, fizzled after less than a month.

When to that comparative dearth of good facilities in the United States was added the perceived need of American soccer to be played outside the parameters of the baseball season, the result was some National Challenge Cup matches being played in memorably fierce winter weather. In the first year of the cup, four teams from Chicago competed on December 6, two on a field at the corner of West Madison Street and Fifty-Second Avenue and the other two at Aviation Field, on the corner of Sixteenth Street and Forty-Eighth Avenue. The *Chicago Tribune* covered both games. Its reporter for the first game described the field as "frozen hard, [with] little snow on it," with a "biting breeze from the north," making playing conditions "slippery and windy," and "combination play difficult."[68] The reporter at the second match described the contest as "a frigid proposition" between "thinly-clad kickers," and noted that two players had left the field in the second half "to escape turning into icicles."[69]

Conditions were no better elsewhere. A week after the second of the Chicago matches, two local Detroit clubs, Roses FC and Packard FC, played a cup match at Maloney Park. The match attracted "over 700 persons" on a "cold raw day," a correspondent for the *Detroit Free Press* reported. "Anyone who has the impression that the game is gentle," the reporter noted, "is far from the facts. On the contrary, the men are in consistent danger of being kicked when they charge for the ball, while it is no joke to be spilled on a hard field in the light and airy costume of the sport."[70] Nor was a cup match that same year, played on Long Island between Yonkers, of the New York State Amateur League, and the Fulton Athletic Club from Brooklyn, a more comfortable experience for players or spectators: a reporter there noted that when the referee whistled the end of the first half, "six players were trying to kick the ball out of a big puddle" as spectators, "armed with umbrellas and raincoats, stood around the field ankle deep in mud."[71] Still, the USFA forged ahead through the winter with cup rounds, resulting in numerous weather-related postponements. In Chicago the two teams that had won on December 6, 1913, did not play their next round match until March 8, 1914, two months after it had initially been scheduled.

In February 1914 the Niagara Falls Rangers came to Detroit to play Roses FC of that city, which had defeated Packard FC the preceding December, in the next round of the USFA Cup. The ground at Packard Park in Detroit, where the match was staged, "was covered by about a foot of snow, which made it very hard for the players," the *Detroit Free Press* reported. "The Roses in the first half should have been at least three goals up but failed to take advantage of the opportunities, the deep snow being a great handicap," and eventually Niagara Falls, which "proved the better snow wallowers," prevailed.[72] This earned Niagara Falls a home match in the next round against Pullman FC, one of the victorious Chicago clubs. But weather conditions prevented the match, scheduled in Buffalo, from being played for two months, and when it finally did take place, it was on a waterlogged field in the falling snow. Niagara Falls had sought to cover the field with coke screenings before the match, but it was still noticeably slippery at game time.[73]

As the first National Challenge Cup progressed to its semifinals, weather became less of a problem, but the location of matches proved a subject of controversy. At that point in the history of the tournament, semifinal and final matches were to be played on neutral sites, with the USFA officials—in this instance Cahill, in his capacity as honorary secretary—determining the locations. The semifinals in 1913–14 pitted New Bedford against the Brooklyn FC and the Niagara Fall Rangers against Celtic, another Brooklyn club. Cahill selected Pawtucket for the first match and Paterson for the second, both choices being based on the long history of association football in those communities, which, Cahill felt, would result in "football intelligent" fans who would patronize the games.[74] He turned out to be correct about the Pawtucket semifinal, which attracted nearly 5,000 spectators even though a Pawtucket club was not represented, but not about the semifinal held in Patterson, where only 1,000 spectators attended the match, held at the Patterson baseball stadium. When it came to the final, Cahill chose Pawtucket, even though two Brooklyn teams were playing against one another. The match attracted over 6,000 spectators and resulted in the USFA ending its first year with a surplus of $779.18, not an inconsiderable sum for the time. A Pawtucket paper lauded Cahill for having "demanded that the final be played in [New England]." He had had "to fight his way through strong opposition to do so," the correspondent maintained, and the USFA "thr[ew] the entire responsibility on Cahill's shoulders and order[ed] him to stage the game," knowing that "if it was a failure the blame would rest on his shoulders," but "if it was a success, the teams and the officials would grab a share of the honors." The final "was a success from every standpoint," the reporter concluded. "Everything possible to make the contest a good one for the spectator was provided."[75]

THE CHALLENGES FOR SOCCER IN EARLY TWENTIETH-CENTURY AMERICA: A SUMMARY

By 1916 the National Challenge Cup final would attract nearly 10,000 spectators.[76] But the state of soccer in early twentieth-century America remained behind that in the UK in every respect. Although the USFA had avoided the Football Association's controversies about professional and amateur players. it had not made much progress on the other elements that, taken together, had enabled soccer in the British Isles to grow and to flourish.

Nothing like the British command-and-control structure of football organization had emerged in the United States. There were several reasons why the Football Association's structural model for promoting and expanding the game did not surface in America. First, when association football first established itself as independent from the Rugby School version in the 1860s, the only other popular sport in England was cricket, which demanded not only a significant amount of equipment but considerable patience on the part of both players and spectators. Association football thus had a large space as a recreational activity in England, and it initially developed in that capacity. The founders of the Football Association were, as we have seen, interested in establishing the game not as an admission-charging spectator sport but as one played by men in their spare time and according to a common set of rules. English football thus first emerged in the late nineteenth century as a recreational pursuit, its only official competition being the FA Cup, which, because of the way its matches were organized, did not require most of its entrants to be engaged in the competition for lengthy periods.

When association football first came to be played in the United States, it was played in particular communities, such as Fall River, Pawtucket, Kearny, Harrison, Chicago, and St. Louis, all of which were then home to a considerable number of workers from the UK or, in the case of St. Louis, Italy, with a degree of familiarity with association football. At the time when association football began to be played in the United States, and the American Football Association and its American Cup were established, there was no tradition of soccer played in prep schools or colleges. Nationally, then, not many people longed to continue to play soccer after high school or college.[77] Consequently no movement to standardize the game's rules marked the early years of organized soccer, and teams from different localities continued to employ different styles of play.[78]

And whereas association football developed with only rugby and cricket as alternative forms of recreation, American soccer emerged in the late nineteenth century under the distinct shadow of baseball. By 1876 professional baseball had become established in the United States in the form of the National League, which would endure throughout the remainder of the century, competing with rival leagues such as the American Association and the Western League, which eventually became the American League and would be absorbed into Major League Baseball in the early twentieth century. From the outset American baseball leagues were profit-seeking enterprises, run by individuals who often owned teams in connection with their businesses and who unabashedly sought to control players' salaries and ability to move from one team to another. Many baseball teams were owned by brewers, who used games to sell their product. From the start, then, the owners of American baseball teams were keenly conscious of spectators, gate receipts, and profits. There was also no tradition of plowing revenue back into their clubs.[79]

And baseball, being a weather-dependent sport, was played in the United States in the spring, summer, and early fall. As a spectator sport, it grew rapidly in the late nineteenth century, establishing itself as one of America's primary professional sports, along with horse racing and boxing. It would grow even more rapidly in the early twentieth century, as the National and American Leagues began an organized coexistence culminating in a World Series featuring the champions of those two leagues, with clubs beginning to invest in new steel-and-concrete stadiums to seat many thousands of fans, and owners making a conscious effort to reduce the sport's connections with gambling.[80] The frequent comments by early twentieth-century soccer enthusiasts in the United States that the game might flourish as a winter sport were prompted by baseball's strong presence as a spectator sport in all three of the other seasons.

Aspirations for soccer to emerge in America as a national pastime played in the winter months may have been fueled by its long having been played in the winter months in the UK. But, as the USFA's experiences with playing National Challenge Cup matches in the winter of 1913–14 demonstrated, it was one thing to play soccer in damp and raw conditions in an English winter and another altogether to play it in the frozen, snow-covered fields of the United States. And although there were of course regional variations in weather around the UK, with some regions typically having harsher winter conditions than others, that was nothing compared to the variations in weather in the United States. While it certainly was possible to play soccer on the West Coast or in the South over the winter, both the Northeast, clearly the regional center of early American soccer, and the Midwest, where the game had established a foothold and begun to grow in the late nineteenth century, were largely inhospitable environments for outdoor sport from November through March.

The baseball model of franchise organization had been for-profit competition: baseball leagues only combined when their owners thought it economically sensible to do so. Major League Baseball did not employ the command-and-control approach of the Football Association and the Football League. It had no central organization overseeing leagues until the 1920s, when—in response to the "Black Sox" scandal when players on the Chicago

White Sox agreed to lose the World Series to the Cincinnati Reds in exchange for payments from gamblers—baseball owners appointed a commissioner who, despite his authoritative oversight status, worked for the owners.[81] Nothing like the Football Association's Committee or Council ever surfaced in American baseball. Because there was no model of structural organization in American sports comparable to that in the UK when the American Football Association came into being, soccer in the United States developed through independent leagues that had no connection with one another.

The absence of any English-style central overseeing body for American soccer meant that under the AFA and the USFA, soccer leagues in the United States came into and went out of existence at the will of the clubs of which they were composed, the motivations of which were dictated by a combination of owners' desire for profits and the willingness of a critical mass of players to form and maintain a club. Although one of the chief priorities of the USFA, at its formation, was to organize clubs in leagues, and leagues in some sort of central organization, it was largely unsuccessful in achieving the latter goal, primarily because the vast distances on the American continent made the coordination of different regional leagues difficult. One might contrast the relative ease with which FA Cup matches and Football League games were played in England—given the comparatively short distances between cities, the large number of clubs affiliated with the Football Association, and the conscious desire of the teams in the league to establish rivalries among clubs located relatively close to one another—with the great difficulty the USFA had in attracting teams from different areas of the country to its 1913–14 National Challenge Cup. When Thomas Cahill mandated that those first Challenge Cup semifinals and finals be held in southeastern New England, he was attempting to make the matches accessible to a large body of potential fans. It was apparent that the geographic barriers that had made the consolidation of regional leagues difficult would also pose a formidable challenge to the efficient staging of cup competitions in the United States.

Perhaps most fundamentally, the absence of a central organizing body for soccer in America made it much more difficult for the distinctive ethos of English association football to take root. That ethos had three chief components: the eventual replacement of a strong tradition of amateurism with professionalism in the top-tier leagues, illustrated by the increased number of full-time professional players on the rosters of clubs in those leagues; the identification of football clubs with small communities, often city neighborhoods, towns, and counties; and a strong desire to standardize and make uniform the rules of the game.

American soccer never had such an ethos. As noted, the issues of professionalism and amateurism were not part of the early history of the sport in the United States. The market for professional players was not substantial, American clubs commanding nothing like the gate appeal of clubs in the UK, and few players from overseas came to America to play soccer professionally in the late nineteenth and early twentieth centuries. Most American soccer players were in fact from overseas, but they were amateurs, blue-collar workers in particular communities who played soccer for recreation. When professional players imported from the UK did join American clubs, they were tolerated, yet they never amounted to anything like a majority of those who took the field in the years up to World War I.

American soccer clubs were indeed identified with communities, but the allegiance of those clubs could shift, and their identities lacked constancy. The early clubs, we have seen, were composed of players from industrial cities or towns with large immigrant populations, typically generated by a particular form of factory work. Sometimes, as with Fall River or Kearny or Patterson or Brooklyn, multiple clubs were established in the same community. In contrast to their counterparts in the UK, US clubs passed in and out of existence according to the presence or absence of a critical mass of players or the goals of a particular factory owner. Since the leagues with which those clubs were affiliated were simply efforts to further regular competition among clubs, tiers of leagues were not established, nor was promotion and relegation. And to the extent that an American model of sports franchising existed in the late nineteenth and early twentieth centuries, it was the owner-dominated model of organized baseball leagues: lacking central oversight, with clubs entirely composed of professional players and teams overtly operated to generate revenue, whether in the form of gate receipts or concessions. Thus at the time when the USFA made efforts to combine soccer leagues in a centralized organizational format, no similar model existed in American sport; there were no compelling reasons that those involved in the operation of clubs should surrender their autonomy to a command-and-control organization.

Finally, there was no tradition of youth soccer in America outside the very few communities in which it had taken root. Boys regularly played baseball, "touch" gridiron football, and, beginning in the first decade of the twentieth century, basketball as recreational activities. The dramatic growth of youth soccer in the United States in the twenty-first century has revealed that the sport is in some respects an ideal one for young boys and girls: inexpensive to play; comparatively safe, especially when compared with gridiron football; not requiring a premium on size or strength, unlike gridiron football or basketball; and not subjecting young players to overt failure in front of their peers or spectators, as when young batters strike out or fail to catch balls or make accurate throws in baseball. Yet youth soccer was generally not played in America for much of the twentieth century, all but ensuring that there would rarely be a critical mass of persons in any given community sufficiently familiar with the sport to, later in life, participate in it recreationally or appreciate it as spectators. As we will see in subsequent chapters, the general absence of youth soccer in America had negative ripple effects for the growth of the sport, limiting the number of persons inclined to play, even when colleges and high schools began to offer it. ⚽

Chapter Three

Association Football Comes to America II

Decades of Marginality

THE FIVE DECADES from the 1910s through the 1950s featured two world wars and an economic depression that adversely affected both the performance of American professional sports teams and attendance at their games. Nonetheless in those decades the playing and watching of professional sports for profit dramatically increased in the United States, and some professional sports established or cemented themselves as culturally resonant activities.

Historians regularly describe the 1920s as a golden age of American sport.[1] The description typically alludes to the growing attractiveness of amateur and professional sports to spectators during the decade, a time when some of those sports, notably baseball and college gridiron football, became lucrative enterprises. This chapter considers the reason that, given the growth of several American spectator sports after the end of World War I, soccer did not experience a comparable growth in popularity. To get at the root of the question, one needs to take a closer look at the status of all amateur and professional sports in early twentieth-century America. Two inquiries are central to this investigation: the place of sports in the culture of high schools, colleges, and universities, and the connection of sports to social and economic trends in the nation during the first five decades of the twentieth century.[2]

THE EMERGENCE OF MAJOR AMERICAN PROFESSIONAL SPORTS, 1900–1960

The biggest success story in professional sports in America in the first half of the twentieth century was Major League Baseball. Its structure as established in 1903—two leagues with season-long pennant races, capped by a World Series (championship tournament) between the National and American League pennant winners—remained in place, unchanged, until 1960. The number of MLB franchises remained constant between 1903 and 1953, with the same teams operating in the same cities notwithstanding their respective level of success, both on the field and at the gate. MLB's core practices included the granting of territorial rights to each major-league club, which prevented prospective competitors from creating new clubs within established territories; the reserve clause, which, like the retention and transfer practices in English League football, forced players on major-league rosters to accept the terms of contracts offered them by their club's management each year or retire from the game; and the resultant creation of a buyers' monopoly for the purchase and sale of players, under which a club could pay players whatever it chose, and trade or sell them to other clubs, without their having any choice in the matter.

Although the legality of the reserve clause and MLB's territoriality practices were challenged in the courts over the course of those decades,[3] they were not overturned, even though they were clearly inconsistent with American antitrust laws, and comparable restrictions had not been allowed to stand in other professional sports.[4] The constancy of major-league baseball franchises would also reveal itself as anomalous over time. Some cities with two franchises, such as St. Louis, had smaller populations than other cities with just one team, such as Detroit; some cities in geographic regions where major-league baseball had regularly been played, such as Baltimore, Buffalo, Indianapolis, Milwaukee, and Kansas City, were never offered the opportunity to establish major-league franchises, even though existing clubs such as the St. Louis Browns, Philadelphia Phillies, and Washington Senators regularly fielded weak teams with poor attendance; and over the course of the decades the populations of cities such as Atlanta, Dallas, Houston, Los Angeles, Miami, Minneapolis–St. Paul, and San Francisco came to outdistance several of the cities with major-league franchises. In 1940, for example, the population of Los Angeles, a city without a major-league team, stood at 1,504,277, while that of St. Louis, which had two teams, was 816,048.[5]

When the first movement of franchises in took place in 1953 and 1954, with the Boston Braves relocating to Milwaukee, the St. Louis Browns to Baltimore, and the Philadelphia Athletics to Kansas City, major-league baseball was clearly established as the "national pastime," the predominant American professional sport in terms of fan interest, attendance, and revenue. But other professional sports leagues also had become established since the 1920s. The first of those, chronologically, was the National Hockey League (NHL), which had formed in 1917 as a cluster of Canadian teams. In 1924 the NHL acquired its first American franchise, the Boston Bruins, and by 1926 had six franchises from American cities in a ten-team league.[6] In 1920 a professional gridiron football league, the American Professional Football Association, was created with fourteen member franchises, all of them in small midwestern cities. The league changed its name to the National Football League in 1922 and established a franchise in Chicago, but otherwise remained a regional small-city operation until 1933, when it was reorganized in two five-team divisions, with all of the teams representing large cities except for Green Bay, Wisconsin, a town that was one of the early sites and had a strong football tradition.[7]

In 1946 the owners of the major ice hockey arenas in the northeastern and midwestern United States and Canada formed the Basketball Association of America (BAA) in an effort to garner more revenue from their arena operations. Although there were two other professional basketball leagues in operation at the time, the National Basketball League (NBL) and the American Basketball League (ABL), the BAA was the first to play in large arenas in big cities. After two years of competition among the leagues, during which some franchises from both the NBL and the ABL moved to the BAA, a "merger" between the NBL and the BAA took place in 1949, with the resultant league being called the National Basketball Association (NBA). The 1950s featured a consolidation of franchises and movement toward larger cities in professional basketball, and the NBA became solidly established.[8]

Between the 1920s and the 1950s, then, four professional sports leagues had come into being and refined their operations, so that by 1950 all those leagues had teams in comparatively large cities. As the decade of the 1950s opened, professional sports teams still tended to cluster in the Northeast and Midwest, reflecting population tendencies, but as population began to shift to southern and western regions after 1960, professional sports franchises would follow.

FACILITIES AND SPECTATORS

THE SPECIAL CASE OF GRIDIRON FOOTBALL

In the United States, the center of a professional sports team's operations was its stadium or arena. That was true not only for all the major professional sports but also for the most commercially successful amateur sport of the early and middle twentieth century, college gridiron football. The financial success of college football teams was typically connected to their having geographically convenient, accessible, and spectator-friendly places in which to play their games. In the first five decades of the twentieth century all of the major professional sports and gridiron college football rose to prominence in part because they had established spectator-friendly stadiums and arenas that could attract and accommodate large numbers of paying, and concessions-buying, spectators and generate revenue. As we will see, during those same decades professional soccer leagues and colleges failed to create specific, spectator-friendly stadiums.

The construction of stadiums and arenas for sports teams came in waves. All of the major-league baseball teams replaced their wooden ballparks, which were vulnerable to fire and often lacked outfield seating, with steel and concrete stadiums between 1908 and 1923.[9] College football was next: after World War I a boom in the construction of stadiums for college and university football teams occurred, most of them financed by contributions from alumni and friends of the institution. Although those stadiums were principally designed for football games, which only occurred once a week in the fall months, they were built with the idea of attracting large crowds: many of the spectators for college gridiron football games had no direct affiliation with the college, but were still willing to pay to watch games. With those stadiums in place, home football games became one of the principal ways in which colleges and universities raised revenue.[10]

In the case of both professional hockey and basketball, games were played at indoor arenas. The NHL and the NBA learned, in the years after their formation, that locating franchises in larger cities and building arenas there were prerequisites to economic success. By the 1940s technology enabled artificial ice to be laid over the top of an existing basketball floor and then removed, permitting basketball and hockey teams to use the same arena. Arenas such as the Boston Garden and Madison Square Garden in New York tended to be built above railroad and subway stations so that spectators had convenient access to them.[11]

The construction of stadiums and arenas for professional sports was in keeping with larger social and economic trends in the United States in the first five decades of the twentieth century. The emergence of the automobile as a mode of transportation available to most Americans made it possible for teams to locate their football stadiums, and subsequently baseball stadiums, outside city centers, where they could still be reached by car if not easily by public transportation. Coupled with the extensive public transit systems in most cities, automobiles increased the ability of Americans to pursue leisure activities, including attending sports events. Subsequently the growth of media, which came to include radio and television as well as newspapers over the course of the decades, increased public awareness of sports events. Games came to be broadcast on radio and eventually television, and newspaper sports pages had carried accounts of them since the 1920s.

The early twentieth-century growth of college gridiron football, which was unique among college sports in rivaling the professional sports' spectator appeal in that period, deserves further comment. Several scholars have attempted to explain the transformation of gridiron football from a game played at a few elite colleges to one that after World War I captured the imagination of a large segment of the public, resulting in the establishment of gridiron football teams in virtually all American colleges and universities, the formation of leagues and conferences in all sections of the country, the creation of "bowl" games, featuring intersectional matchups between teams with outstanding records at the close of their seasons, and regular attention to teams and players in the media.[12] Among college sports, gridiron football, at least until the 1960s, was singular in receiving the amount of public attention that it did.[13]

The cultural status of gridiron football in the four decades after 1920 is all the more intriguing because of its very limited appeal as a recreational activity. The demands of the game severely limit the number of people who can play it, restricting it not only to men but to particularly large ones. From its origins it was recognized as a violent sport, emphasizing physical contact and requiring its players to initially wear headgear and subsequently shoulder, knee, and thigh pads as well. Although in its early twentieth-century version the occasional long-distance run or pass occurred, most of its plays consisted of players on opposing teams running into one another until the one carrying the ball was tackled to the ground.

Spectators at gridiron football games also have more difficulty identifying players, and sometimes discerning plays, because of the protective equipment and the tendency of many plays to be short clashes among multiple individuals. And unlike all the other team spectator sports that underwent striking growth after 1920 in America, gridiron football is played under nearly all weather conditions, the only exception being during lightning strikes. Given that feature of the game, the distance of most spectators from the field, and the difficulties they might have in discerning players' identities and actions taking place on the field, one might have expected gridiron football to be one of the less attractive college sports to spectators in the early and middle years of the twentieth century. And yet, in terms of both spectator participation and interest in the fortunes of individual college teams, it was clearly the most attractive.

Scholars have advanced various reasons for the unexpected cultural resonance of college gridiron football in early and mid-twentieth century America.[14] Those reasons might be encapsulated as follows. As more public universities and "comprehensive" public high schools were created in the late nineteenth and early twentieth centuries, attendance at college and engagement with college sports as a participant or spectator became more commonplace, as did the introduction of sports as activities organized by high schools rather than voluntary clubs or associations. Colleges had self-consciously introduced athletic sports by the last decades of the nineteenth century and first decades of the twentieth as counterweights to the intellectual demands of course offerings and as efforts to channel the physical passions of students, most of whom at the time were male, into healthful activities. As the industrializing tendencies of American society produced fewer jobs emphasizing physical labor, particularly among college graduates, some academicians became concerned about the possible loss of "masculinity" in the educated male sectors of the population. Integrating physical activities, in the form of organized sports, into the college experience would be beneficial, they believed. Meanwhile comparable attitudes resulted in high schools introducing organized sports into their curricula and encouraging local communities to support "varsity" high school teams.[15]

That attitude was, of course, gendered. Early twentieth-century coeducational colleges and universities or public high schools established few women's sports teams, although many single-sex women's colleges and some single-sex girls' private schools did. In a gendered college and high school universe, the figure of the male football player, who in most cases needed to be large, tough, and physically gifted, appeared as an embodiment of masculinity, someone who female students might find attractive and male students might vicariously admire. As college and high school football teams became established, their players became the objects of campus rituals such as pep rallies, cheers from the student body orchestrated, at coeducational institutions, by both male and female cheerleaders, and excursions of fans to away games.

One of the most remarkable features of college gridiron football's early twentieth-century growth in America was the emergence of strong support from the residents of the city or town in which a team's college or university was located. In one respect that support mirrored the close affiliation of English association football clubs with localities. But the players in an English football club—even "imported" professionals—typically lived, and often worked, in that locality, while players on American college football teams were students at the college. Living at a college, taking classes and engaging in social and athletic activities within its boundaries, they had little contact with local residents, especially those not affiliated with or alumni of the college. And yet support for college football teams from unaffiliated local residents, who helped fill large football stadiums and thereby contributed revenues to colleges and universities, was a defining feature of gridiron football's growth in twentieth-century America. Resident supporters of college football teams served as "boosters" of the teams and their localities, flocking on Saturday afternoons to throng outside stadiums, eating and drinking before and after games, accompanying teams on their trips to other universities, listening to games on local radio stations, and following the exploits of teams and players in local newspapers.[16]

As some team sports became established as major attractions for paid spectators in the United States, the ambivalent attitude toward professionalism in association football that existed in England in the late nineteenth and early twentieth centuries did not, on the whole, emerge. Baseball, gridiron football, and basketball had all been played in colleges before American professional leagues were established in those sports, and only in the case of football was there any widespread resistance to playing the sport for profit.

In the United States in the early twentieth century a cadre of prospective professional baseball players unaffiliated with colleges or universities, similar to the cadre of late nineteenth-century association football players in the United Kingdom, emerged. Christy Mathewson, the acclaimed pitcher of the New York Giants in the early years of the century, was among several professional baseball players who had attended college, but he, along with many of those players, left Bucknell University before graduating to sign a professional baseball contract.[17] By the 1920s minor-league baseball franchises were established, and major-league clubs began to form affiliations with them, signing young players and assigning them to their minor-league affiliates to groom them for places on major-league rosters.[18] The players they signed were often high school graduates, or sometimes persons of that age who had dropped out. From the opening of the twentieth century through the 1950s, it was comparatively unusual for a major-league baseball player to have played baseball in college before turning professional.

There was thus no widespread concern about professionalism in baseball, though it was played on the college level; the two versions of the sport were not regarded as competing with one another. Nor was there any widespread concern about professionalism in ice hockey or basketball. Ice hockey was played at comparatively few American colleges during the years when the NHL was establishing itself in larger American cities. Most of the players in the league were Canadians, and few had attended college, many being signed by clubs as teenagers and assigned to minor-league teams in Canada. Basketball was introduced in colleges early in the twentieth century and spread rapidly; by the time the NBA had solidified itself in the late 1940s, there was sufficient interest in the college game that two nationwide season-end tournaments, the National Invitation Tournament in New York and one run by the National Collegiate Athletic Association, had become well-attended and lucrative events. Although in the early years of the NBA some of its players never attended college, emerging from a fairly substantial pool of semiprofessional basketball players associated with athletic clubs in cities,[19] by the 1950s the overwhelming number of NBA players had joined the league after successful careers on college teams.

Only in gridiron football did resistance to professionalism emerge. That came when the NFL, shortly after its founding, began to consider recruiting successful college players before they had graduated. At its founding, American professional gridiron football differed from baseball and hockey in its pool of potential players. Although football was increasingly played in high schools as well as colleges by the 1920s, high school players, unlike their counterparts in baseball and hockey, were not coveted by professional football clubs because the vast majority of them had not reached their full growth potential, and added height and weight was a distinct advantage for football. Consequently there were no minor leagues in which younger football players could hone their skills for NFL competition. Instead, the vast majority of players on NFL teams came to them from college.[20]

We have seen that gridiron football began in American colleges and universities strictly as a recreational pursuit. But its appeal to spectators prompted colleges to charge admission for games, build audience-friendly stadiums, form leagues and conferences to encourage the game's popularity, seek to attract audiences from outside the immediate confines of their institutions by publicizing games in newspapers, and generally treat football as a revenue-raising sport. This trend was well under way by the 1920s, with college football becoming second only to baseball in attendance and newspaper coverage. Some outstanding college players received publicity that went beyond their leagues and regions.

FIGURE 3. An aerial photograph of Memorial Stadium, University of Illinois, on its dedication, October 18, 1924. Memorial Stadium was characteristic of the large gridiron football stadiums constructed by colleges and universities in the 1920s, a decade in which college football emerged as one of the major spectator sports in the nation. Photo 0001027, University of Illinois Archives.

A primary example of that sort of player was the University of Illinois running back Harold "Red" Grange. A graduate of Wheaton High School in Wheaton, Illinois, a suburb of Chicago, Grange became a member of the UI's football team his sophomore year.[21] By his junior year he was a star, named to the recently created All-America football team of outstanding players throughout the country.[22] That year, on October 18, 1924, in a game against Michigan, Grange's performance—he ran for four touchdowns in twelve minutes and would subsequently run for another and pass for a sixth[23]—would gain even more national attention.

After his spectacular junior-year performance in the 1924 Michigan game, Grange left the University of Illinois at the end of the season, not having earned a degree, to join the NFL's Chicago Bears for the 1925 season. Grange's decision was widely criticized on two principal grounds, one of which may appear surprising to contemporary American followers of college and professional football. The first was somewhat reminiscent of the critiques of professionalism in association football. Grange's decision to play football for pay rather than for sport was said to be somewhat unseemly, disparaging the value of a college education.[24] At the same time it was said to be misguided, because the quality of play in the NFL was inferior to that of the leading college teams. Grange would have had better competition on the football field, that line of comments suggested, if he had remained at Illinois, playing Big Ten opponents.[25] The reaction to Grange's turning professional suggests that in at least one of the indigenous American sports begin played in the 1920s, an amateur ethos had been established.

THE CONTINUING MARGINALITY OF SOCCER IN THE GOLDEN AGE OF AMERICAN SPORT

Our attention, in this portion of the chapter, has been directed at surveying the growth of other American team sports in the early and middle years of the twentieth century, in order to place the status of soccer in those years in context. But the tremendous growth of college gridiron football from the 1920s on, coupled with the emergence of the NFL as a going concern, needs to be mentioned as one of the factors that retarded the development of soccer in America.

Gridiron football was a direct competitor to association football from its origins. As we have seen, it was played at the same time of year and initially at the same places, colleges and universities. The two games sprang from the same root, the version of English football that survived as the game of rugby. Gridiron football was initially a rougher version of rugby football, emphasizing running with the ball more than kicking it, and more extensive physical contact, and association football became a different version of the rugby game, eventually altogether eliminating running, hacking, and tackling with arms. The comments quoted in the preceding chapter, reflecting the perception among some early twentieth-century observers that gridiron football was a dangerous sport and soccer a much safer one, suggest that early twentieth-century commentators did indeed identify gridiron and association football as competitors.

Thus as gridiron football expanded significantly in American colleges and became established as a professional sport, it arguably reduced the opportunities for soccer to establish itself in either venue. Although only a limited number of college students could play intercollegiate gridiron football successfully, some of those might well have been successful college soccer players. But to the extent that soccer teams existed at colleges and universities, they garnered only a minuscule amount of attention compared to football teams. Since they were not revenue-raising operations, colleges and universities had limited incentives to provide financial support to soccer teams in terms of facilities, recruitment of players and coaches, or publicity. In contrast to football teams, college and university soccer teams were largely anonymous entities, attention to them confined to a limited circle of players and supporters.

The marginal status of soccer on college campuses during the years when many other college sports were expanding meant the means for developing professional soccer players in the United States in the early and mid-twentieth centuries was essentially nonexistent. In gridiron football and basketball, colleges and universities served as the major areas from which players on American professional teams in those sports were recruited. In contrast, players in most American professional soccer clubs came from the semiprofessional ranks, where most players were blue-collar workers in industries identified with particular ethnic communities. There was not a significant pool of such players. Professional European players had few incentives to move to America, where both the level of professional soccer and its economic success was inferior to that of the leagues in Great Britain and western Europe; and most semiprofessional American soccer players relied in part on income from their jobs and could not afford to play professional soccer full-time. Given the limited number of prospective professional soccer players from ethnic communities, the absence of a large pool of college soccer players in the first five decades of the twentieth century ended up being a major barrier to the development of a high level of play in professional American soccer leagues.

At the close of World War I, as we have seen, three markers of the state of professional soccer in the United States existed. The first was administrative control of the game. In 1913 the United States Football Association came into existence just as the American Football Association was being largely displaced by its rival, the American Amateur Football Association, which secured FIFA recognition the following year. The USFA's only conspicuous enterprise was running the National Challenge Cup, starting in 1914, and seeking to encourage professional clubs from different sections of the country to enter the league. Although that effort would eventually produce a truly intersectional competition, in the years between 1914 and 1919 nearly all the clubs entering were from the Northeast, with a club from Brooklyn winning the tournament in 1914, one from Fall River winning in 1917, and Bethlehem Steel winning the next four years.[26] By 1919 the USFA had persuaded St. Louis clubs to enter the cup competition, and St. Louis would win the cup in 1920 and 1922, as well as being a finalist in 1921, 1923, 1926, 1929, and 1932.[27]

The National Challenge Cup competition would represent American professional soccer's second marker. It was held every year from 1914 through the 1950s, and although eastern teams continued to appear as finalists in most of those years, clubs from St. Louis, Detroit, Chicago, Cleveland, and Los Angeles won the competition or made it to the finals in thirty-four of those forty-six years.[28] In addition, the American Cup existed until 1922, and some clubs who entered the National Challenge Cup also continued to play in that competition.[29] The American Cup, however, was clearly a regional event, one dominated between 1913 and 1922 by Bethlehem Steel and clubs from northern New Jersey.[30] Attendance at National Challenge Cup matches reached a high of over 100,000 in 1922–23, in which 132 clubs entered the competition, and that year the USFA generated $112,000 in receipts. But receipts declined sharply thereafter. Although the decline may have initially been connected to worsening economic conditions in the 1930s, it continued into the 1950s, when prosperity had returned.[31]

The third marker was the presence of professional soccer leagues. In 1919, among the several semipro leagues in existence, three stood out in terms of the quality of the teams and the relative consistency of play. Those were the National Association Football League, whose founding in 1895 by a group of clubs clustered in northern New Jersey was recounted in chapter 3; the Southern New England Soccer League, which, we have also seen, was created by clubs in Boston and southeastern Massachusetts in 1907; and the St. Louis League, created in 1915 and composed of only four clubs, but whose teams would do exceptionally well in the National Challenge Cup after they first entered it in the 1919–20 competition, reaching the final five years in a row between that year and 1924 and winning the championship once.[32]

Comparisons of those markers with the state of English football around the same time, and with the state of other American college and professional sports, serve to demonstrate the marginal status of professional soccer in the United States as the golden age of American sport dawned. The Football Association had canceled the FA Cup and international matches in July 1915 in response to the outbreak of World War I, only allowing league clubs to continue to play informal matches, with no player remuneration, a policy it would continue until the end of the war.[33] In addition, differences between FIFA and the Football Association over the playing of matches between clubs from England, Scotland, and Wales and clubs from countries affiliated with the Central Powers had led to the withdrawal of the association from FIFA in 1920.[34] But once the Great War concluded, English domestic football rapidly came back to life, and continued to grow: by 1922 the Football League had expanded to four divisions, comprising a total of eighty-six clubs, more than double the number in 1915. That number increased the next year to eighty-eight.[35] In 1953 the official historian of the Football Association would describe the state of the game in the 1920s:

> The overhanging shadows had passed. [Association] Football, rising up once more, stepped into the brave new world. The new era that followed was to bring an even greater enthusiasm for the game. Players and clubs multiplied and grew like mushrooms in the night; crowd

> attendance soared skywards; the financial aspect reached heights undreamed of a few years back.[36]

SOCCER IN AMERICAN COLLEGES

In the United States, as we have seen, nearly all of the individual sports and the teams they comprised expanded their spectator appeal in the 1920s, while two professional sports leagues, the National Hockey League and National Football League, established themselves and began to experience healthy growth. College football enjoyed tremendous growth and became a lucrative enterprise, with college teams emerging as the primary revenue-raising operations for their respective universities' athletic departments.[37] In contrast, soccer remained a sport played in relative obscurity at only a handful of colleges and universities. As early as 1911 the National Collegiate Athletic Association (the successor to the Intercollegiate Athletic Association), in the wake of the tours by the Pilgrims and Corinthians and amid the popular perception that gridiron football was perhaps too dangerous a game for college athletes to play, established its Committee on Association Football,[38] and in the next two years college newspapers as well as *Spalding's Official Soccer Football Guide* (a publication on American soccer issued annually between 1904 and 1924 by the A. G. Spalding Sporting Goods Company in St. Louis) claimed that soccer was spreading faster on campuses than any other sport.[39] But although the Intercollegiate Soccer Football Association (ISFA), dedicated to expanding and facilitating soccer competition among colleges, had existed since 1906, soccer failed to establish itself outside a group of eastern colleges.[40] Moreover, financial support for soccer teams was meager[41] and spectator attendance at matches very low.[42] A committee of the ISFA would determine the "national champion" at the end of a season, but there was no postseason tournament and the committee was dominated by alumni of the University of Pennsylvania.[43] By 1939, eighty colleges and universities had intercollegiate soccer teams, but there was still no postseason tournament.[44]

One of the strongest indications of the relative stature of gridiron and soccer football on college campuses in the three decades after 1920 was the gap between the rules under which American collegians played and those employed everywhere else. The rules of college gridiron football were identical to those of the professional version: the sport, after all, had been invented on American college campuses. But in 1925 intercollegiate soccer matches were divided into twenty-two minute quarters, while the rest of the soccer world employed two forty-five minute halves. There were no overtime periods in association football, but American colleges had instituted them even before the start of World War I. In 1949 two referees were instituted in college soccer, but the rest of the soccer world, including American professional leagues, continued to have only one. One-handed throw-ins were permitted in college soccer for a brief time in the late 1940s, and in 1950 college soccer replaced throw-ins with kick-ins. Most significantly, college soccer allowed liberal substitution of players, progressing from two in 1913 to five in 1934. In 1954 a limit on resubstitutions was removed, meaning that players could be subbed in and out through the entire length of games at will.[45]

Another sign of gridiron football's influence was the positioning of college soccer players on the field. Association football had emphasized fluidity of play, with players moving back, forth, and sideways to gain space to receive and make controlled passes. Offensive and defensive players were not rigidly stationed in designated areas; although they concentrated on particular areas in the field, they were free to move out of them as play required. The inexperience of many American college soccer coaches, few of whom had played association football, led them to analogize to gridiron football in determining team formations on the field. As in the UK until the mid-1920s, the formations consisted of a goalkeeper, two fullbacks, stationed deep on either side of the defensive portion of a field, three "halfbacks," spread across the midfield, and five forwards. There was a tendency in American soccer, as it developed in colleges, to have only the halfbacks venture into the offensive portion of the field, and then only as support for forwards. The offensive players, two wings, stationed near the sidelines in the offensive end, two "insides," who typically played behind the wings in the offensive midfield, and a "center forward," stationed in the center of the offensive portion of the field, rarely entered the defensive portion of the field.

American college soccer teams typically moved down the field in "formation," somewhat like a football team in possession of the ball. A "forward line" of players moved about the field in something like unison, with the wings and center forwards in advance of the insides, and insides followed by halfbacks. Wings typically dribbled the ball down sidelines until they met resistance from a defender (usually a fullback) and then "crossed" the ball to the center of the field, where it would hopefully be possessed by an inside or center forward. The game emphasized long passes from insides or halfbacks to wings or center forwards, which ideally would send the ball flying safely over the heads of the defenders and allow the recipients of the passes to run unobstructed toward the goal. When compared with soccer played elsewhere, the American college version was much less flexible and encouraged the specialization of positions. Wings and center forwards, for example, were discouraged from coming too far into the defensive portions of their teams' fields, lest they be out of position to receive long passes.

The positioning of college soccer players, and the offensive and defensive formations associated with the American college game as developed in the decades after 1920, meant that any soccer player who had played the game in college would need to make a considerable adjustment were he to join a semipro team. As late as the 1920s teams such as those of the University of Pennsylvania and Penn State University scheduled games against semi-pro clubs such as Bethlehem Steel or Altoona,[46] and on one occasion the Penn State college newspaper quoted the Penn State coach as noting that "professional soccer teams used a close style of play, emphasizing dribbling and short passes, while college booters depend upon long passes and aggressiveness to score goals."[47]

Thus even the mild growth of college soccer in the years from 1920 through the 1960s was unlikely to have had any positive effects on the development of professional soccer in the United States. The college game operated independently from the professional version, except for those rare times in the early decades of the twentieth century when college teams scheduled matches against professional clubs. This meant that even the limited pool of college players in the United States was, practically speaking, unavailable for recruitment by professional teams. College players played a different game, under different rules; because of their expectations about playing time and substitution, they had not trained under the same conditions as had professional players; and the level of play in colleges was not high, mainly because of a combination of a limited number of coaches with playing experience and the unfortunate tendency of college teams to analogize the positioning of their players to that of gridiron rather than association football. When the Penn State soccer team, which had compiled an outstanding record for the previous two years, was invited to tour Scotland in the summer of 1934, it lost all its matches to local clubs—and by considerable margins.[48] After one contest an Inverness newspaper reported that "the Americans were outclassed in every department. . . . The general impression amongst the large crowd was that the visitors have a lot to learn about the game." Penn State had "not yet acquired the proper method of tackling," the correspondent felt; "their shooting was weak, and their combination [play] left much to be desired."[49]

THE AMERICAN SOCCER LEAGUE AND THE UNITED STATES FOOTBALL ASSOCIATION

In the midst of what, in retrospect, was an unpropitious environment for American professional soccer in the golden age of the 1920s, the first ambitious effort to create a professional soccer league, the American Soccer League (ASL), began play in the fall of 1921. The ASL was a combination of clubs from the two most prominent early twentieth-century semiprofessional leagues, the National Association Football League, which had originally been centered in northern New Jersey but by 1921 had expanded to include clubs from the New York area, Pennsylvania, and Holyoke, Massachusetts, and the Southern New England Soccer League, centered in southeastern Massachusetts and Rhode Island.[50]

In its initial season, 1921–22, the American Soccer League was composed of two clubs from southeastern New England and six others. The former set of clubs were J & P Coats, from Pawtucket, and Fall River United. The others were Philadelphia FC (actually the Bethlehem, Pennsylvania, club), New York FC, from New York City, Todd Shipyard from Brooklyn, clubs from Harrison and Jersey City, New Jersey, and the Holyoke Falcos from western Massachusetts.[51] The common denominator of all of the clubs was that they were located in cities with industrial factories, textiles in the case of Pawtucket, Fall River, Harrison, and Holyoke, various other types of manufacturing in the others. That feature of the league would, as it turned out, contribute to its demise in 1933.

All of the clubs in the American Soccer League were semiprofessional, with some players, even if nominally employees of firms, being paid exclusively to play soccer. Most of the members of the US team in the first World

Cup of 1930, where the United States defeated Belgium and Paraguay in early rounds before losing to Argentina and then to Brazil, were players in the league,[52] suggesting that its level of play was at least moderately high.

There were three distinctive features of the American Soccer League during its years of operation. The first was that although the impetus for its formation was similar to that of the English Football League—creating an organization whose members could play against one another on a regular basis, establishing rivalries, and hopefully boosting attendance—its members never achieved the stability of English league clubs. In the eleven full and partial seasons in which the league recorded standings, clubs entered and withdrew from the league nearly every year. Not a single club remained in the league for all of those seasons, and only three, Bethlehem Steel, the Fall River Marksmen, and J & P Coats from Pawtucket, were in the league for more than half of the seasons.[53] New clubs replaced exiting clubs in the same cities on some occasions, but on others a club from a new city would replace one that had withdrawn. In short, instead of the stability fostered by regular, long-term rivalries among the same clubs that marked the English leagues, the American Soccer League was marked by a constant turnover of club franchises and cities. The changes in clubs were not primarily a function of the league's expansion from an original eight teams to twelve, beginning in the 1924–25 season. Of the eight clubs that founded the league, three withdrew after the initial season,[54] two of them being replaced by clubs in the same city, which established a pattern of at least one new club replacing another, and regularly two or three clubs being replaced, in every year of the league's existence.

The second distinguishing feature of the American Soccer League was that from its origins it was an effort to compete with, rather than complement, the United States Football Association. A similar purpose may have contributed to the formation of the English Football League, some of whose most successful clubs were chafing under the Football Association's emphasis on the FA Cup competition, but the league and the association eventually coexisted. The USFA never achieved a comparable coexistence with the ASL; indeed for much of its existence the ASL openly defied the USFA's efforts to regulate it. That was ironic, since the person who had been the guiding force in the USFA's replacement of the American Football Association as the principal body administrating US soccer, and in securing

FIFA recognition of the USFA, was none other than Thomas Cahill, also the leader in the formation of the American Soccer League.[55]

We have seen that Cahill, with the support of his employer, the A. G. Spalding Sporting Goods Company of St. Louis, had become heavily involved with the activities of the American Amateur Football Association when it was first created to challenge the American Football Association in 1912. When that successful challenge resulted in the USFA succeeding the AFA as the acknowledged representative of professional soccer in the United States, Cahill was named honorary secretary of the USFA, a position without remuneration but with ample administrative duties. Some of those duties involved attempting to make peace among sectional semipro leagues; others centered on Cahill's relations with the USFA president, G. Randolph Manning, who was a strong supporter of the Football Association, whereas one of Cahill's goals was to develop American soccer as an independent entity featuring American-born players. After clashing with Manning over the United States' failure to send a soccer team to the 1920 Olympics—Manning believed that Cahill had undermined that effort—as well as over the USFA's decision not to follow the Football Association's withdrawal from FIFA in 1920 after it refused to play matches against clubs from the former Central Powers, Cahill concluded that he would be better off leaving the USFA. In an interview with the *St. Louis Post-Dispatch* in November 1920, he said that he had "several things in mind" for American professional soccer, but could not "accomplish these . . . if I am tied down to the secretaryship." Among his plans were "to put the game on a paying basis" and "to form a national soccer league." To accomplish the latter goal, he acknowledged, "a lot of money is needed," and he was determined to raise it.[56]

After Cahill announced that he was leaving the USFA, that organization attempted to entice him to stay by awarding him a $2,000 honorarium and membership for life,[57] but Cahill resigned and immediately began fundraising for what a year later would become the American Soccer League.[58] He approached clubs in the National Association Football League and the Southern New England Soccer League, setting a franchise fee of $2,000 and pledging to play games on Sundays (thought to be an ideal day for spectators, although states such as Massachusetts and Pennsylvania prohibited Sunday play), and to make arrangements for ASL clubs to play matches in baseball parks or athletic stadiums, where spectators could sit under cover.[59] Through his numerous contacts with owners of enterprises that sponsored semiprofessional clubs, Cahill was an ideal person to organize the ASL, and he served as the league's secretary even after the USFA reappointed him as its secretary after his replacement, James Scholefield, disappeared in November 1921 along with $1,200 of the association's assets, and was not found until three years later, living under a different name and working as an accountant in Greensboro, North Carolina.[60]

Between 1922 and 1924 Cahill served as secretary of both the USFA and the AFL, years in which the league, despite its regular turnover of clubs, did sufficiently well to expand to twelve clubs for the 1924–25 season. A signal of Cahill's prominence was that he was asked to manage the US entry at the 1924 Olympics. But both the USFA and the AFL showed signs of internal turbulence during those years, much of it centering on Cahill.

In the 1922–23 final of the National Challenge Cup, held in Harrison, New Jersey, 10,000 spectators attended. But the match, between a club from Patterson, New Jersey, and the St. Louis–based Scullin Steel club, ended in a tie, and Scullin Steel, a number of whose players also played professional baseball, said that it could only play a rematch in St. Louis because the baseball season was about to open. The USFA, which had a longtime policy of staging cup finals in the northeast, refused. An effort by Cahill to resolve the matter failed, and the USFA declared Scullin to have forfeited the final, infuriating USFA members from St. Louis, who retaliated at the USFA annual meeting by helping vote the existing USFA president, George Healy from Detroit, out of office. Healy was replaced by Peter Peel from Chicago, with whom Cahill had had antagonistic relations during Peel's earlier USFA presidency from 1917 to 1919. After Peel's election, he was named Cahill's deputy on the 1924 Olympic committee.[61]

It was not long before Cahill and Peel were at loggerheads on that committee, Cahill claiming that Peel had been "insulting and domineering" toward him, and Peel suggesting that Cahill sought to run the entire Olympic operation himself.[62] Matters came to a head at a meeting of the committee the evening before the National Challenge Cup final in 1923. After criticizing Cahill at the meeting, Peel loudly pronounced when it adjourned that he could "take care of Cahill mentally or physically at any time." When Peel made his remarks, Cahill was in the process of cutting a plug of tobacco with a pocket knife. After hearing Peel, Cahill, according to his account, advanced toward Peel, putting the knife away and taking off his glasses. Two other persons intervened to prevent a physical confrontation, and Cahill left the room.[63] Peel subsequently asserted that Cahill had assaulted him with a knife in a statement to a Chicago newspaper, who printed Peel's version of events.[64] The USFA subsequently dismissed Cahill as its secretary for "insubordination and incompetence" and removed him as head of the 1924 Olympic effort, stating that he had "displayed a flare of temper which could not be passed without notice." Peel claimed that "the recent actions of the ex-secretary, . . . when he showed his true colors, were a culmination of many such acts to which national officers were subjected by Cahill in the past." Cahill's removal, Peel concluded, "marks the end of his tyrannical reign, and soccer fans and followers will undoubtedly relish his relegation to the scrap heap."[65]

But Cahill survived. In the 1924 meeting of the USFA a compromise was reached: Cahill apologized for losing his temper and was awarded a $2,000 honorarium and retained as a life member, although he was not reappointed as secretary. Three years later, after the existing secretary decided not to continue, Peel announced that he would consider all applications for that position "on their merits," with "all previous history of this organization" being "lost sight of," a clear signal that Cahill could be considered a candidate, and Cahill was subsequently reappointed.[66]

In the years between 1924 and 1927 Cahill devoted his efforts to the ASA, with initial success. The league seemed to be on firmer ground by 1924, and in an effort to increase its revenues that year, it declined to have its clubs enter the National Challenge Cup competition and staged its own tournament, accompanied by clubs from St. Louis. The result demonstrated how dependent the National Challenge Cup's financial success was on having the stronger professional clubs participate. In 144 Challenge Cup matches in the 1924–25 competition, the USFA drew less than 56,000 fans, whereas the ASA/St. Louis Professional Cup competition drew almost 52,000 for only 11 matches.[67] In 1925 the *St. Louis Post-Dispatch* commented that "the shadow of Cahill's newly built American Soccer League fell athwart the USFA and blotted it out."[68]

Cahill had a clear agenda for American professional soccer: to build soccer-specific stadiums to house spectators watching games in the winter or, at a minimum, rent baseball stadiums for that purpose; to recognize the competition that gridiron football represented and the need not to stage matches on Saturday afternoons in cities where college football games were being played; and to build up a cadre of American-born soccer players to make professional soccer less dependent upon foreign players and immigrant audiences.[69] Despite Cahill's efforts, none of those goals were realized by the mid-1920s, the most propitious time for American professional soccer's growth after the end of World War I. The ASL struggled to avoid Saturday-afternoon matches because some states prohibited athletic contests on Sundays, and the workweek for many blue-collar jobs extended through Saturday mornings. And, partially because of the state of soccer in colleges and partially because the appeal of professional soccer was largely confined to cities with immigrant populations, developing a substantial pool of American-born talent proved elusive. The dominant clubs in the ASL continued to have a number of foreign-born players on their rosters.

As Cahill struggled to achieve his goals for the ASL, a palace revolt was brewing. When revenues did not increase in the 1925–26 season, some New England clubs considered withdrawing from the league and forming one of their own, possibly including Canadian franchises. In 1926 the incumbent president of the ASL, Fred Smith, was replaced by Bill Cunningham, a sportswriter for the *Boston Post*, with the expectation that Cunningham would serve as a national commissioner of professional soccer leagues in the United States, akin to the commissioner of major-league baseball.[70] Cunningham was also named secretary of the league, and Cahill was "retained in an advisory capacity, with a salary to be determined at a later date."[71] It turned out that this position did not consist of any major responsibilities, and Cahill resigned, telling the *St. Louis Post-Dispatch* that he "considered the offer of an 'advisory' post a demotion and a reduction in salary, and it looked as if these fellows thought I had reached the end of my usefulness."[72] By 1927 he was temporarily out of professional soccer, and when he returned to the USFA as secretary a year later, he warned that the ASL was a "grave danger" to the USFA.[73]

Initially the USFA, under Cunningham, had sought to placate the ASL by giving its clubs greater latitude to institute changes in the game, such as shirt numbers and player substitutions.[74] The ASL had begun to disregard

FIFA's rules on the signing of international players, and in 1927 FIFA threatened to expel the USFA because of the ASL's activities. When the USFA supported FIFA, some ASL owners, led by Charles Stoneham, who owned the New York Nationals in the ASL and the New York Giants in baseball's National League, proposed that the ASL withdraw its clubs from the 1928–29 National Challenge Cup. Stoneham's ostensible rationale was possible conflicts between cup matches and the ASL's schedule, but his action was understood by both sides to be a challenge to the USFA's authority to control American professional soccer.[75]

When Stoneham's proposal was issued to the ASL clubs, it was accepted by a majority, but four clubs who had opposed it— Bethlehem Steel, the New Bedford Whalers, the New York Giants, and the Newark Skeeters—refused to withdraw from cup competition and were suspended by the league. The USFA responded by suspending the ASL, depriving it of official sanctioning by FIFA.[76] Then Cahill, by now fully estranged from the leadership of the ASL, moved to form a rival league, the Eastern Professional Soccer League, which included the clubs barred from the ASL and several clubs from the New York City area, including New York Hakoah, which fielded a very strong team mainly composed of Jewish players from Vienna, one of the leading European centers of association football. Bethlehem Steel, New Bedford, and Hakoah were the dominant clubs in the EPSL, which was only in existence for one season.[77]

At this point a soccer war had begun in earnest. The ASL was declared an "outlaw" league by the USFA for its 1928–29 season. The USFA enlisted the support of national federations of other countries and put pressure on the ASL to cease its defiant posture. In early October 1929, the "war" was settled; the ASL, which had begun its second "outlaw" season without the four EPSL clubs, agreed to reinstate them and operate as before, calling itself the Atlantic Coast League, which included Bethlehem Steel, New Bedford, and the New York Nationals, as well as Hakoah, in a 1929–30 season.[78] Cahill declared in early 1929 that the ASL rebels had "absolutely failed in their effort to wreck the USFA,"[79] but the sports editor of the *New York Telegram*, writing that same year, saw things differently. "At present," he claimed, "there are three or four contesting leagues and associations" in professional soccer. "They put on games which draw less than 100 spectators on numerous occasions." They "bicker, yap, fight and tear each other's reputations to shreds." They had even gone so far, he suggested, as attempting to deport overseas players on the ground that they were "nonartists" under the immigration laws.[80]

OVERSEAS PLAYERS IN THE ASL

The *Telegram*'s comments pointed up the third distinctive feature of the American Soccer League. From its origins it had concentrated on recruiting players, and in some instances entire teams, from overseas rather than seeking to fill club rosters with American-born players. There were two reasons for this emphasis. One was that the owners of ASL clubs sensed that in the 1920s, with the Football Association barring its clubs from playing games against clubs from the former Central Powers, and the rebellion in Ireland reducing contacts between Irish and English football clubs, there were enhanced opportunities to recruit players from the United Kingdom. They responded by offering some of those players high salaries. Secondly, the ASA recognized that its principal spectators for matches would come from ethnic communities in the United States. Its teams were overwhelmingly from cities with established immigrant populations, where association football had been played since the late nineteenth century. Two American cities with strong concentrations of native-born players, Chicago and St. Louis, never joined the ASL, primarily because of its distance from the eastern cities from which the league had sprung. The ASL was, despite Cahill's strong interest in developing American-born professional players, very much peopled by players who had either been born overseas and retained their citizenship in other nations, or players from first-generation immigrant families who had grown up in ethnic communities.

The settlement of the "soccer war" might have resulted in improved fortunes for the ASL in the 1930s, but the onset of the Great Depression, which particularly affected the industrial enterprises that hired immigrants, sponsored clubs, and contributed to the salaries of some players, shrunk the revenues of clubs to the point of no return. In 1930 the Bethlehem Steel franchise, arguably the club with the longest run of consistent success in the ASL since its founding, disbanded.[81] A year later the ASL itself ended its schedule in the middle of the year, and the St. Louis league was on the verge of collapse.[82] In 1935 the *St. Louis Post Dispatch* pronounced a kind of obituary, not only for that league but for American professional soccer itself:

> Soccer was an infant left on the doorstep of the United States. It has been raised rather haphazardly and has been kicked around carelessly because no niche for it could be found. For six months of the year . . . soccer is shouldered aside by baseball. In the fall, when its next best opportunity comes along, the country goes mad over college football. In the winter . . . icy fields and biting winds drive supporters of soccer to the indoor sports of hockey, basketball, track and skating. There is, therefore, no place in the United States sports calendar into which this really fine game can fit. Because it came along after all our American pastimes were fully developed, it is now practically an outcast, almost a pariah.[83]

Although adversely affected by the Great Depression, professional baseball, football, and ice hockey would emerge as profitable enterprises after World War II,[84] but professional soccer nearly disappeared from view. A successor to the ASL, with the same name, came into being in 1933, but it was even more markedly an ethnic league, its clubs clustering in northeastern cities with immigrant populations, bearing names such as the Kearny Scots, the Kearny Irish, the Philadelphia Ukranian Nationals, New York Hakoah, and Brooklyn Hispano.[85] For financial reasons it eschewed the recruitment of overseas players, so its rosters were composed primarily of American-born players from immigrant households. Its only significant revenue events were matches between clubs from overseas on tours and local teams. In nearly all respects the second version of the ASL, which remained in existence until 1983, was evidence of the distinctly marginal status of American professional soccer for much of the twentieth century.[86]

SOCCER'S MARGINALITY IN THE GOLDEN AGE OF AMERICAN SPORT

Why did professional soccer fail to enhance its visibility and attractiveness to American fan bases in decades in which some other professional team sports succeeding in so doing? Some reasons have been advanced throughout this chapter.

If we recall the factors contributing to the phenomenal growth of association football in England, and subsequently throughout the United Kingdom, in the late nineteenth and early twentieth centuries, it is noteworthy that none of them were features of professional soccer in America. First and foremost among those was the control of football, throughout England and into Scotland, Ireland, and Wales, by the Football Association and its affiliated associations and leagues. Over time the FA standardized the rules of the game; dealt with the issues of importation and professionalism of players; established a cup competition that continued to attract more clubs and generate more revenue; tolerated the formation of the English Football League; countenanced the initiation of the retain-and-transfer system that prevented clubs from getting into bidding wars for players but also allowed them to profit from transfer fees if they chose to do so; oversaw the leagues' establishment of tiers of divisions, with promotion and relegation, thereby retaining a constant affiliation between clubs and towns, counties, cities, or regions while maintaining incentives for all clubs in a league to compete throughout the season; and initiated the creation of national teams playing international matches.

There were several side effects of this command-and-control management style. Club franchises remained in continuous existence over time because their owners had no ability to move them without FA or Football League permission, and few financial incentives to do so, since their constancy promoted local fan bases and generated rivalries with other clubs. The combination of FA Cup competition and league competitions allowed stronger clubs to generate more revenue for themselves, but the FA to retain revenue from the last stages of cups. The retain-and-transfer system prevented wealthier clubs from accumulating the most competent players and allowed weaker clubs to buttress their finances by attaching transfer fees to their gifted players. Perhaps most significantly, those engaged in the ownership and management of club franchises were expected not to use revenues they generated for personal gain, but to plow them back into the franchise. Owning or managing a football club was not regarded as a means of acquiring wealth.

It may be startling, when a comparison of the management structure of association football in the UK with that employed for professional soccer clubs in America is made, that virtually none of the features associated with English football crossed the Atlantic. There never was a command-and-control structure for professional soccer in the United States comparable to that in England. Soccer clubs in the States were initially semiprofessional ventures mainly affiliated with industrial enterprises. They may well have been first designed not as profit-making ventures but as recreational opportunities for workers, most of whom were recently arrived immigrants. But when they developed the potential to generate revenue, they were treated by their owners as businesses. If the communities in which they were located failed to support them at the gate, they were moved, sold, or disbanded. When some club franchises in particular regions formed leagues to facilitate play and generate revenue, the clubs kept the proceeds of matches. The members of leagues passed in and out of existence, as did leagues themselves, without any oversight by a national body comparable to the Football Association or Football League, even though both the AFA and the AAFA were initially modeled on the FA.

Promotion and relegation among clubs in a league was never initiated. Nor was a retain-and-transfer system. Players passed between clubs seemingly at will, and clubs came and went frequently. In that atmosphere it was harder both to forge connections between clubs and localities—although some communities, such as Fall River, New Bedford, Pawtucket, and Kearny, managed to do that—and to develop player loyalties to clubs, since players could leave at any time and clubs might vanish.

Most strikingly, perhaps, the organizational bodies overseeing professional football in America instituted nothing like the Football Association and Football League's control over clubs participating in the sport. Initially the Football Association controlled all of the activities of affiliated clubs in England, and when a group of clubs from northern cities revolted against that practice and formed the Football League, the FA tolerated that development rather than resisting it. In the United States the AFA and the USFA essentially did nothing except establish the National Challenge Cup and become affiliated with FIFA. When the ASA came into being, it was without the USFA's support, and the two organizations were primarily competitors during the years they overlapped. Although the USFA seems to have attempted to establish rules for the ASA after its formation, when the ASA challenged those by withdrawing from the National Challenge Cup, the USFA responded by allowing the ASA to set its own rules and practices. An important semiprofessional league in America, the St. Louis league, had no connection to either the USFA or the ASA, even though its clubs regularly and successfully participated in the National Challenge Cup.

The USFA had no control over the development of soccer in colleges and universities, and the college game developed along different lines, making it harder for professional clubs to recruit college players. When the ASA began recruiting overseas players and FIFA objected to its recruiting practices, FIFA had to threaten the USFA with suspension to introduce any pressure on the ASA. The ASA twice defied the USFA by withdrawing its clubs from participating in the National Challenge Cup in the 1920s, making it clear how much the USFA needed quality clubs in its competition to generate revenue, and how dependent it was on the cup competition to keep itself afloat.

Why were the early twentieth-century governing bodies of US professional soccer so ineffectual? Why were the owners of professional clubs—hardly lucrative operations at their founding—disinclined to accept any command-and-control oversight of their operations, and the governing bodies apparently so reluctant to seek to impose one? To be sure, there was no American tradition of command-and-control management of sports franchises. Owners of professional baseball, football, and hockey teams were entrepreneurs. Some were independently wealthy individuals with aspirations to be thought of as sportsmen, but others were eager to make profits. Yet major-league baseball owners accepted something of a command-and-control structure, agreeing to restrict their ability to move franchises and initiating a reserve clause system that depressed player salaries and limited players' opportunities to move from one team to another. No such restrictions were placed on the owners of American professional soccer clubs. Despite Thomas Cahill's considerable energy, awareness of the organization of English and European soccer clubs, and keen sense of the obstacles that American professional soccer faced in becoming an established sport, the USFA did almost nothing to control the structure of professional soccer leagues during his tenure. It seems to have directed most of its time toward infighting among its executives or efforts to defend itself against the ASA.

Then there was the interconnected question of weather, sports seasons, and stadiums. From the early decades of the twentieth century persons interested in promoting semiprofessional soccer as a revenue-generating activity seem to have been assumed that the sport could only be played in the "winter" months ("winter" stretching from the close to the opening of the baseball season) because baseball had established itself as the predominant

American spring and summer game. Something like that seasonal approach to sport existed in England, with cricket being regarded as a summer activity, and association (or rugby) football as winter ones. But when association football began to become established in pockets of the United States in the early twentieth century, those interested in the game's growth were surely aware what playing soccer in the winter meant. Those first pockets were in the Northeast or Midwest, regions with harsh winters. If one were to seek in those regions to play soccer through the fall, winter, and early spring, there would be ice or snow on the ground, frigid temperatures, and generally hostile conditions through much of that season. It would be difficult to play matches in those conditions, and difficult for spectators to watch them.

This would seem to mean, as Cahill repeatedly maintained, that successful professional American soccer franchises could not thrive without adequate stadiums, meaning places where spectators could watch a game in relative comfort, sheltered from the elements. But although Cahill spoke wistfully of the USFA constructing a model stadium that could seat up to 50,000 spectators, perhaps completely covered in the fashion of Sweden's Stockholm Olympic Stadium,[87] nothing like that ever materialized in the early twentieth century. The only stadiums available to soccer clubs were owned by baseball clubs, and their configuration did not suit soccer particularly well. Some athletic fields had a modicum of cover, but rarely enough to provide ample shelter. Gridiron football stadiums were out of use for most of the fall. And no soccer-style stadiums were built in America in the first half of the twentieth century, although they existed in many other countries.[88]

The final factor worth considering involves Cahill's desire to "Americanize" of the sport, and the connection of that "Americanization" to ethnicity. Cahill believed that soccer in the US could not grow without the participation of a significant pool of American-born players. He wanted the USFA to mount campaigns, which he referred to as "propaganda,"[89] to establish soccer in high schools and to build up the game in colleges. Other than Cahill himself in an occasional speech, nobody in the USFA or the ASA seems to have been concerned with developing American-born players. The first version of the ASA consciously recruited foreign players, and its clubs, nearly all of them located in cities with ethnic identities, played to audiences largely composed of immigrants or their first-generation offspring. Most of the resident American players in semiprofessional clubs or leagues were from immigrant families. In the next chapter we will see that in decades in which US restrictions on immigration tightened and in which a fair amount of nativist attitudes were expressed in public discourse, the association of professional soccer with immigrant groups certainly discouraged the sport's introduction in public high schools, and very likely contributed to its marginality.

One can only imagine what might have been had the priorities of the AFA and the USFA been different. Suppose those organizations had mounted in the 1920s, when the American economy was on an upward path, campaigns to raise money for soccer-only stadiums. That money was raised for college football stadiums, and it did not come only from graduates of those colleges. Would American audiences had been receptive? And, if so, would skillfully constructed soccer stadiums have generated a comfortable experience for spectators in soccer's winter?

Or suppose those who directed the AFA and the USFA had convinced soccer club owners to adopt a command-and-control management structure comparable to that of the Football Association. Suppose they had been convinced to maintain clubs for long intervals in particular communities, to plow profits back into those clubs, to form clubs into leagues divided into different levels of competence, featuring promotion and relegation, and to adopt retain-and-transfer systems or other devices limiting clubs' ability to bid for players' services or players' ability to move from club to club. Suppose the presence of clubs established over long periods in communities had generated interest in soccer among youth in those communities, resulting in an expanding pool of American players.

There were uphill battles for professional soccer in the United States in the golden age of the 1920s and succeeding decades. But there had been an uphill battle for gridiron football in colleges and universities prior to World War I, and yet that sport—which far fewer persons were suited to play and which was arguably a far less spectator-friendly sport than soccer—had grown, and when a professional version began in the 1920s, it eventually flourished. Professional hockey and basketball ended up having comparable histories. It seems plain, from contemporary experience, that multiple professional sports are capable of coexisting in America. So a fascinating puzzle surrounding the distinct marginality of soccer in the twentieth century's golden age of sport, and succeeding decades, remains. Was the marginal status of American professional soccer predetermined, or was it the product of myopia and incompetence on the part of governing bodies and the resultant failure to address issues necessary to soccer's growth in the United States? Had the enticing prospects of "the beautiful game" been ignored, or obscured, by those ostensibly responsible for its development? Or were there cultural intangibles lurking about, intangibles that resulted in gridiron football becoming a ritual of fall life in America while soccer remained in the shadows? That last question will continue to occupy us in succeeding chapters, the next of which takes a closer look at the state of men's soccer in American high schools and colleges in the three decades beginning in the 1920s.

Chapter Four

Men's College Soccer in the Twentieth Century

WE SAW IN the last chapter that one of the factors retarding the growth of soccer in the United States for much of the twentieth century was the inability of most American communities to establish a critical mass of persons who played and understood the game. When soccer was played and followed, that tended to be in particular cities and towns, such as St. Louis, Chicago; Pawtucket, Rhode Island; Fall River, Massachusetts; and a few towns in northern New Jersey, which combined large immigrant populations from European nations where soccer had been played with particular industries, such as textiles, that recruited European workers. Outside those places, soccer was neither a recreational nor a spectator sport.

One result of the limited connection of Americans to soccer, either as participants or fans, was the inability of professional soccer leagues to staff their clubs with players who had learned the game in the United States or to elicit broad bases of fan support. The teams in early and mid-twentieth-century soccer leagues tended to be distinctly local in character, associated with local businesses, and featured players on their rosters who were either citizens of other nations or immigrants who had learned the game elsewhere.

This chapter continues an inquiry begun in previous ones: Why didn't the English and continental European models through which soccer grew and developed as a participatory and spectator sport in the UK and western Europe become established in America? As we have seen, those models linked association football, as a recreational sport, to voluntary clubs and associations, establishing close connections among those entities, localities, and spectator fan bases. As association football grew within the UK from its London roots, clubs and associations formed for the purpose of playing football morphed into teams with distinct groups of local supporters, and rivalries among those teams emerged. The initial expansion of the Football Association and the emergence of the Football League were associated with an emphasis on the close connection of clubs to localities and fan bases. And when association football grew to the point where it could accommodate tiers or divisions of leagues, it emphasized the ties of league clubs to localities by keeping the local identities of clubs, regardless of their level of performance, intact through promotion and relegation. This meant that the connections between clubs and particular local fan bases were not at risk of being severed by a club's moving to another locality or going out of existence.

There was, however, another side effect of association football's being organized in the UK and western Europe through voluntary clubs and associations:[1] those clubs and associations provided a form of organization for youth soccer and encouraged boys and young men to play the sport. Anyone in a particular locality capable of playing football competently could do so by associating himself with a local football club. He did not need high social status, or wealth, or an ample amount of education to do so, and he was implicitly encouraged to begin playing the sport at a young age. We have seen that association football did not begin in England as a working-class sport—its origins were in public schools and universities, and it was initially played by "gentlemen"—but as it expanded, it did so through the same model through which it came into being, voluntary clubs and associations formed by people who wanted opportunities to play the game. Those clubs and associations came to include persons from all ranks of life. The early controversy over, and eventual acceptance of, professionalism within association football circles signaled the increasing tendency of the sport to detach itself from its upper-class origins.

There were two effects of the centering of soccer in the UK in voluntary clubs and associations. One was to cement the connections between football clubs and the localities in which they emerged, with respect both to fan support and to the identities of players, as association football grew and spread within the UK. Those who sought to join voluntary clubs and associations tended to live (or work, if they were professionals recruited from other locations) within a small radius of their club's headquarters, and the same was true of those who became nonplaying supporters of the clubs. The extent to which this local emphasis remains a defining feature of association football in the UK can be seen in the clubs that regularly make up the English Premier League, a first-division entity that arguably showcases the world's highest-quality soccer. The Premier League currently has twenty clubs. Of those, four are from various areas of London, two from sections of Liverpool, and two from the greater Manchester area. The remaining clubs are scattered over England and in some cases represent comparatively small cities, such as Wolverhampton, Bournemouth, and Brighton.[2]

The other result of UK soccer having been centered in voluntary clubs and associations was to encourage boys and young men to engage in it as a recreational activity. The comparative ease with which the game could be played—it only required some appropriate pitch with goalposts, goal lines, and sidelines, a soccer ball, suitable footwear, and at least twelve players—contributed to the growth of recreational youth soccer. But so did the existence of local football clubs and associations that organized teams to participate in FA and league matches, serving not only as bases for local fan support of clubs but also as aspirational entities. A young man living in a community that hosted a football club might grow up not only rooting for that club but hoping someday to play for it. Therefore, communities in the UK with football clubs—and, as mentioned, there were a lot of them—did not need specially organized youth soccer leagues to inspire young men's interest in playing soccer.

We have noted that professional soccer in the United States did not develop along the same lines as in the UK. Although the United States Soccer Federation was recognized by FIFA in 1913 as the controlling body for American soccer, the latter was never able to establish the command-and-control structure of the Football Association. Professional and semi-professional leagues came into and went out of existence for much of the twentieth century; promotion and relegation were never established, resulting in unsuccessful clubs disbanding or moving to other locations; and the leagues were unable to control the activities of club owners. The success of professional or semiprofessional teams largely turned on the fortuity of their being associated with localities with large immigrant populations. In such an atmosphere, professional soccer in the United States was unlikely to thrive, and it did not.

But it was not simply the organizational structure of early twentieth-century American professional soccer that contributed to the sport's failure to grow. We noted in the preceding chapter that for much of the twentieth century another factor hindered soccer from flourishing in the United States, either as a recreational or spectator sport. That was the organization of the sport of soccer, along with other team sports in the United States, by schools and colleges rather than by voluntary clubs and associations. This chapter delves deeper into the connection of team sports to high school and college education in twentieth-century America. It suggests that the delegation of the growth of soccer as a recreational sport in the United States to high schools, colleges, and universities, combined with the very limited attention paid to soccer by those who ran those institutions, largely kept soccer on the sidelines as a game that a great many Americans played or watched. This chapter focuses only on soccer played in high schools and colleges by young men; a separate chapter traces the history of women's soccer in the United States.

THE TRANSFORMATION OF AMERICAN PUBLIC EDUCATION IN THE EARLY TWENTIETH CENTURY

Higher education in the UK and western Europe was, and deep into the twentieth century continued to be, the province of a comparatively small segment of the population.[3] Although the cost of university education remained noticeably lower in the UK and western European nations than in the United States, barriers to entry to universities remained quite high. Nothing like the mid- and late twentieth-century proliferation of private and public colleges and universities in the United States, including community colleges with negligible admissions standards, occurred in western Europe and the UK. And to this day, widescale admission to universities in those nations—the equivalent of American colleges offering exclusively undergraduate education—has not generally surfaced in the UK and western Europe; instead admission is based on rigorous comprehensive examinations that unabashedly disqualify many students from matriculating at universities at all. In addition, sitting for those examinations is discretionary; a good many secondary school students elect not to take them, and some are even discouraged from doing so. This results in the default posture for most such students being that they will not attend a university.[4]

Secondary and higher education in the United States took quite a different path, beginning in the late nineteenth century.[5] Prior to then the American educational system had roughly resembled that of the UK and western Europe. There were some institutions of higher education, typically but not exclusively private, most of them affiliated with particular religious denominations, and all of them catering to persons of high social status.[6] Secondary education was not required in most states, but a few private secondary schools existed, modeled on the English public schools, that also catered to a high-status clientele. Not only did most Americans not attend colleges or universities, they did not complete the equivalent of a high school education.[7]

In nineteenth-century America, public education evolved in three distinct phases. In the eighteenth century, aside from efforts by reformers to develop literacy among "paupers and servants," public education was confined to a few New England states, notably Massachusetts and Connecticut, whose legislatures supported it as a form of indoctrinating the citizenry in particular religious dogmas. Between 1800 and 1825, some New England states passed laws requiring compulsory "education," by which was meant that parents had an obligation to teach their children to read and write.[8] Only Massachusetts mandated compulsory attendance at school, and that law was not rigorously enforced until the 1850s, when Massachusetts authorized its townships to arrest "habitual truants" who failed to attend.[9]

It was a considerable step from compulsory literacy to compulsory school attendance, but between 1825 and 1850 several states moved in that direction by establishing free public schools that were designed to educate all children, not merely those of paupers. In those states, children were induced, if not compelled, to attend public schools. By the 1850s every state in the Union had established free public schools, and children's attendance at them had become routine.[10]

As late as the American Civil War, however, only Massachusetts and Connecticut required attendance at public schools, and that mandate pertained only to children of certain ages for certain times of the year. In 1852 Massachusetts compelled all children between the ages of eight and fourteen to attend school, but this only for a minimum of thirteen weeks a year. By 1866 compulsory school attendance had been extended to children between the ages of seven and sixteen, and for at least six months. This still meant, however, that a student could drop out of school at seventeen and, until reaching that age, spend six months of the year outside the classroom.[11]

Between the end of the Civil War and the close of the nineteenth century, however, compulsory public education spread beyond New England to most of the rest of the nation. The processes by which federal public lands in the western half of the continental United States were distributed in the middle and later years of the nineteenth century, and settlers were encouraged to move westward to occupy those territories, were intimately connected to the spread of public education in the territories as they became states. By 1900 compulsory public education, and the presence of public universities, had become entrenched in most of the nation.[12]

The impact of widespread public education in the United States would eventually have profound effects on social mobility and the criteria associated with occupational and professional success. It was also to have an unintended consequence: the way in which, with one exception, team sports were established and organized in the twentieth century. The principal way in which those sports came to be organized was through schools and colleges rather than through voluntary clubs and associations.[13] In two of the three sports that became the principal participatory and spectator team sports of the early and middle twentieth century, gridiron football and basketball, persons who had excelled in playing those sports in high school often continued to play them in college, and when professional gridiron football and basketball leagues emerged in America, the players recruited to play in those leagues were successful college players. Gridiron football and basketball, unlike soccer, were indigenous American sports, "invented" in the United States and not, until comparatively late in the twentieth century, played elsewhere in the world.[14] American-born players with college experience would thus form the basis of professional gridiron football and basketball leagues when those leagues were launched, gridiron football in the 1920s and basketball after World War II.

Baseball was slightly different in that it had emerged earlier as a professional sport that was sufficiently attractive to spectators to allow its top leagues to establish franchise clubs with the potential to become financially successful. A prospective career in professional baseball thus could be lucrative for gifted young players, and in the first fifty years of major-league baseball's existence it was uncommon for conspicuously successful high school players to continue to play baseball in college rather than sign with major-league clubs.[15] When major-league baseball became entrenched in the early twentieth century, it developed a system of minor leagues, whose clubs were typically affiliated with the major-league franchises, partially to raise revenue but principally to allow the major-league clubs to develop young players.[16] A player signed by a major-league club out of high school was usually not playing at a level that would enable him to go directly to the major leagues; instead, the club was banking on his potential and his getting good instruction and experience in the minors. For at least the first half of the twentieth century, major-league teams were more confident about the level of competition and coaching that young players would get in the minors than on college teams. The opportunities for high-school-age players to enter the minor leagues served to open up baseball to a wider pool, since the pool could include young men with no aspirations to go to college.[17]

The result was that college baseball teams, which began to emerge along with other college team sports in early and mid-twentieth-century America, did not function as "farm clubs" for professional teams as did college gridiron and basketball teams. Nonetheless baseball, along with gridiron football and basketball, came to be regularly played by high school teams. Unlike in the UK and western Europe, where team sports were largely played and organized through clubs and associations,[18] the leading indigenous American team sports of the twentieth century, baseball, football, and basketball, were invariably played in high schools, both public and private.

What accounted for this difference between the organization of team sports in the UK and western Europe and that in America? The answer to that question is the unintended consequence alluded to earlier and briefly discussed in the preceding chapter. When, after 1890, public high schools and public as well as private colleges and universities proliferated in the United States, those educational institutions began to sweep athletic activities into their purview rather than allowing students to participate in them voluntarily, and independent of institutional supervision, as they did in the UK and Europe. The group of Cambridge-based football enthusiasts who first sought to standardize the rules of what would become association football in the late 1840s and the group of London-based players who established the Football Association in 1863 had no official connection to any particular secondary school or university. They had simply gotten together, as participants in a sport, to organize it in some fashion.

That way of integrating athletics (including team sports) with university education in the UK and western Europe was consistent with the prevalent attitude toward mixing all nonacademic and scholarly pursuits. In the late nineteenth and early twentieth centuries, public school and university educators in the UK believed that a healthy mix of academic and nonacademic activities was beneficial for young men. But they also believed that academic inquiries were a university's primary mission, and emphasized that conviction by putting the university's imprimatur on those inquiries rather than on nonacademic pursuits. Universities in the UK and western Europe thus declined to sponsor team sports in the late nineteenth and twentieth centuries despite their students' engagement in those sports, notably rugby, association football, cricket, and rowing. The only physical activity that administrators explicitly brought within university activities in those years was gymnastics, apparently because some of them believed in a close connection between gymnastic training and the development of mental faculties. In some European institutions, educators avoided even tacit encouragement of voluntary team sports for students, on the ground that such sports competed with gymnastics.[19]

While this attitude toward athletics remained in place in UK and other European universities (and in English public schools as well), those institutions also remained conspicuously elitist, serving only a small, normally affluent sector of the populations. In the United States in the same time period, however, public secondary schools and public colleges and universities were becoming symbols of an approach to education that emphasized the inclusion of large numbers of students in "comprehensive" schools that offered not only academic programs but extracurricular activities. One assumption made by proponents of this approach, we have seen, was that public high schools could be not only academic preparatory grounds for colleges and universities but also places where students could develop social and practical skills helpful in careers in the business world.[20] That assumption reflected the fact that despite the growth of colleges and universities in the United States from the 1890s on, most graduates of American public high schools did not attend college during the first half of the twentieth century.[21]

The emergence of public comprehensive high schools in the late nineteenth century followed from a recognition that "work," for children and adolescents, had changed with increased urbanization and industrialization. When the United States was overwhelmingly a rural society, with individual households serving as commercial as well as domestic entities, the work children and adolescents did in connection with their households was economically valued. Children and adolescents could and did contribute to the solvency and profitability of households. But as the United States became more urban and more industrialized after the Civil War, and occupational opportunities expanded, more adult family members found work outside their households, using their wages to help support their families. There was correspondingly less need for households to function as commercial economic units as well as domestic ones, and the labor of children and adolescents within the household became less vital to its solvency.[22]

At the same time institutions of higher education had begun to proliferate, and degrees from those institutions had come to be regarded as facilitating entry into business and the professions. Attendance and performance at secondary schools came to be seen as training for college, so more children and adolescents were encouraged to go to school rather remain at home, where their work was less valued and their leisure time regarded as wasteful, if not potentially worrisome. The comprehensive high school was created to accommodate children from households making the transition from a rural to an urbanizing and industrializing environment. It was designed not merely to prepare students to attend college but to allow them to develop social and practical skills suited to the business world.

The changing orientation of public high schools introduced more students to extracurricular activities, and in the early twentieth century educators in both high schools and colleges sought to assume control over those activities, including sports. The reason for this shift in emphasis from voluntary to school-sponsored extracurricular activities was a fear among educators and administrators that if the experience of high school students was confined to academic training for only a portion of the day, they might not use their leisure time profitably. They might engage in dangerous sports or activities; they might form groups involved in inappropriate social conduct; or they just might waste their leisure time.[23]

In addition, school-sponsored athletic teams could enhance community solidarity by providing cities, townships, or counties with entities whose activities could be supported by persons who were not direct participants in the sports involved. Encouraging students to pursue school-sponsored sports thus had the dual advantage of providing students with healthful activities and boosting community support for a comprehensive high school.[24]

The result, in many American communities, was the creation of varsity[25] high school teams in some sports, notably baseball, gridiron football, and basketball, and the enlistment of members of the community—including the local officials involved in high school governance, whether through townships, counties, or school boards—in the welfare of those teams. High school baseball, football, and basketball teams became a focus of community solidarity and support, attracting interest from local residents whose only connection to a comprehensive high school was its placement in their hometown.[26]

A similar phenomenon emerged with respect to major team sports in American public universities in the early twentieth century. Educators in those universities moved to assume control over their athletic activities, hiring coaches for university teams, financing their equipment, training, and facilities, and organizing matches against teams from other universities. A wave of construction of university football stadiums designed to host very large numbers of spectators drawn from the surrounding communities amounted to a self-conscious effort to establish varsity teams in major sports as symbols of community and regional pride and solidarity.[27]

CONTROLLING COLLEGE SPORTS: THE NATIONAL COLLEGIATE ATHLETIC ASSOCIATION

In the same period, college and university officials moved to establish control of the sports they were offering as part of the college experience. The method they adopted bore a striking resemblance to that of the Football Association in its years of solid growth: a central command-and-control organization whose goals included standardization of a sport's rules; the management of that sport's development through affiliated local associations that operated autonomously but were ultimately beholden to the central body; and the staging of competitive matches between clubs in those associations and of nationwide cup tournaments, both designed to increase recreational and spectator interest in the sport as well as raise revenue. The institution that American colleges and universities established to perform those functions was the National Collegiate Athletic Association (NCAA).[28]

We have seen that gridiron football emerged at some northeastern universities, notably Columbia, Harvard, Princeton, Rutgers, and Yale, in the 1870s and 1880s. In 1880 Walter Camp, who worked for a New Haven watchmaking firm after attending Yale and playing football there from 1875 to 1882 (the last three years after he had graduated), persuaded the Intercollegiate Association, which had been formed in 1876 to standardize the rules of football, to adopt some rule changes.[29] Camp's suggested rule changes eliminated the rugby scrum as a means of initiating play, replacing it with a "line of scrimmage" between offensive and defensive teams. An offensive team could retain possession of the ball indefinitely unless it was kicked or fumbled to the defense. Initially that change was not a success: offensive teams were rarely able to gain yardage, since forward passes were not allowed at the time, so games consisted of the offensive teams continually being pushed back on their side of the field.

Camp responded in 1881 by initiating another rule change. The new rule divided the field into five-yard intervals and required an offensive team, in order to retain possession of the ball, to gain five yards in three attempts. Players were allowed to throw the ball sideways, run with it, or kick it forward in an effort to gain those yards. No tackling below the waist was initially permitted, but another rule change initiated by Camp in 1888 changed that. "Blocking"—running interference between a ball carrier and defenders—was also permitted. As a result of those changes, teams began to mass players in formation opposing one another, with offensive players seeking to block defenders as their teammates sought to advance the ball down the field, and defensive players seeking to tackle the ball carriers. The game became a mass of players on both sides, pushing and shoving one another in an effort to move the ball.

In the late nineteenth and early twentieth centuries, gridiron football was not played with helmets or other protective devices. Players wore long-sleeved shirts, the equivalent of knickers, high socks, and wool caps, along with cleated boots. Given the lack of equipment and the evolution of the game into a pushing and shoving match, gridiron football had become a quite dangerous sport by the turn of the twentieth century. Eighteen deaths and 159 serious injuries occurred in football games in the year 1905 alone,[30] and Columbia, Northwestern, the University of California, and Stanford either suspended play or abolished the sport on their campuses after that year. That also happened to be the same year in which President Theodore Roosevelt summoned representatives from Harvard, Princeton, and Yale to a conference on violence and safety in gridiron football, and the chancellor of New York University organized a conference of thirteen eastern colleges with football teams to consider whether the sport should be reformed or abolished.[31]

That conference was followed by a second one, held in December 1905 and attended by representatives of sixty-two colleges and universities, but not Columbia, Harvard, Princeton, Rutgers, or Yale.[32] Two central issues emerged at this conference: safety and the eligibility of players. Although gridiron football teams were affiliated with universities, there were no limits to the amount of time a player could play for a team so long as he had some affiliation with its university. Camp himself had played seven years for Yale, the last three as a graduate of the institution.[33] Universities were not only permitting players who were not or were no longer full-time students to play, but they were creating financial incentives for them to do so. Out of that conference the Intercollegiate Athletic Association of the United States was created, an institution whose purpose was to standardize the on-the-field and eligibility rules of gridiron football. In 1910 that body changed its name to the National Collegiate Athletic Association.[34]

The NCAA would ultimately assume control over all forms of intercollegiate athletics, including women's as well as men's team sports and individual sports such as tennis and golf. It eventually became a cartel, an institution designed to create a monopsony (a buyers' monopoly) among its members by restricting the number of games that teams for its member institutions could play in a given season, and the number of games that could be broadcast on the radio, and later televised.[35] Moreover, the NCAA has established strict rules on the recruiting and financial aid given to athletes, which have the effect of transferring the rewards of athletic success from players to schools and their coaches. The remuneration of athletes, in the form of scholarships covering room and board, is set at fixed levels.[36]

The NCAA has been a controversial institution for much of its history, particularly after the 1960s, when the emergence of television had a dramatic effect on the revenue its members received from the broadcasting of athletic contests.[37] This chapter, however, focuses on its contribution to the marginalization of soccer in colleges, and tangentially in high schools, in the twentieth-century United States.

THE INITIAL ORIENTATION OF COLLEGE AND HIGH SCHOOL ATHLETICS

The NCAA had its origins in three interlocking developments. One, as we have seen, was the effort of educators in late nineteenth-century American colleges and public high schools simultaneously to introduce athletics into the student experience at those institutions and to control that experience through the management of sports teams by school and college personnel, rather than by voluntary clubs and associations whose affairs were conducted by students. That development led not only to the creation of college-sponsored sports, administered by persons affiliated with the college (sometimes coaches hired specifically to manage an individual sport, more typically faculty members who doubled as coaches), but also to the comparable creation of high-school-sponsored sports, also managed by school faculty members or coaches hired by the school.

One effect of that development was the identification of certain team sports as central to a college's or school's athletic program. Over the first two decades of the twentieth century, three such sports would come to occupy central roles: baseball, the most established American team sport at the time; basketball, which could be played indoors and thus was an ideal activity for months in which cold weather interfered with outdoor sports; and gridiron football. All three had been created in America, and as such implicitly signaled the ability of residents of the United States, most of whom traced their families' origins to other nations, to demonstrate their independence from the countries from which they had come. Baseball and basketball had been "invented" in America, and gridiron football, we have seen, represented a self-conscious modification of the English sports of association football and rugby.

The identification of baseball, basketball, and gridiron football as the team sports most central to the athletic programs of US colleges and high schools was also based on the assumption that members of the communities in which those colleges and schools were situated would want to follow the fortunes of their teams in those sports. Visible and successful college and high school teams in those sports were thought capable of garnering followers in their communities, not only from students, faculty, and staff at their respective institutions but from other persons who were, or felt, connected to the teams, either as alumni of an institution, friends or relatives of players on the teams, or simply members of a community that took a vicarious interest in the teams' welfare.

As a result, in the early twentieth century colleges and universities increasingly emphasized baseball, basketball, and gridiron football in their athletic programs, as did high schools.[38] This was due partially to the perceived attractiveness of those sports to followers and spectators in regions associated with those schools, but also to the fact that being on a high school varsity baseball, basketball, or gridiron football team roster allowed students to identify themselves to colleges as prospective players in those sports. And those tendencies had ripple effects in communities with visible varsity teams in the major sports, stimulating a further emphasis on teaching and playing those sports among youth in those communities. In short, more boys and young men began playing, as well as following, baseball, basketball, and gridiron football in early twentieth-century America.[39]

Gridiron football, however, had a dimension that the other two major early twentieth-century sports lacked: it was dangerous.[40] Some of the rule changes the NCAA initiated were designed to enliven gridiron football and make it safer. Those included requiring at least seven players to be on the line of scrimmage when the ball was put into play, thereby reducing offensive teams' ability to create interlocking wedges of players to run interference for a runner; expanding the yardage that an offensive team had to gain to retain possession of the ball from five to ten yards; giving offenses four rather than three chances to gain ten yards; and eventually allowing passes to be thrown beyond the line of scrimmage in any direction and to any length.[41]

Beginning in 1906, the IAA initiated new eligibility rules. Student athletes were required to be full-time students at the institution for which they played. Giving students direct or indirect financial aid for the sole purpose of their engaging in athletics was decried as inconsistent with the ideal of amateurism, as was giving prospective student athletes financial incentives to matriculate at a particular college. Students could only participate in athletics for three years, and if they transferred from one institution to another, they could not play the sport they had played at their previous institution for a year. First-year students (typically called freshmen) were not eligible to play on any varsity athletic teams.[42]

When those rules were initiated, they only applied to gridiron football. Although the NCAA had ambitions to extend its control over college athletics to include additional team sports, and would eventually do so, bringing men's basketball, baseball, track and field, and swimming within its purview between 1910 and World War II, its character as an institution was determined by its early association with gridiron football. That was so because, as college sports proliferated in the years between the two world wars, only gridiron football both posed significant dangers to those who played it and was subject to a variety of unethical recruitment and retention practices. Baseball and basketball, which were also widely played in colleges and universities in those years, were susceptible to unethical practices—college baseball players regularly played in summer leagues and were often covertly compensated for doing so, and basketball players were recruited through many of the same unethical methods that the NCAA was seeking to curtail with respect to gridiron players[43]—but were not positively dangerous. The NCAA was founded as an organization primarily devoted to promoting safety in a risky sport: it was only after rule changes in gridiron football had improved the game's safety after 1910 that the NCAA turned its focus to maintaining amateurism in college sports.[44]

And as it did, a different dimension of the NCAA's effort to control the recruitment and retention of student athletes surfaced. Gridiron football's popularity in colleges and high schools in the years after World War I, as we have seen, generated the construction of large football stadiums all over the United States. Even though college conferences affiliated with the NCAA limited the number of games that gridiron teams could play in a season and spaced out those games on a weekly basis, the revenues colleges and universities amassed from charging admission to home games and taking a percentage of the receipts from road games were considerable. From the 1920s onward, universities received most of their athletics income from gridiron football and men's basketball games.[45]

Beginning in the 1920s, members of the NCAA, which grew from fewer than 100 institutions in its initial decade to 210 in 1945,[46] recognized that if they rigorously policed the expenditures institutions spent on recruiting and retaining athletes in revenue-raising sports, and at the same time promoted varsity teams in those sports as attractions for alumni and members of communities as well as faculty and students, the major sports teams of colleges and universities could become profit-making operations. The beauty—and, to some, the hypocrisy—of that approach (labeled by economists as cartel behavior, designed to reduce the outputs expended by major sports teams and increase the inputs those teams received from others[47]) was that by policing unethical behavior in the recruitment or retention of student athletes, NCAA member institutions appeared to be seeking to uphold the idea of amateurism in college sports.

They may well have been doing that, but they were also limiting the money that colleges and universities spent on student athletes. By setting limits on the number and value of athletic scholarships, forbidding student athletes from earning money from other sources while playing a sport, clamping down on gifts or other compensation to athletes from college and university "boosters," and requiring all student athletes to be full-time students, thereby preventing them from engaging in part-time work, NCAA member institutions were essentially transferring virtually all of the revenue that college athletic teams generated directly to themselves. Coaches, athletic departments, and colleges or universities received that revenue; players did not, even though it was players that spectators paid to watch, players who risked injury, and players whose exploits raised revenue for major college sports teams.

The NCAA thus came into being, and flourished, as a unique product of a widespread effort to ensure that athletics in the late nineteenth and early twentieth centuries was integrated into the school and college experience of students, instead of being associated with voluntary, student-run clubs and associations; of the apparent "crisis" that college officials faced in the simultaneous popularity and dangerousness of gridiron football in that period; and of the perhaps fortuitous interaction of the NCAA's rhetorical commitment to amateurism in college athletics with the growth of gridiron football as a spectator sport in the 1920s, which made it an important source of revenue for NCAA member institutions. It now remains to show how the status of men's college soccer in the early twentieth century was adversely affected by the same developments that combined to make the NCAA a force in college athletics.

SOCCER, THE NCAA, AND HIGH SCHOOLS

Soccer might have had a chance to become established at American colleges and universities during the first half of the twentieth century. As colleges and universities proliferated in that period, they could have included soccer among the team sports they offered, and the NCAA could have swept soccer into the sports that its member institutions sought to regulate through their on-the-field rules and recruitment and retention practices. Neither development took place.

In 1906 some eastern colleges at which soccer was played at a semiofficial level, most of them in what came to be called the Ivy League, formed the Intercollegiate Soccer Football League (ISFL), an entity designed to organize matches among its member institutions. The colleges involved were Columbia, Harvard, Haverford, Princeton, the University of Pennsylvania, and Yale. Between 1906 and 1925, with the exception of 1918, a champion of the ISFL was determined, based on the win-loss records of matches. In that interval Haverford won or shared the championship seven times; Penn, six: Princeton, three; and Columbia, Harvard, and Yale twice each.[48] In 1926 the ISFL became the Intercollegiate Soccer Football Association (ISFA), which included a larger number of member colleges, most prominent among them, in terms of performance, Penn State. Between 1926 and 1958, with the exception of the war years between 1941 and 1945, the ISFA selected the Outstanding Soccer Team for that year, but not, until 1950, based on on-the-field competition: a committee of representatives of participating members made the selection.[49]

Even after the ISFA established in 1950 the Soccer Bowl, involving four teams, the Outstanding Soccer Team was not invariably the winner of that tournament. In 1950 the squad at the College of West Chester was selected as the year's Outstanding Soccer Team, even though in the Soccer Bowl finals Penn State had defeated Purdue.[50] And the participants in the Soccer Bowl were themselves selected by an ISFA committee.[51] As we have seen, even as Penn State began to establish itself as a soccer powerhouse in the 1920s, the ISFA committee was slow to recognize it as the year's Outstanding Soccer Team, giving it the award by itself only once between 1926 and 1935. Given Penn State's outstanding performance in those years—the team never lost a match once in the 1930s—its grudging recognition by the ISFA committee might have had something to do with several members on the committee who were either affiliated with or graduates of the University of Pennsylvania, which won or shared four Outstanding Soccer Team awards between 1930 and 1933.[52]

As late as 1939, only eighty American colleges and universities had men's soccer teams,[53] and their seasons remained short, with virtually no interregional matches and no postseason tournaments. And even those institutions that did field a soccer team gave that program paltry financial support, especially as compared to the support given to gridiron football and men's basketball teams after 1920. As for the NCAA, it remained largely indifferent to soccer, not sponsoring a postseason championship until 1959.

In public high schools the marginality of soccer was even more marked. As late as the 1969–70 academic year, when men's soccer had begun to expand considerably in colleges, ten high school varsity sports outranked soccer in terms of the number of schools fielding a team and the number of students participating. In addition to football, baseball, and basketball, the varsity sports that outranked soccer included track and field, cross-country, golf, wrestling, tennis, swimming, and volleyball.[54] The dramatic expansion of the number of colleges and universities offering soccer in the 1960s had not been marked by a corresponding expansion in the number of high school youths exposed to the sport. When the first NCAA men's soccer tournament was held in 1959, only eight teams participated. By 1969 that number had been increased to twenty-four.[55] But only a very few public high schools in the United States were offering soccer as a varsity sport.[56]

There were two additional factors that emerged in connection with the early twentieth-century takeover of sports by colleges and high schools and the designation, made by faculty and staff members, of certain sports as "varsity" sports, which served to retard the growth of professional soccer in the United States. The first was the continued and widespread perception of soccer as an "ethnic" sport, played largely by groups of recent immigrants who had learned the game outside the United States.

When public comprehensive high schools considered whether to offer particular sports as part of their curriculum, and particularly which sports to designate as "varsity" and therefore to subsidize in the hope of attracting attention and supporters to their matches, soccer was rarely chosen. Only in communities in which there was already a strong tradition of soccer as a popular recreational and spectator sport did public high schools offer soccer teams. And since soccer was not offered at the vast majority of American high schools, there was no reason for most communities in the United States to develop youth soccer programs.

The second factor was the disinclination of those who engaged in the administration of the ISFL, the ISFA, and ultimately the NCAA to establish rules for soccer that conformed to the Football Association rules adopted, with some modifications over time, by FIFA. American colleges and high schools established their own soccer rules, arguably making the experience of soccer players on their teams quite different from that of other soccer players around the world, including those in professional and semiprofessional leagues in the United States.

One difference between the rules of American colleges and high schools and the rest of the soccer world was comparatively trivial: colleges and high school adopted a system of "counting down" the number of minutes in a given period of a game, analogous to the timing of the periods of play of North American ice hockey. The time of a period began with its designated minutes and then was counted down until it reached zero. Since soccer play is continuous, with no time-outs given for substitutions or other matters, the time of play within periods often closely approximates real time, although some stoppage time can be added to compensate for unexpectedly halted play, such as when an injured player needs to be treated on the field.

In association football matches in the UK, western Europe, and Latin America, and in FIFA matches—indeed, everywhere but in college and high school games in the United States—time in a soccer match is "counted up," meaning that a period begins with zeros on the clock and moves upward until the period is over, or a designated amount of stoppage time (also counted up) is exhausted. Although there was otherwise no difference between the way time was counted in American college and high school soccer matches and the way it was counted elsewhere, the difference was sufficiently annoying to fans of the American men's professional league Major League Soccer, which after its founding in 1996 adopted the "counting down" approach in its matches, that when MLS executives polled fans about changes they would welcome in the way MLS games were conducted, they overwhelmingly voted to change MLS's counting system to match the rest of the world.[57]

Although the choice to count down or count up had no significance beyond a technique by which the passage of time in a given period of a match was recognized, it symbolized the independence with which American soccer leagues tended to react to efforts on the part of other bodies to make uniform the rules of the sport. American colleges and high schools were comparably independent.

The principal rule differences between soccer played in colleges and high schools in the United States did not involve the offside rule or the width of goals, two areas in which the professional North American Soccer League, after it came into being in 1968, contemplated rule changes designed to promote offense. Instead, the new rules US colleges and high schools imposed involved the length and configuration of periods in matches and substitution. In both instances the differences between American colleges and high schools and the rest of the soccer world might not at first glance appear significant, but in terms of preparing American male high school and college players to play professional soccer, in the United States or elsewhere, they were.

The first major difference between match play in American high schools and colleges and elsewhere came in the length and configuration of the periods. Throughout the rest of the soccer world, including semiprofessional and professional soccer leagues in the United States, matches were played in two periods of forty or forty-five minutes, with continuous play, sometimes with stoppage time added. No voluntary stoppage of play was permitted, except on rare occasions where very hot weather dictated it. "Continuous play" thus meant that most players were moving up and down the soccer field without resting for the entire duration of a half. A short break was then taken, and play resumed for one more continuous period of forty or forty-five minutes.

Soccer matches in American colleges and high schools were played in quarters rather than halves, typically for twenty-two minutes at the college level and about seventeen minutes at the high school level (the total playing time for colleges was eighty-eight minutes, and for high schools, seventy). Breaks were taken after the quarters.[58] This meant that the interval of continuous play was significantly shorter for college and high school players in the United States, meaning that players did not necessarily build up the level of stamina required to be on the field continuously for forty-five minutes.

In addition, there was a dramatically different rule about the substitution of players in US colleges and high schools. Initially the rules of the Football Association, as they came to be adopted by FIFA-affiliated associations and confederations throughout the world, permitted no substitutions at all, not even when players were injured to the degree that they were unable to perform. Eventually the no-substitution rule came to be slightly modified in two situations, when goalkeepers were injured and when matches were played in extreme heat. Then some FIFA members sought permission to introduce limited substitutions, such as one per half or one per game. After initially resisting the change, FIFA approved it. By the twenty-first century almost all FIFA-affiliated soccer leagues and associations had settled on a rule of three substitutions over the course of an entire match, with players who were substituted out being ineligible to return to play. With that rule in place, many teams choose, when a player is injured, not to replace him immediately but to continue the match with fewer players until it is determined whether the injured player can recover enough to return. In short, the current worldwide rules for professional soccer discourage substitution and make a team's three substitutions coveted and strategically utilized.

But American colleges and high schools used different substitution rules. The substitution of one player per match seems to have been permitted when soccer was first played in colleges, and in 1913 the ISFL allowed two substitutions, one as a "legitimate reserve" and the other "to be allowed . . . in case of injury sustained by a member of the regular eleven, subject to the approval of the referee."[59] And over time the rules became increasingly liberalized. A rule change instituted by the ISFA in 1934 permitted up to five substitutions per match, and, most strikingly, allowed three resubstitutions, meaning that some players could come in and out of the same game. In 1954 the limit of five substitutions was retained, but all substituted players were eligible to return. And in 1964 up to sixteen players could be substituted over the course of a match.[60]

When American private and public high schools began offering soccer as a varsity sport more regularly after the middle of the twentieth century, unlimited substitution was treated as the norm. High schools' adoption of the liberal substitution rules stemmed partly from the ethos of high school soccer in the United States; soccer was perceived less as a training ground for professional soccer players than as a sport to which men not physically developed enough to play gridiron football could turn.[61] Liberal substitution meant that in any given game and throughout the season more young players would get the opportunity to play on the field and feel "part of the team," and also that a coach could mix and match players of differing abilities, allowing those whose skills were developing to be exposed to more experienced players. Unlimited substitution currently remains in place for private and public high school soccer in the United States.[62]

When taken together with the division of playing time into quarters rather than halves, resulting in breaks from continuous play every twenty minutes or so,[63] American college and high school soccer's liberal substitution rules transformed the experience of playing soccer for teenage boys and young men in the United States. For many of those players, "continuous play," as the rest of the soccer world understood it, did not exist. Many players on college and high school teams did not play continuously for even twenty-odd minutes without a break. They could be on the field for intervals, then substituted, and in high school matches players could return to play at any time. College players who were taken out had less opportunity to reenter, but after 1934 they were permitted to do so. With matches divided into twenty-odd-minute quarters, no players had the experience of being on the field for forty-five minutes straight, as in the rest of the soccer world.[64]

The American rules for the duration of the game and substitution affected both the assembling of varsity soccer teams and coaching strategies. With ample substitution allowed and continuous play limited in duration, coaches could instruct a player entering a game as a substitute to play at a rapid pace rather than conserving energy, since that player likely would not be on the field for long. And since the substitution rules allowed more players to participate in a given game, soccer teams could have more players on their rosters, which was not only useful for substitution but provided a larger pool of players for practice scrimmages. Whereas in the rest of the soccer world a team roster often consisted of a starting eleven, who were expected to play most of the match if not the entire one, and a few replacements, American college and high school team rosters typically included at least one replacement player at every position. It was common for replacements to be inserted not only to allow them to play rapidly for short intervals but also to allow the players they replaced to do the same.[65]

In sum, the physical demands of college and high school soccer in the United States would come to be quite different from those in the rest of the soccer world. Instead of being expected to run around on a field continuously for forty-five minutes, much like basketball players exposed to long "minutes" of running up and down the court without resting, many American players experienced a game of short bursts, followed by breathing spaces in which a player was removed from a match or a quarter ended. As anyone who has trained at soccer will attest, this produced a different form of conditioning, something akin to the difference between how one would train for sprinting and long-distance running.

Because of their quite different rules regarding duration of play and substitution, American colleges and high schools conditioned soccer players differently from the way they were conditioned in all other soccer leagues. This meant that when American professional and semiprofessional clubs sought to recruit players, most of the available pool of native-born players consisted of persons who had played and trained for a game that did not much resemble the sport they would be expected to play in professional leagues. Given the dissonance between the sort of soccer played in college or high school games in the United States and that played in professional leagues, it is no surprise that when the United States entered teams in the 1930, 1934, and 1950 World Cups, not a single player on those teams' rosters was recruited from an American college or public or private high school.[66]

CONCLUSION

It would be an overstatement to say that American educators took over the management of soccer for adolescent boys and young adult men in the early twentieth century and did nothing with it, but by no means a gross one. The transfer of the management and development of youth soccer from clubs to private schools, colleges, and a few public high schools certainly had the effect, on the whole, of retarding rather than furthering the growth of soccer as a participatory and spectator sport in twentieth-century America.

As we have seen, college soccer in the early twentieth century encountered competition as a fall sport with gridiron football, a competition that soccer lost, at least in terms of spectator appeal and social standing on campuses. One of the first decisions made by the ISFL was to schedule soccer games in the spring semester in order to avoid direct competition with gridiron football or rugby, but that move did not enhance the game's popularity as a spectator sport. When the NCAA came into being as a result of the early twentieth-century crisis about safety and ethical practices in gridiron football, the governing body quickly recognized the revenue-raising potential of that sport, began to assume more direct control of it, and ultimately established cartel practices that served to cement the importance of gridiron football on college campuses, which also contributed to the continuing marginalization of soccer.

Meanwhile the comprehensive public high school movement had gotten under way, transforming high schools, whose attendance was initially not compulsory in most states, from academically centered institutions, catering to the comparatively small number of students who were preparing to enter college, to centers serving diverse members of the community in which they were situated, offering extracurricular as well as academic activities, and seeking to train students not only for college but for the business world. Comprehensive public high schools began to create varsity teams in certain sports, seeking not only to provide activities for their students but to establish those teams as objects of community support. In nearly all such high schools, varsity teams were fielded in the leading "indigenous" sports of baseball, gridiron football, and men's basketball. In almost no such schools, we have seen, were varsity soccer teams established. From the point of view of high school educators and their community boosters, that emphasis made sense. All of those sports were not only perceived of as "American" but also played in nearly all colleges and universities in the United States. If a student aspired to play a sport in college, playing one of the three major sports in high school was a step in that direction. And since soccer, which for much of its early history in the United States was perceived of as an ethnic sport played by immigrants, was not offered in most American public high schools, college-level teams struggled to field competitive varsity teams for some time after an increasing number of young men chose to attend college.

The absence of participation in soccer at the high school or college levels for most American men for much of the twentieth century had ramifications that went beyond the particular experience of those persons. Because most American men had limited exposure to soccer, they were unlikely to have played the game as youths, to become fans of college or professional soccer teams in the United States, and to encourage their children to pursue the sport recreationally.[67]

Those factors created, for most of the twentieth century, a paradoxical relationship in American communities between participation in and vicarious support for the major indigenous sports. Baseball, as most parents of young children exposed to the game recognize, is a very difficult sport for boys to master, requiring considerable hand-eye coordination. There are comparatively few rewards and many prospects for humiliation in youth baseball. And yet for most of the twentieth century, parents routinely encouraged their sons to play baseball and to engage in organized baseball activities such as Little League or Babe Ruth League. Moreover, parental attendance at youth baseball games, and the engagement of members of communities with high school baseball games, was a regular phenomenon.[68]

Baseball may be difficult to play as a youth sport, but those who play it do not have to possess above-average physical size or strength to have a chance to succeed. The same cannot be said for gridiron football and basketball. Size and strength clearly matters in gridiron football, so much so that at the high school level a player with very little athletic ability can function well as an offensive or defensive lineman simply by being big, heavy, and therefore difficult to move out of the way. In basketball, although some very gifted smaller players can succeed, being tall and physically strong is a distinct advantage. Basketball further limits the opportunity of a great many young men to aspire to varsity status, in that the game's starting squads comprise only five players, so there is no need for teams to carry large rosters.

And yet, with the entrenchment of baseball, gridiron football, and basketball as varsity sports in American high schools and colleges for nearly all of the twentieth century, most young men in the United States were encouraged to play those sports as youths, even though the nature of those sports ensured that relatively very few of them would ultimately succeed as varsity athletes, whether in high schools or in colleges. Still, for nearly a hundred years, beginning at the outset of the twentieth century, a great many American families encouraged their male children to participate in baseball, basketball, and football—in some cases more than one of them, or all three.

Perhaps that very recognition of the obstacles facing most youths who aspired to succeed in baseball, gridiron football, and basketball eventually inclined a certain class of American parents—largely affluent white professionals—to identify soccer as a youth sport. In any case, that recognition came late in the twentieth century, in the 1970s, when recreational American team sports were revolutionized by the passage of Title IX, which offered girls and women equal opportunities to participate in high school and college athletics. Only one of the major indigenous sports offered in high schools and colleges for much of the twentieth century, basketball, had anticipated women playing the sport at all, and for several decades of the century women's basketball was a distinctly different sport from the men's game, ensuring that coeducational youth basketball could not exist.[69]

Soccer, as we will see in a subsequent chapter, was different in that there were no obvious physical barriers to women playing the game. Women's soccer was barely offered at all, and never in the form of a varsity sport, in private schools or colleges until the 1960s, but that was for reasons unconnected to physiography. After Title IX signaled that there would be opportunities for girls and women to play the sport in high schools and colleges, a certain sector of parents—caricatured as "soccer moms," who knew little about the game but found youth soccer attractive as a recreational activity for their male and female children alike, as well as a pleasant social activity in their communities—began to recognize that soccer had some distinct advantages over the established indigenous sports as a recreational pursuit for youths. It was comparatively inexpensive in terms of equipment; playing it did not require an elaborate facility or a specially designed space; it could be played, although usually not too successfully, at a quite early age; it was far less dangerous than gridiron football; it could accommodate more players than basketball; it had far fewer pauses in the action of a game than baseball; and it could be played by both boys and girls, indeed by boys and girls together, up to high school.

Perhaps most important, youth soccer was an activity in which radically different levels of skill were not easily apparent in the earlier years of childhood, and where, in later years, there were opportunities for players with different skill sets to perform different roles and yet be integrated into a team. In the earliest years of youth soccer, children of both sexes tend to swarm around one another on the field, chasing after the ball, one child sometimes breaking out of the swarm, running down the field along with the ball, and maybe shooting it at the goal. Meanwhile the "goalkeeper," instructed to stay in the area near the goal, may become distracted by a blade of grass, a dandelion, or another player with whom he or she is socializing, and might or might not seek to prevent the breakaway from resulting in a score. The whole spectacle tends to be a mixture of spontaneous racing around a field and spontaneous idleness. Rarely do any players come in contact with one another so as to cause injury. No one is typically singled out, except in the occasional breakaway, and no one usually "fails" in front of their peers and adult spectators. Parents without much experience with or appreciation for soccer can typically attend without having to watch the action on the field closely: hence the reputation of youth soccer games as opportunities for social interchange among parents with children of comparable ages.

When one reflects upon the emergence of youth soccer in the United States in the late twentieth century, two thoughts come to mind. One is that youth soccer activities, which are typically created and managed by volunteer organizations within communities and not connected to public elementary or secondary schools, resemble in their organizational form the clubs and associations that served to organize association football in the UK and Europe. To the extent that those clubs and associations tended to cater to members of working-class families in overseas nations, youth soccer in the United States from the late twentieth century on has been sociologically different: the parents encouraging their children to participate in youth soccer have been from less diverse and more affluent sectors. But the voluntary dimensions of youth soccer in America resemble the longtime organization of the sport in the UK and western Europe.

The other feature of the emergence of youth soccer in America, especially when taken together with the dramatic effect of Title IX on opportunities for girls and women to play the sport at a varsity level in high schools and colleges, has been that it has served, over time, to build up a critical mass of Americans with at least a passing knowledge of the game. In addition to all the young men and women that have played youth soccer, as well as played soccer in high schools and colleges since the last decades of the twentieth century, a series of parents, in connection with a community youth soccer organization, have sought to coach youth teams in soccer leagues or at least to pay closer attention to the sport their children are seeking to learn. Over time, "soccer moms" and "soccer dads" have begun to familiarize themselves with a sport that they never played as youths and to which they may have never paid attention.[70] To the extent that a critical mass of knowledgeable fans is a necessary condition for professional soccer to become established in America, the emergence of youth soccer may have gone a long way toward building the knowledge base.

One cannot fairly recount the history of men's college soccer in the United States without acknowledging the proliferation of the sport since the opening of the twenty-first century.[71] All told, however, this chapter has been another exercise in identifying factors that contributed to the recurrent, and seemingly puzzling, marginality of soccer as a sport in the United States in years in which it was expanding and flourishing throughout most of the rest of the globe. Although one cannot claim that without the transfer of adolescent and young adult male soccer from volunteer clubs and associations in the United States to colleges and ultimately to public high schools, that form of soccer might have flourished, stimulating the emergence of a successful men's professional soccer league, the transfer certainly did nothing to help the growth of soccer as a recreational or spectator sport in twentieth-century America, and very probably hindered that growth.

Chapter Five

Association Football Comes to America III

Efforts to Escape the Doldrums, 1950–1995

AS SHIPS MAKE the passage between northern Europe and Asia, around the Cape of Good Hope, there is a segment off the northwest coast of Africa where they may well encounter a dead calm stretch, where the wind drops almost entirely. That stretch, often referred to as the doldrums, is the product of a zone of low pressure some five degrees north and south of the equator, and thus a common feature of this particular passage. When the only ships undertaking this route were under sail, reliant upon the wind to make their way, entering this stretch could be a dangerous proposition. Once there, ships might lie becalmed off the African coast for long periods, their crews sometimes suffering from extreme heat while they waited for enough wind to carry them south or north. Sailors associated "the doldrums" with depressed spirits and a bad omen for the voyage. When, through either unusual wind patterns or the fortuitous presence of a storm, a ship was propelled safely beyond the stretch, sailors remarked with relief that they had "escaped the doldrums."

As we have seen, soccer in the United States, at both the collegiate and professional levels, lay mired in the doldrums from the 1920s through the 1940s. Gridiron football on college campuses had eclipsed soccer to the point that there were very few college soccer conferences and no postseason tournament, the "national champion" being determined by a committee of the Interscholastic Football Soccer Association. Although participation on college soccer teams grew steadily in the 1930s, not until the 1960s would the college game explode, so that by 1984 soccer would be played at more colleges than gridiron football.[1]

Professional soccer, at least from the mid-1930s through the 1950s, was even more obscure. The second version of the ASL was essentially a semiprofessional regional league, resembling those in New Jersey and southeastern New England earlier in the twentieth century. Games were largely attended by members of ethnic communities, clubs came and went, and newspapers rarely covered matches. The only significant revenue for the league came when it sponsored American tours for European clubs, who played games against ASL clubs in the summer.[2] In the 1950s, attendance at US Open Cup matches averaged less than 3,000.[3]

Most depressing of all for soccer aficionados in the United States in those years may have been American audiences' apparent inability of to understand or appreciate the game. Formidable weather conditions for spectators; the unfamiliarity of most Americans, few of whom had played soccer at high schools or colleges, with the intricacies of the game; and the relative scarcity of scored goals all made the experience of watching soccer daunting or off-putting for many Americans. Two comments in the early 1960s by Arthur Daley, the Pulitzer Prize–winning sports columnist from the *New York Times*, serve to capture American spectators' difficulties in relating to soccer. In one, Daley, who by the 1960s had a regular column entitled "Sports of the Times," which he commonly devoted to baseball, wrote, "About thirty years ago this reporter was assigned to cover a soccer championship in the outer fringes of Brooklyn. It was a grim day in the dead of winter with no transportation, no shelter, no spectators, and no score. They played three overtime periods. It was enough to scar a man for life. This reporter hasn't witnessed a soccer game of his own free will since."[4]

Seven years later CBS televised its first soccer game, a match between the Baltimore Bays and the Atlanta Chiefs in the National Professional Soccer League, an "outlaw" league in its first season (it had unsuccessfully competed with another league, the United Soccer Association, to secure recognition from the USFA and the Canadian Soccer Association). CBS signed a contract with the NPSL to broadcast games in 1967, and resolved to televise them in color at a time when National Football League games were still being televised in black and white. After the first telecast, Daley wrote, "The soccer game whisked into view sharp and clear, with the orange uniforms of Baltimore—or did they wear the red?—and the other uniforms of Atlanta in sharp contrast to the deep green grass of the Baltimore Stadium field. Everyone was an unknown and the action had no compelling interest. A flick of the wrist, and Richie Allen was hitting a home run for the Phils, Charlie Smith was making a super-spectacular stop of a liner and [Wilt] Chamberlain was wolfing in rebounds."[5]

Daley's references to MLB players and NBA star Wilt Chamberlain highlighted the fact that when the National Professional Soccer League (NPSL) played its first matches, on April 16, 1967, it was at that time of the year competing directly with baseball and basketball teams for sport fans' attention. Because of the hurried starts of both the NPSL and its competitor league, the officially sanctioned United Soccer Association, and the dearth of competent American players, both leagues' initial seasons featured an emphasis on foreign players, eliciting Daley's comment that "everyone was an unknown." The rosters of NPSL teams were composed of very few Americans, and those of the USA none, because that league simply brought clubs from other countries to the United States during their summer break and associated them with American cities. The Wolverhampton Wanderers appeared as the Los Angeles Wolves; Stoke City as the Cleveland Stokers; Cagliari of Italy as the Chicago Mustangs; Bangu of Brazil as the Houston Stars; and Cerro of Uruguay as the New York Skyliners. The NPSL's season lasted into September, but the USA's was limited to six weeks between late June and the middle of August.[6]

Daley condemned the action he had observed in the Baltimore-Atlanta game he watched on CBS as having "no compelling interest." The game ended with Baltimore scoring a late goal to win 1–0, hardly an unusual score for top-tier European soccer matches at the time; first-division European leagues emphasized defense, which was only accentuated by a rule that defensive players could kick balls backward to goalkeepers, who were allowed to field the passes with their hands and then throw or kick the ball back out in the opposite direction. That rule gave defenders concerned about opposing forwards challenging them for possession the option of turning matters over to their goalkeepers, making it difficult for offenses to sustain attacks long enough to take a shot on goal. Defenders also proved adept at committing what came to be called "cynical" fouls, in which they tackled players who threatened to dribble past them, resulting in free kicks for their opponents that could more easily be guarded against. American audiences, not used to watching sports with comparatively little scoring, apparently failed to gauge the value of those defensive tactics, concluding that much of the action on soccer fields did not seem to be leading anywhere.

Jack Goud, the *New York Times* television critic, had also witnessed the CBS telecast in April 1967, and he echoed Daley's comments about the lack of any action with "compelling interest." "Occasionally," Gould wrote, "there were moments of exotic footwork and team coordination that explain the success of soccer elsewhere," but "on the whole," he felt, "the patches of excitement were so infrequent that it took a notable sense of duty not to sample competing sports attractions on other channels."[7]

Both Daley's and Gould's comments serve to capture the state of American professional soccer just it was launching new leagues. The matches were largely fielded by unknown players, almost exclusively from outside the United States, and were played in a legacy of stadiums that were poorly configured for soccer; the action failed to galvanize American audiences. To all of this was added the absence of any extensive experience on the part of most Americans in playing or observing the game, and the conundrum that soccer games either had to take place in the American winter, causing spectators great discomfort, or compete with basketball and hockey in the spring, college and professional football in the fall, and baseball in both of those seasons. All this suggested that even with television contracts in place, US professional soccer, as it sought to revitalize itself in 1967, was not likely to escape the doldrums.

THE 1950 AMERICAN TEAM'S WORLD CUP

The depressed state of American professional soccer in the three decades after 1920 also affected the formation and stature of the US men's World Cup team after the FIFA-sponsored World Cup tournament became established in 1930. One of the central episodes in the history of twentieth-century American soccer, the US team's participation in the 1950 World Cup competition in Brazil, serves to illustrate the gap between American professional soccer and the state of the game in other nations at mid-century.

In 1930 and 1934 the United States sent teams to the World Cup competitions. The players on those teams were drawn from the American Soccer League, which was still active in the 1930–31 season and had resumed play, with a different set of clubs, in 1933–34.[8] In order to qualify for the World Cup in 1934, the United States needed to play a match against Mexico in Italy, which it won, but then the team lost 7–1 to Italy in its only World Cup match, which that year was a single-elimination event.[9] The 1930 team, in competition where there was no qualifying, fared better, defeating Belgium and Paraguay before losing to Argentina and Brazil.[10] For the 1950 World

Cup the qualifying was more extensive, but not demanding: the top two of the three teams entered in the North American Championships, held in Mexico City in September, 1949, would receive invitations to the cup. Cuba, Mexico, and the United States were the entrants. The American team lost twice to Mexico and drew with Cuba in its first game against them, but subsequently beat Cuba by three goals and advanced to the World Cup after Cuba lost to Mexico for the second time.[11]

The US 1950 World Cup team consisted of a mix of players from the American Soccer League and semiprofessional clubs. Of the seventeen players selected for the team, only four were from ASL clubs.[12] Tryouts for the team had been held in New York, Chicago, St. Louis, and Los Angeles in 1949, and the final roster reflected the still-parochial locations of soccer in the United States and its distinctly semiprofessional status in the years following World War II. Six players from St. Louis, all of whom played for sponsored clubs connected to their employment, were joined by two semiprofessional players from Fall River, two from Pittsburgh, and two from Chicago. The four professional players were from the Philadelphia Nationals, New York Brookhatten, and Brooklyn Hispano in the ASL. Only one of them played soccer full-time, but they were paid for their efforts in cup competition, whereas the semiprofessional players only received expenses. The large number of players from St. Louis was a product of that city's having active soccer leagues and the president of the USSF, Walter Geisler, being a resident of that city.[13]

Not all of the players on the US team roster were American citizens. Three of the starters, all from professional clubs, were citizens, respectively, of Haiti, Belgium, and Scotland. Two of them had jobs in the United States (a dishwasher in Manhattan and a paper stripper on Long Island), and the third apparently lived off his salary.[14] All of the players on the roster were first- or second-generation immigrants. Of the eleven starters, four were of Italian extraction (all from St. Louis); two, John and Eddie Sousa from Fall River, were of Portuguese descent; and the others had families who had emigrated from Belgium, Germany, Haiti, Ireland, and Scotland.[15] The 1950 US World Cup team was emblematic of the state of American professional soccer at the time, all of its players being from immigrant communities, some of them being citizens of other nations who had been recruited to play soccer in the United States,[16] none of them earning a substantial living from soccer, and all of them joining a World Cup team that played in virtual obscurity. The American press sent only one representative to the 1950 tournament in Brazil, a sportswriter for the *St. Louis Post-Dispatch* who paid his own way to the event.[17]

In 1946 the British rejoined FIFA, and in the interval between that year and the 1950 World Cup the English national team had emerged as a world power, losing only four of the thirty games they played against European competition.[18] They were placed in the same bracket as the United States in the early rounds of the cup, the other two teams being Spain and Chile.[19] England and Spain were overwhelming favorites to move beyond the bracket, and England among the favorites to win the cup. London bookmakers, a week before the tournament began in late June 1950, listed England's odds of winning at three to one, roughly comparable to those of Brazil. Spain, Italy, and Uruguay had the next most support, being quoted at between six and twelve to one. The United States was listed at five hundred to one.[20]

In the first matches in the US team's bracket, those odds appeared to be holding up, with England comfortably beating Chile, 2–0, and the United States losing to Spain, 3–1.[21] The US-Spain match was, however, closer than the final score indicated, the US team scoring first in the eighteenth minute and holding that lead until the eightieth minute, when Spain tied the score and then went on to add goals in the eighty-second and eighty-fifth minute.[22] But as the US team prepared to play England on June 29, four days after its match with Spain, its odds of winning the cup remained at five hundred to one.[23]

The match with Spain had revealed that the US team was capable of playing rugged, aggressive defense, preventing opponents from advancing from midfield into areas near the goal. Its formation—five forwards, three halfbacks, and two fullbacks—was characteristic of American professional soccer but not of European leagues, which featured more fluid 3-2-2-3 formations, employing fewer forwards but anticipating that wing halfbacks would move into the offensive end of the field. The Americans typically employed a "wall" of halfbacks and fullbacks in midfield, designed to form an obstacle to the circular downfield movement of European clubs. The team relied on its goalkeeper to collect balls hit over the top of defenders. Should the US team score first in a game, it would seek to impose the wall for the remainder of play. That had proven effective against Spain, but eventually the US players tired under relentless Spanish pressure in the Brazilian heat—no substitutes were allowed in Cup games at the time—and the Spanish had broken through.

When the US team sought to employ the same tactics against England, the English players responded by controlling possession with measured passes and effective dribbling, moving deep into the American end of the field and attempting shots at the US goal. For one reason or another, however, the English shots repeatedly misfired, some members of the English press later suggesting that the grass on the field—the game was held at a relatively primitive stadium in Belo Horizonte, a mining city three hundred miles north of Rio de Janeiro, where only first-round matches were to be played—was so patchy, uneven, and high in places that it prevented players from getting off effective shots.[24] That suggestion was echoed by the English manager, Walter Winterbottom, in an interview forty-six years later:

> Why we had to play [in Belo Horizonte] God only knows, but the pitch was in dreadful shape. The grass was high and thick, it was Bermuda grass growing in small clusters and it spreads and sends the ball up. We hadn't had any practice on it. . . . What is happening is the ball is teed up and you are hitting shots over the bar. . . . Maurice Smith . . . was doing statistics on the match and he said we hit the woodwork eleven times.[25]

Meanwhile the American players had virtually no possession of the ball for the first thirty minutes of the first half, and took only two shots on goal in that interval, whereas the English took more than a dozen shots, at least two of which got by American goalkeeper Frank Borghi only to bounce off a goalpost.[26] In the thirty-seventh minute, after a US throw-in at midfield, Walter Bahr, the American left halfback, began streaking into the English zone, with no initial resistance from English players. When an English defender challenged Bahr, about twenty-five yards from the goal, Bahr took a shot on goal that headed to the goalkeeper's right side. The shot had too little pace to represent more than a routine save for English goalkeeper Bert Williams. But as the ball was nearing Williams, positioned not far from the penalty area, in front of the goal, American center forward Joe Gaetjens dove forward toward the ball, eventually landing about eight feet from where Williams had been stationed. Gaetjens's head grazed the ball, directing it to the left of Williams, who stumbled as he sought to pivot to change direction. Gaetjens's header passed by Williams into the back of the goal, giving the United States a 1–0 lead.[27]

Over fifty minutes remained in the match. For most of that time the English team controlled play, with the Americans trying to fend them off. With eight minutes to go, Stanley Mortensen, the fastest player on the English team, broke away, heading alone toward the US goal. Charley Columbo, the American "stopper" (center halfback), chased Mortensen. When it became clear, as Mortensen approached the penalty area, that Columbo was not going to catch him, Columbo dove headlong in Mortensen's direction, crashing into him just outside the penalty area. The play was not just a foul but very likely merited a red card, disqualifying Columbo, but the referee only awarded a free kick to England. Alf Ramsey, one of the gifted English forwards, took the kick, chipping the ball over the heads of the American players standing in front of their goalkeeper, onto the head of Englishman Jimmy Mullen, who had run past the Americans. Mullen headed the ball toward the goal, and Borghi allowed it to get past him, then lunged backward, attempting to slap the shot wide of the net before it crossed the goal line. Although the referee signaled that Borghi had effectively blocked the shot, American fullback Harry Keogh, over forty years later, thought that the ball might have gone beyond the line before Borghi made contact with it.[28] A flurry of dribbling by John Sousa, ending in Sousa's kicking the ball off the foot of an English player to retain possession for the United States in the final minutes, ended the game.[29]

The American team's victory was stunning, but the team failed to get beyond the first round, losing to Chile in its next match as Spain beat England to advance. The cup was a disaster for the English team, foreshadowing its decline in international stature for the next decade and a half. "Probably never before has an English team played so badly," the *London Times* reported.[30]

The American triumph was barely noticed in the United States. According to one account,[31] the *New York Times* received a wire notice, an hour before the paper for the day was to be printed, that the United States had beaten England 1–0 at the World Cup in Brazil. Fearful that the report was a hoax, the *Times* staff declined to run a story on the game at all. The next day, June

30, 1950, the United States entered the Korean War, and the small amount of World Cup information filtering back to America largely disappeared from public consciousness in the States, although the American team's win over England was front-page news in Europe and Latin America.[32]

Although the US team's 1950 defeat of England in the World Cup has become one of the celebrated pieces of lore in the history of American men's soccer, its principal role in this chapter is as an illustration of the continued marginal status of the soccer in the United States in 1950. Although the team that defeated England was managed by a college coach, Bill Jeffrey from Penn State, it did not have a single college player on its roster. Nor did it have a majority of players from the second version of the American soccer league, and it included only one full-time professional, who was not a US citizen. All but one of its players were drawn from either the ASL, which was a semiprofessional league at the time, or local semiprofessional clubs. Not only were American colleges not producing high-level soccer players in the late 1940s, when tryouts for the US World Cup team took place, but the ASL itself was not producing a sufficient number of quality players to make up the entire team. Many of the starters on the team were from local leagues in St. Louis.

The next thing that stands out about the US World Cup team's effort in 1950 is that even though the competition that year was held in the western hemisphere, there was virtually no coverage of it in American media. As mentioned, the only media representative from the United States in attendance at the tournament had chosen to pay his own way. Although the US team's stunning upset was recognized as a huge international soccer story by European and Latin American media, it received almost no attention in the United States. This was even though the team involved was not simply a club in an obscure American semiprofessional league but the US national team, participating in the world's largest and most celebrated international soccer tournament. Finally, when the players made it back to the United States between July 8 and 10, six to eight days after they had lost their final World Cup game to Chile and been eliminated from the tournament, only family members greeted them at the airport. Two of the team members, Joe Maca and Eddie Sousa, held jobs they were supposed to have reported back to some days earlier, and feared they would be fired. After their stint in World Cup competition, all of the players on the US team continued to play soccer, two of them, Gaetjens and McIlenny, doing so as full-time professionals in France and the UK, respectively, and the remainder in semiprofessional leagues. All the semiprofessional players continued to work in a variety of jobs, with little recognition of their having been on a US national soccer team.[33]

THE EMERGENCE OF TELEVISION AND US SOCCER

Then, in the 1950s, a development occurred that raised the possibility of American professional soccer escaping the doldrums. The 1950s was the decade of television in the United States. When the decade opened, only 9 percent of American households had a television set; by 1960, a whopping 90 percent of households owned at least one.[34] Before 1952 the price of a television set ranged from $129 to $1,295, at a time when the average price of a new car was $2,200.[35] By 1953 the average price of a television set had dropped to around $200.[36] Once coaxial cables were laid from coast to coast, television networks could be established, so that duplicate programs could be broadcast on local affiliates of the three major networks, the Columbia Broadcasting System (CBS), the National Broadcasting Company (NBC), and the American Broadcasting Company (ABC).[37] Initially television programming was heavily local, but with the advent of network programming the number of "live" telecasts receded. The two principal forms of live television programming were news shows and sports coverage.

The networks quickly found that televised sports events could attract large audiences. The spectacle of immediate viewer access to live sports was one that had not previously existed on American media, and it proved irresistible to some audiences. By the mid-1960s all of the established professional sports leagues in the United States—baseball, gridiron football, and basketball—had secured contracts with television networks to broadcast games. The dramatic impact television could have on a professional sport was underscored in 1964, when the fledgling American Football League, launched as a rival to the four-decade-old National Football League, secured a television contract with NBC, for which the network paid $36 million. That influx of money assured that the AFL would be solvent for at least the duration of the contract, and two years later the AFL, which had established teams in some cities without NFL franchises, successfully pressured the NFL into a merger in which some AFL teams became members of the newly created league, which was now organized into two conferences, the National and American Conferences, most of the former AFL teams being placed in the latter conference.

Television contracts also stimulated expansion in both professional hockey and professional basketball. After the National Hockey League was able to secure a contract, it doubled its size from six teams—two of them in Canada—to include cities on the West Coast, which television executives believed would increase its visibility. And in 1968 the American Basketball Association was created as a rival to the National Basketball Association; it also made use of a television contract to expand into cities without NBA franchises and eventually to force its merger with the NBA.[38]

Although the British Broadcasting Company had televised an association football match as early as 1937,[39] and an international match and FA Cup final in 1938,[40] television coverage of English football was slow to develop, for several reasons. The BBC, which had a monopoly on television broadcasting in the UK until the 1950s, had only two channels, one of which was available only in the London area. Lights that made it possible to hold night games were not introduced until the mid-1950s, and the television audience for day games was not large. When the ITV television network began as a competitor to the BBC in the mid-1950s, the new network saw televised football as a way of gaining audience share. In response the BBC instituted a Saturday-evening program, *Sports Special*, on which it showed brief highlights of various soccer matches.

That program ran until 1963, and in 1960 ITV signed a contract with the English Football League under which it paid £150,000 to broadcast twenty Football League matches, all of them to be played in the evening. Although one game, between Blackpool and Bolton Wanderers, was broadcast that year, ITV withdrew from the arrangement after two visible Football League clubs, Arsenal and Tottenham, refused permission to televise their games, fearing that putting matches on television might adversely affect attendance.[41] Meanwhile the BBC moved cautiously toward televising games, introducing *Match of the Day*, a program that evolved from *Sports Special*, in 1964 and switching that program from BBC 2 to BBC 1, where it could be seen across the nation, in 1966. Not until 1983 would ITV and the BBC sign a joint two-year contract with the league, for £5.2 million, to televise matches.[42]

One difficulty that would plague the efforts of American television networks to broadcast soccer matches was not a concern for English broadcasters. The BBC was a public corporation that gained its revenues from licensing fees rather than commercial advertising, so when it broadcast live sports events, they were not interrupted by commercials. When ITV was created in the 1950s, it was in the model of American television networks that featured commercial advertising and began to include advertisements on its programs.[43] But live soccer matches presented what appeared to be an endemic difficulty for television broadcasters who wanted to include advertising in their programming.

Action in soccer matches is nearly continuous. There are breaks in play when the ball is knocked outside sidelines, or players are injured, and referees allow some limited substitution in those intervals, but clubs are not permitted to call strategic time-outs, so time routinely runs consecutively for forty-five minutes in each half, with "stoppage time" to make up for unanticipated delays. Then there is a break between halves, lasting approximately fifteen minutes. One might compare that flow of action with baseball, where teams change places on the field after each half inning, a process that typically takes about a minute and half; or football, which allows each team a specified number of time-outs in each half and also features "changes of possession," wherein one team succeeds another on offense, a process not unduly affected by minor delays; or basketball, which also gives teams a specific number of time-outs per half or quarter. Only ice hockey resembles soccer in its nearly continuous action.

In the television broadcasts of every other American professional sport, commercial advertisements are inserted during breaks in the action. This is true even in hockey, with television networks having persuaded clubs to take a few "commercial breaks" in action that would otherwise have been continuous. Advertisements fit nicely into the changes between half innings in baseball, and "TV timeouts," designed to take place when there are brief breaks in play, are now routine features of football, basketball, and even hockey broadcasts. But from the time when soccer games first came to be broadcast on television, live action has not been interrupted by commercials.

In England the absence of commercials in televised sporting events was for many years unremarkable, since many of the broadcasts were on BBC.

But when ITV, and subsequently the satellite service Sky Broadcasting, began to bid for the rights to broadcast top-tier league matches, the issue came to the fore, since both of those services relied on commercial advertising for revenues. As the prices for broadcast rights skyrocketed in the late 1980s, clubs in the top division of the Football League recognized the transformative potential of those rights for their own revenues. That led in 1992 to all of the clubs in the league's top division withdrawing to form a new league, the Premier League, and negotiating a new television contract. The eventual winner of exclusive rights, Sky Broadcasting, paid £191.5 million for a five-year contract in 1992, and £670 million for another four years in 1996.[44]

That was a considerable investment, requiring some recouping through advertising revenues. A solution, which avoided commercial advertisements interrupting Premier League matches, was for advertisers to pay clubs to display their companies' names or logos on club uniforms. The standard player uniform for a top-level soccer team now features, in addition to the player's name and number on the back, the name and logo of a sponsoring company on the front. Occasionally the name or logo will be that of the company that owns the club, as with the New York Red Bulls in Major League Soccer, whose uniforms bear the logo of the Red Bull soft drink company, but more commonly the name or logo on a club's uniform will have no apparent connection to the club, sometimes being that of a corporation from another country. In any case, the sponsors of club uniforms seem to believe that fans and television viewers' continuous exposure to their logos during soccer matches makes for good advertising.

All of the issues surrounding the emergence of television, its potential impact on professional sports, and the peculiar difficulties of adapting soccer to commercially based American television networks would play a role in the first major effort of American professional soccer to escape the doldrums. By the opening of the 1960s European clubs commonly went on North American tours in the summer months, when their leagues were inactive, and in some instances attendance at such clubs' games, typically held in baseball stadiums, was high. In 1960 New York area sports promoter Bill Cox decided to create a "league" of European clubs, called the International Soccer League, with the idea of offering matches in the United States during the comparatively limited summer break from European league play. The clubs would enter into competition with one another and sometimes with an "American" all-star club, made up of players from various international clubs who had American antecedents.[45] Although attendance at International Soccer League games was uneven, matches in cities with no strong history of professional soccer, such as Los Angeles, sometimes drew large crowds. Cox's theory in starting the league was that if American audiences were exposed to top-flight soccer, they would come to appreciate the game. Although the league lasted for only five years, ceasing play in 1965, it served to demonstrate that European-based players had comparatively easy access to American markets, and thus might become part of a pool of players for future professional soccer leagues in the United States.

During the years in which Cox's league was in operation, the United States Soccer Football Association, as it had come to be known after 1945, was aware and resentful of its presence, since the ISL was competing with the tours of European clubs that the USSFA had sponsored for decades. After the ISL folded in 1965, the USSFA, recognizing television's potential for professional soccer in the United States, let it be known that it would welcome the creation of a new coast-to-coast professional league, hopefully one that could secure a television contract. Eventually two groups of sports promoters responded. One included Cox. Another was represented by Jack Kent Cooke, then part owner of the Washington Redskins; Judge Roy Hofheinz, the owner of the Houston Astros baseball team, who in 1965 had built the first domed baseball stadium, the Houston Astrodome; and Lamar Hunt, the founding owner of the Kansas City Chiefs, who also had been influential in the formation of the American Football League.[46]

In 1966 the USSFA created a committee to consider proposals from the groups and make a recommendation at its annual meeting in July of that year. This set off the sort of chaos that had marked the launching of professional soccer leagues in the United States from World War I on. The USSFA approached FIFA on the matter, but although FIFA was interested in the establishment of a major American soccer league, its leadership resisted sanctioning a league before it had any players, FIFA recommending sanctioning individual clubs on their merits once they had been staffed, which would have resulted in a merger of the groups. The groups resisted that overture, and the USSFA resolved to sanction only one group.[47]

Before the USSFA meeting took place, however, the Cox group decided to move on its own. Ignoring the USSFA and dealing directly with FIFA, the group announced the creation of the North American Professional Soccer League, which would commence play in the fall of 1967. In response the USSFA resolved to sanction a rival league organized by the remaining promotional group. In exchange for its approval, the USSFA asked to be paid $25,000 per franchise plus 4 percent of gate receipts and 2 percent of television revenues, should they materialize. The syndicate led by Cooke agreed to those demands, and in July 1966 the USSFA sanctioned the Cooke group, whose league was to be called the North American Soccer League (NASL) and would start play in the spring of 1968.[48]

Now Cox's group took action. It announced that their new league, the National Professional Soccer League (NPSL), would begin play in the spring of 1967, a full year ahead of the start of NASL play. They also negotiated a long-term contract to televise games with CBS, which would pay them $1 million a year for exclusive rights to broadcast the games. The contract was one-sided, allowing CBS to choose whether to show games or not, but it seemingly gave the NPSL a decisive advantage over the NASL. Although FIFA then sought to encourage the two leagues to merge, the USSFA resisted, continuing its support for the NASL. Once assured of the USSFA's support, the NASL resolved to commence operations in 1967, even though its clubs had no players. It did so by entering into agreements with European and South American clubs to play matches in the United States after their seasons had ended. This was the same approach Cox's International Soccer League had taken, but the NASL believed that their revived effort would eventually lead to viable American-based franchises emerging, largely staffed by European and South American players.[49]

Both the NASL and the NPSL played seasons in 1967, the former changing its name to the United Soccer Association (USA) before starting play. Rather than importing whole teams from Europe and South America, the USA recruited players from those continents, some of them highly visible international players but most of them at the end of their playing careers. Although the attendance for some initial matches was relatively large, it quickly dwindled, and by the end of the 1967 season it already was apparent that the United States could not sustain two major professional soccer leagues. The USA and the NASL merged, resulting in twelve of the seventeen clubs that had played in 1967 folding. After the 1968 season, CBS canceled its contract with the NASL.[50]

It appeared that the same problems that had plagued American professional soccer since the early years of the twentieth century were still in place when the NPSL/USA and NASL sought to get off the ground. Neither league featured American-born players because there were very few such players in US colleges and universities, or semiprofessional leagues, who could compete with foreign players, even those whose best playing days were behind them. The result was that American audiences were exposed to foreign clubs or players with whom they had little familiarity, and the leagues found themselves at the mercy of foreign clubs and players. Few foreign clubs were inclined to send their top players to the United States for out-of-season games, and those that did agree to do so insisted upon fees that the executives of US professional leagues could not always recoup from gate receipts, resulting in all the clubs in both leagues initially losing money. Since foreign players were only inclined to play in the United States if they were paid well and if their careers in Europe or South American were on a downslide, the American leagues ended up overpaying those players without necessarily getting high-level performances out of them in return.

The potentially lucrative presence of a television contract did not pan out. CBS found it difficult to televise games in baseball stadiums, which were not well configured for soccer, and it was even more difficult to solve the problem of inserting commercials into uninterrupted action. Once CBS had established a regular Sunday *Game of the Week* broadcast, it equipped referees with an electronic device that alerted them when the network wanted action stopped in order to insert a commercial. A network employee would be stationed on the sideline to signal the referee once the commercial had ended. The idea was to get referees to prolong incidental delays in action in order to produce commercial breaks. The system seemed to work until the referee of a match between clubs from Pittsburgh and Toronto admitted to the media that he had "made up" eleven fouls to produce commercial breaks, and indicated that referees had met with teams before matches, encouraging them to "cooperate" to deliberately delay play. The Federal Communications Commission eventually investigated CBS for "misleading" soccer audiences.[51]

As CBS's problems with positioning cameras in baseball stadiums to most effectively capture the action of a soccer match suggested, the endemic problem of where and when professional soccer games were to be played in the United States was still extant in the late 1960s. Some baseball teams, such as the New York Mets, refused to rent their stadiums for soccer matches on the ground that play would damage the ballfields.[52] In other cities soccer clubs played in huge stadiums, like the Los Angeles Coliseum or Chicago's Soldier Field, which only accentuated the low attendance at soccer matches. Although both the NASL and the USA leagues initially played in the summer because of their dependence on European clubs and players, doing so brought American professional soccer into direct conflict with major-league baseball, which was experiencing a decline in attendance in the late 1960s but still had very deep roots in the United States.[53]

Finally, there was the question of how any major American professional soccer league would be structured. Not only the early attempts at such leagues, but both the NPSL and NASL in their infancy, were enterprises created in the typical American fashion: franchises run by individual entrepreneurs for profit, not necessarily tied to particular localities and serving, in some respects, as competitive as well as cooperative mechanisms for their peers. There had been no tradition in the United States of command-and-control management of soccer leagues, and the structure of early twentieth-century professional leagues reflected that situation. Clubs, and leagues, were started by individual entrepreneurs; they were for-profit enterprises; their associations with cities were fortuitous and sometimes fleeting; they came into and went out of existence rapidly; the owners of clubs rarely thought of plowing back profits into club operations or facilities.

The creation of the NASL and NPS, which took place at approximately the same time as the formation of the American Football League and the American Basketball Association, was very much in the same American "free enterprise" tradition. The promotional groups bidding for sanctioning from the USSFA in 1966 were made up of individual investors seeking to hold stakes in individual clubs. Their ventures with their league partners were cooperative only in the sense of trying to get a league off the ground: once it was in operation, the expenses, gate receipts, and revenues of individual clubs would control their future. When all the clubs in both the NASL and USA lost money in the 1967 season, that affected different club owners differently. Some, such as Lamar Hunt, the owner of the Dallas Tornado, were prepared to absorb losses for an indefinite duration; others, such as the owners of the New York Generals, Boston Beacons, and Washington Whips, were not. After just one season the latter three clubs, despite being in large cities, had ceased to exist.[54]

THE NASL APPARENTLY TAKES ROOT

It would take several more years for American investors in professional soccer clubs to recognize that something like the Football Association's command-and-control structure would have to be implemented for a professional soccer league in the United States to thrive. But despite the difficulties that plagued the two new leagues at their inception and caused the USA to fold after one season, the National American Soccer League persisted, and a decade after its inaugural season appeared to have truly gained a foothold in American sports culture.

Three developments contributed to that possibly surprising state of affairs. First, soccer began to grow substantially in American colleges and universities, resulting in the pool of prospective US-born players expanding for the NASL. In response the NASL made a conscious effort to recruit American players for its clubs, reasoning that US audiences would be more likely to become attached to homegrown players than to imported ones, some of whom spoke little English and made no effort to become permanent residents of the United States. Second, the relative affluence of the club owners who remained in the NASL after its size was dramatically reduced after the 1967 season—the league went from seventeen to five clubs in 1968, and continued with no more than nine clubs through 1973[55]—enabled clubs to continue to bid for the services of visible foreign players, sometimes paying them quite high salaries, which enhanced the league's level of play. Third, the increased television broadcasts of foreign and international matches in the United States, including World Cup competitions (none of which were held in the United States until 1994) and Olympic matches, made American audiences more familiar with soccer and its international stars.

The culmination of those developments came in the summer of 1975, when the New York Cosmos, which had replaced the Generals as the New York City entry in the NASL in 1971, signed the Brazilian superstar Edson Arantes do Nascimento, known around the world as Pelé, to a contract after he had retired from Brazilian league and World Cup play.[56] Pelé had first visited the United States in the summer of 1966 on a tour with his club,

Santos, to the delight of large crowds: he was the highest-paid and most visible soccer player in the world at the time. By 1975 Pelé, who had been playing professionally from his teens, was thirty-five years old. He was paid nearly $7 million by the New York Cosmos, who successfully proposed that the NASL renegotiate the allocation of their away-game receipts as a means of financing Pelé's contract.[57]

The NASL had expanded the previous year, going from nine clubs to twelve, including new teams in Denver, San Jose, and Seattle, and the return of previous West Coast franchises in Los Angeles and Vancouver. Initially this resulted in a spike in attendance in the new cities, but by the conclusion of the 1974 season the numbers of spectators in those cities had dwindled. Still, the league continued to expand the next season, reaching twenty-one teams. The boost in attendance generated by Pelé's signing was significant, but largely confined to games involving the Cosmos, initially not a successful team despite Pelé's presence. One feature of expansion was that some cities, such as San Jose and Vancouver, did not have major-league baseball stadiums, resulting in their soccer clubs playing in minor-league parks or high school football stadiums, the smaller size of which actually turned out to be more suitable for viewing soccer.[58]

For the next two years the NASL continued to expand, although some franchises dropped out. In 1976 the Cosmos signed Italian star Giorgio Chinaglia at the astonishingly low salary of $750,000. Chinaglia, whose US-born wife wanted to raise children in America, had become disenchanted with Italian football in 1974, when he was removed from the Italian World Cup squad for making an obscene gesture when he was substituted. Chinaglia was only twenty-eight years old when he signed with the Cosmos, and he quickly became a dominant player in the NASL.[59] With him on the roster, the club's fortunes revived in 1976 and 1977; in the latter year it won the league championship, which marked Pelé's last appearance with the club.[60] Meanwhile, when the New York Giants football team moved into a new stadium in East Rutherford, New Jersey, the Cosmos rented space there from the Giants. The two teams' schedules rarely overlapped, and the artificial turf surface at East Rutherford proved adaptable to soccer. Attendance at Cosmos matches began skyrocketing in the 1977 season, peaking in a quarter-final playoff match with the Fort Lauderdale Strikers that drew 77,691 spectators.[61] Even though the number of NASL franchises dropped from twenty-one to eighteen between 1976 and 1978, attendance throughout the league increased to the point where it appeared that professional soccer had truly become established in the United States.[62]

But just six years later the NASL had folded. Several developments contributed to that result. A massive imbalance between the Cosmos and other clubs emerged as, boosted by their substantial attendance, they began spending more money to purchase international players or secure them on loan. With some exceptions, the attendance of other clubs did not grow sufficiently to allow them to expend large sums for foreign players, but many owners continued to offer high salaries in the hope of competing with the Cosmos' level of play.

Although ABC responded to the increase in NASL attendance by offering the league a television contract in 1978, it resolved not to renew that contract two years later.[63] The reason was that American audiences, even in 1981, when a major-league baseball strike made the NASL the only professional team sport to which fans could turn during the summer, seemed incapable of watching soccer on television with interest, despite the somewhat ludicrous efforts on the part of the NASL to increase scores in games and discourage draws. Those included raising the number of permissible substitutions, drawing a line thirty-five yards from the goal beyond which players could not be offside, and instituting "shootouts," borrowed from hockey, to resolve tied games. Under the shootout experiment, players could begin to dribble toward a goal from the halfway line, approaching the goal at their own pace, and goalkeepers were free to meet them at any point in the field from that halfway line to the goal area. FIFA, which had paid little attention to NASL rule changes during its years of obscurity, balked at the offside and shootout changes, threatening the NASL with expulsion if they continued, and the league dropped them.[64] But the experiments revealed that American audiences could not get used to the low scoring and defensive emphasis of soccer, and still did not seem to appreciate the long intervals in which players passed the ball back and forth as clubs moved slowly toward their opponents' goals. After ABC stopped televising NASL games, some cable networks briefly broadcast them, but by the early 1980s those telecasts had ceased as well.[65]

Finally, the English Football League, whose players, on loan, had been a major source of NASL rosters, forbade its clubs from entering into loan agreements with the NASL in 1979.[66] The loan agreements had been desirable for both sides because most of the NASL's schedule was in the summer, at times when English league matches were not played, and the loan arrangements allowed English clubs to gain some revenue and NASL clubs to avoid having to pay players full salaries. But as the NASL began to expand and covet foreign players for its rosters, the Football League became apprehensive that loan arrangements might lead to its players being permanently signed by NASL clubs.

When loan arrangements ceased, NASL clubs were thrown back either on entering into permanent signing arrangements with foreign players or attempting to stock their rosters exclusively with American players. Neither was a particularly attractive alternative. Signing foreign players was expensive, forcing clubs to expand large sums on player salaries. Clubs didn't always get value from the players they purchased, some of whom struggled to adjust to playing and living in America. And despite the considerable growth of college soccer in the United States in the 1970s, NASL clubs remained reluctant to sign American-born players. The result made NASL teams less visible to American audiences despite their greater exposure to international soccer after the mid-1960s.

It turned out, in retrospect, that the dramatic increase in NASL attendance spawned by the Cosmos' signing of Pelé had largely come from onetime audiences—fans interested in the novelty of attending a soccer match and seeing an international star—rather than from substantial increases in the fan bases of clubs. In light of the constant turnover of many NASL franchises, even in years when the league expanded and attendance increased, it is hard to imagine, outside a few cities, such increases occurring. Even the Cosmos experienced a swift drop in attendance in the early 1980s.

As the NASL was experiencing the above difficulties, even as it expanded throughout the 1970s, its league structure remained largely a collection of individual entrepreneurs. When Phil Woosnam, a Welsh international player for Aston Villa in the English Football League who had moved to Atlanta to become playing manager of the Atlanta Chiefs in the NPSL in 1967, became the commissioner of the NASL two years later, he immediately launched campaigns to expand the league, hoping to secure a new television contract and increase revenue.[67] The latter goal proved successful; as the NASL continued to expand throughout the 1970s, the entry fee for new clubs increased, reaching $250,000 in 1974 and $1 million by 1978.[68] Woosnam believed that placing clubs in big cities and on the West Coast was essential to sell the league to television executives, and in 1978, after the league had expanded to twenty-four clubs and had its most successful season in terms of attendance, that turned out to be the case, with ABC signing a contract to televise NASL games for the next three years.

But the NASL's structure remained a collection of independent owners, none of whom had ever made any profits from their soccer clubs. In some cases, as with the Cosmos, the poor financial performance of a club was a result of the large salaries it offered European players, whose presence helped increase the visibility and performance of their teams but failed to attract enough spectators to offset their pay.[69] In other cases clubs suffered financially when their attendance dropped, so their owners resolved to sell them to other groups.

A dramatic illustration of the latter was the Philadelphia Atoms club, which was started in 1973 by Tom McCloskey, the owner of a construction company in the Philadelphia area. McCloskey resolved to create a team that would be a mix of American and foreign players, recruiting the Americans from colleges in the vicinity of Philadelphia, which had been a center of college soccer for much of the twentieth century, and securing the foreign players on loan. The coach of the Atoms was an American, Al Miller, who had enjoyed success as a coach for Hartwick College in New York. Miller endorsed McCloskey's emphasis on combining foreign with American players, and in the Atoms' first season they won the league championship.

But the foreign players on the Atoms, most of whom mainly came from England, returned to the British Isles for the start of the Football League season, illustrating the vulnerability of clubs who sought to combine American players with foreign players on loan. In the succeeding three years, the Atoms were unable to secure quality foreign players, their performance suffered, and their attendance, which had been the highest in the NASL during their initial 1973 season, dwindled sharply. By the close of the 1976 season, McCloskey, who had seen some reverses in his construction business, put the club up for sale. Within four years the Atoms had gone from NASL champions to a nonexistent franchise.[70] And by 1984 the league, which between 1975 and 1980 had fielded teams in Baltimore, Boston,

Chicago, Dallas, Denver, Detroit, Edmonton, Fort Lauderdale, Hartford, Hawaii, Houston, Las Vegas, Los Angeles, Memphis, Miami, Minneapolis, New York, Philadelphia, Portland, Rochester, San Antonio, San Jose, St. Louis, Seattle, Tampa Bay, Toronto, Tulsa, and Vancouver, had dwindled to nine clubs.[71]

AFTER THE NASL'S DEMISE

When one considers the elements of association football in England that contributed to the game's growth and success there, it may be instructive to note that none of those elements could have been associated with any professional soccer league in the United States, from the first American Soccer League of the 1920s through the NASL.

Clubs affiliated with the Football Association, and clubs belonging to the Football League, were command-and-control operations; the association, and subsequently the league, controlled their use of gate receipts and their process for signing and releasing players. Profits made by clubs were plowed back into club operations, and the retain-and-transfer system for players prevented clubs from spending large amounts bidding for players' services. In contrast, the clubs in American professional soccer leagues were owned and operated by individual entrepreneurs, who sought to make profits from their games and reacted adversely when their clubs lost money, readily selling them or moving them to other locations. There were no restrictions on the money clubs could spend to acquire players, and some teams in the NASL spent large sums on the acquisition of international players that prevented them from making profits.[72] The command-and-control structure of English football fostered a continuity of clubs over time, and their close association with localities. That was rarely reached at any point in American professional soccer.

Second, the promotion and relegation system for English football leagues was never instituted in the United States. We have seen that the system had two distinct advantages. First, it ensured that clubs with unsuccessful records in a particular league season would not fold or be moved to other cities, but simply be relegated to a lower-tier league. Although relegation might affect a club's gate receipts, it would not affect its connections to its host locality. And second, promotion and relegation provided incentives for all clubs to compete throughout a league system, despite their records, either to secure promotion or to avoid relegation. This meant that even a match between clubs with undistinguished records, late in a season, might have important implications and thus prove attractive at the gate. Promotion and relegation provided supporters with the continuous hope that a clubs in a lower-tiered league could through effective performance in a league season move to a higher-tiered league, and that a club from a comparatively small city might end up competing with a top-division league's perennial powers, with the potential prestige and revenue that entailed.

In sum, promotion and relegation, combined with the command-and-control structure of English football, ensured that residents of a community who supported a particular club could count on that club's remaining extant over time; that the operators of clubs would continue to improve the condition of their facilities; that player salaries would not unduly escalate; and that the owners of clubs affiliated with the Football Association or the Football League would have a mutual interest in furthering the health of the sport in addition to any personal interest they might have in their club's fortunes. In contrast, the owners of American professional soccer teams had no incentives to continuously operate their clubs in designated communities, or even to retain ownership of clubs if they did not fare well financially. In addition, the absence of promotion and relegation, plus the lack of restrictions on signing or transferring players, meant that talent imbalances could exist among American clubs, with some clubs financially able to sign coveted players and others not, and reduced the incentives for less talented clubs to compete throughout a season, typically resulting in drops in attendance for clubs at the bottom of a league.

But other factors contributed to the doldrums in which American professional soccer ended up for the five decades beginning in 1920. Soccer failed to emerge as an attractive proposition for broadcast and television networks, which, beginning in the 1930s, had begun to cover baseball and gridiron football games regularly on radio, and to extend that coverage to television in the 1950s. Revenues from television contracts made it possible for fledgling professional football and basketball leagues to become financially viable after the 1960s. Professional soccer never generated that level of interest, and when the NASL did temporarily acquire television contracts, the networks involved with them stopped televising games after short intervals.

A fundamental difficulty seemed to lie in the lack of American audiences' enthusiasm for watching soccer games, whether in person or on live television. Even after the NASL resolved to stage its matches in the late spring, summer, and early fall, reducing the spectator discomfort associated with winter matches in earlier leagues, Americans proved fickle in their attraction to soccer, initially showing up in large numbers when an international superstar was introduced in American leagues but not retaining that level of attendance throughout a season. As for television, Americans did not seem to be able to concentrate on soccer matches because so little of the action appeared to be directed toward scoring goals. Since many members of American television audiences had not participated in soccer, they lacked the sophistication to appreciate the subtleties of much of the play on the field.

Here, again, one sees the impact of soccer's being an "ethnic" sport for much of its twentieth-century history in the United States. The ethnic image of the sport retarded its development in American public high schools and colleges, and the ripple effects of soccer's marginal status resulted in comparatively few American-born players reaching a level at which they became attractive to professional soccer clubs in the United States, and comparatively few Americans becoming well acquainted with soccer, either as participants or spectators. That limited acquaintanceship of US residents with the sport was very probably the major reason why even as potentially promising a professional league as the NASL could not survive.

It may have been hard for American professional soccer to escape the doldrums between the 1920s and what would turn out to be the 1990s. But it may seem startling that in decades in which participation in the game, not only at colleges and universities but at high schools, grew remarkably, American professional soccer, after the demise of the NASL in 1984, remained moribund.

Between 1984 and 1996, when Major League Soccer came into being, the state of American professional soccer was as follows. There were three outdoor soccer leagues, the United Soccer League, formed in 1984 after the second version of the American Soccer League, a second-tier semipro circuit, ceased operations that year; the Western Soccer Alliance, created in 1985, whose teams were primarily centered on the West Coast; and the third version of the American Soccer League (ASL III), a semipro league on the East Coast in 1988. The ASL III was conspicuous in initiating something like a command-and-control structure of league operations. In 1990 the Western Soccer Alliance and the ASL III merged to form the American Professional Soccer League, and subsequently the APSL and the United Soccer League would merge to create what came to be called the United Systems of Independent Soccer Leagues, a set of lower-tier leagues that would eventually serve as feeders for Major League Soccer when that professional league became established in 1996. But between 1984 and 1996 none of the professional soccer leagues in operation were comparable, in their drawing power or ambitions, to the NASL. Their clubs were composed largely of American players, and in those years celebrated American college players sought to play overseas after their college careers had ended rather than joining the American leagues.

The years 1984 to 1996 also constituted a period when indoor soccer leagues emerged. There were two such leagues, the Major Indoor Soccer League, created in 1978, and the American Indoor Soccer Association, founded in 1984. Initially the MISL was the dominant league, but it folded in 1992, in part because of competition from the AISA.[73] After the MISL ceased operations a third league, the Continental Indoor Soccer League, was created in 1993. The CISL was a summer league, and the owners of its franchises were primarily owners of National Hockey League or National Basketball Association teams looking to reduce losses from arenas sitting empty in the off-season. It lasted five seasons. After it folded in 1997 the AISA, renamed the National Professional Soccer League II, would emerge as the dominant indoor soccer league in the United States; it is still in existence.[74]

Indoor soccer caught on in the United States as a spectator sport.[75] But American indoor soccer did not much resemble association football. Each side fielded six players, including goalies, and there were unlimited substitutions. Games were divided into three 20-minute periods, as in ice hockey. Playing fields, which were typically laid down over ice in arenas, were surrounded by barricades, in the manner of ice hockey, rather than boundaries, and balls hit off the barricades remained in play. The smaller fields, the fewer number of players, and the ability of players to bounce ball off barricades resulted in far greater opportunities for goal scoring and much higher-paced action on the field. The game amounted to a version of ice hockey played with a soccer ball, and enough American spectators enjoyed watching it to establish indoor soccer as a niche sport.[76] But few overseas soccer players or American collegians with professional ambitions were likely to seek careers in indoor soccer, as those careers would not have been lucrative.

Thus between 1984 and 1996, if indoor soccer is set aside, the state of American professional soccer resembled that of the years between the 1920s and the 1960s, before the first NASL came into being. American soccer leagues were essentially semipro operations. They came and went. They attracted few foreign players. They received almost no media coverage. All of this at a time when English football clubs were attracting television coverage and becoming highly profitable enterprises, and leagues in other countries were booming as well.

It was in this atmosphere that FIFA considered whether the United States should be a candidate to host a World Cup, never yet held in North America. In 1982 Columbia, which had been awarded the cup hosting for 1986, suddenly withdrew, and the NASL, despite opposition from the USSF, scrambled to make a bid, competing against Brazil, Canada, and Mexico. Even though the United States had a large number of stadiums in which World Cup games could be played and an established infrastructure, and would host a conspicuously successful Olympic games in Los Angeles in 1984, FIFA peremptorily turned down the NASL's bid, not even making a preliminary tour to inspect potential playing cites.[77]

But by 1988, despite the folding of the NASL and the absence of any equivalent replacement league, FIFA gave strong consideration to awarding the 1994 World Cup to the United States. Italy would be hosting the 1990 World Cup, Asian nations were not yet prepared to serve as hosts, and the only competitors to host in 1994 were Brazil, whose government had declined to support a proposal made by a group of investors, and Morocco, which had not yet built any stadiums. On July 4, 1988, FIFA announced that by a vote of 10 to 7 the United States had prevailed over Morocco and was awarded the 1994 hosting.[78] Should that event serve to awaken American audiences to soccer, an opportunity for American professional soccer to escape the doldrums might at last be present.

Chapter Six

FIFA and Professional Soccer in the United States

IN CHAPTER TWO we noted the efforts of the AFA and the AAFA to secure recognition from the Federation Internatioonale de Football Association (FIFA), which had been founded in Paris in May 1904. FIFA's founding came at a time when association football was flourishing in the UK and beginning to spread throughout western Europe, and as amateur English clubs were accepting invitations to tour European countries and play matches against local clubs. The impetus for founding an organization that would promote the continued growth of association football in Europe came from a combination of goals sought by proponents: an interest in putting on international matches, a concern that standard rules for the game be established internationally, and a desire to create football associations in European countries along the Football Association model—one association per country that exclusively organized domestic and international matches.

THE STRUCTURE OF FIFA

FIFA is a nonprofit, noncommercial association, registered as such in Switzerland under the Swiss Civil Code.[1] It describes its purpose as "to improve the game of football constantly and promote it globally, particularly through youth and developments programmes."[2] It is taxed in Switzerland in the category of "political, religious, scientific, cultural, [and] charitable" associations with "non-commercial" purposes.[3] As such its only obligations to the Swiss government are to file an accounting of its revenues and expenses on a four-year accounting cycle. It pays no dividends to its members or employees.

From its origins FIFA made it clear that although it invited associations from nations to join it, charging them a minimal entry fee, it would only sanction one such association per country. As the number of associations affiliated with FIFA grew, it organized its association structure into regional confederations, of which there are now six. In chronological order of formation, the confederations are CONMEBOL (the Confederación Sudamericana de Fútbol), founded in 1916, with South American members; UEFA, the Union des Associations Européennes de Football (1954), with members from Europe plus Israel; AFC, the Asian Football Confederation (1954), with members from Asia and Australia; CAF, the Confederation of African Football (1957), with members from Africa; CONCACAF, the Confederation of North, Central American, and Caribbean Association Football (1961); and Oceania, a confederation composed of nations in the South Pacific (1966), including New Zealand and the Pacific Islands.[4] The confederations are not considered part of FIFA: they are recognized by that body but operate independently. However, they receive their status and influence from their formal recognition by FIFA and their affiliation with it, and their policies, especially with respect to the staging of World Cups, are heavily influenced by FIFA. At present there are 209 member nations of the six confederations.[5]

FIFA's policies are set by an executive committee of twenty-four members, either appointed or elected by the confederations. Executive committee members serve four-year terms, and there is no limit to the number of terms they may serve. There are also no age limits to terms of service.[6] The executive committee has a president, a senior vice president, and seven vice presidents (one from each of the confederations and a representative from UK associations), with its remaining members coming from the confederations in a somewhat disproportionate fashion, with more members from UEFA than from CAF or AFC. UEFA is also disproportionately represented on the executive committee, with more members from UEFA and CONMEBOL on the committee than the number of members in those associations would suggest.[7]

Technically speaking, the executive committee merely follows the decisions of FIFA's congress, in which each member association has a single vote. In practice, however, the executive committee makes all of the crucial decisions for FIFA, most notably where to stage World Cups and how FIFA's policies are to be generated and its money spent.[8] Although the executive committee is structured so that no one region can control its votes, in practice this has resulted in strategic alliances between committee members, sometimes for self-serving purposes. Decisions of the committee have also at times been dictated by FIFA presidents: there is a strong tradition of presidential authority in the organization.[9]

Under FIFA's current structure there are a number of standing committees. Among the most significant of those are the Television Advisory Board, the Finance Committee, the Strategic Committee, and the Organizing Committee, which is responsible for individual World Cups. Particularly important are the Emergency Committee and the Bureau Special Projects Committee, designed to make policy when FIFA faces critical decisions or resolves to embark on long-term projects.[10] Although the membership of standing committees is publicized, membership on those committees is not distributed on an equal basis. Some members, many of them on the executive committee, serve on multiple standing committees, most members on just one.[11] As we will see, membership in a standing committee, especially one of the more influential ones, is a primary means by which representatives of confederations affiliated with FIFA exert influence.

Although oversight of FIFA's operations is minimal, that of the associations and confederations associated with it is typically even less. A case in point is the distribution of funds to persons associated with the United States' hosting of the 1994 World Cup. After FIFA awarded the 1994 cup to the United States in 1988, it began campaigning for the ouster of then president of the USSF Werner Fricker and for his replacement by Alan Rothenberg, a Los Angeles lawyer who was the commissioner for soccer when the United States organized the 1984 Olympics. Once Rothenberg was named USSF president, he immediately turned his attention to the organization of the 1994 World Cup, hiring Scott Parks LeTellier as managing director. After that cup's considerable financial success, the USSF awarded Rothenberg $7 million for serving as the World Cup Organizing Committee's chairman, and LeTellier a $500,000 bonus. This was in addition to compensation LeTellier received for his work for the USSF from 1991 to 1994.[12]

FIFA'S PRIMARY GOALS

From its origins FIFA has had two interrelated goals. The first has been to encourage and support the worldwide growth of soccer by fostering player development in individual nations, primarily through the funding of particular programs and facilities administered by its confederations. Money for player development trickles down from FIFA executive committees to confederation officials, who have considerable discretion as to how to spend it, a lack of accountability that has regularly tempted persons of authority in confederations to associate their ability to dole out funds with their campaigns to secure or remain in office. Candidates for the presidency of FIFA have consistently campaigned on pledges to support funding for player development in particular regions, hoping to secure the votes of confederation members from those areas.

FIGURE 4. Joseph "Sepp" Blatter, president of FIFA from 1998 to 2015, photographed on April 20, 2015. Under Blatter's leadership FIFA continued its economic success and domination of international soccer, and also its corrupt practices, revelations of which led to Blatter's being banned from soccer activities in 2015. Press service of the President of Russia, www.kremlin.ru.

The other goal of FIFA has been to sponsor World Cup tournaments on what is now a four-year basis, controlling not only the process by which host nations are chosen but virtually everything else about the staging of a World Cup, including agreements with media and merchandisers to broadcast matches and to produce and distribute memorabilia. FIFA makes a great deal of money from sponsoring World Cups, through not only bids from host nations but also media and merchandising rights. It does so by entering into partnerships with the associations of host nations who successfully bid for World Cups. FIFA pays money to the organizing committees of host nations, and also pays prize money to competing teams and pays the expenses of those teams and of match referees. The host nations are responsible for developing and paying for the infrastructure of World Cup tournaments. Host nations can charge admission for cup matches, and are allowed to amass revenues from some merchandising in connection with the staging of cups, but FIFA retains broadcast rights and most merchandising rights, the latter two areas being the most lucrative ventures associated with World Cups.

FIGURE 5. Jules Rimet, president of FIFA from 1921 to 1954, photographed in 1920. Rimet's presidency was marked by the growing financial success of FIFA from revenues associated with the staging of World Cups. Photo: Meurisse News Agency. Département Estampes et Photographie, EI-13 (2645), Bibliothèque Nationale de France, Paris

The result has been that since 1950—when, after the success of that year's World Cup in Brazil, FIFA's general secretary, Ivo Schriker, wrote to its president, Jules Rimet, "We are rich!"[13]—FIFA has made a considerable amount of money from its control of World Cups.

FIFA AND SOCCER IN THE UNITED STATES

From the early twentieth century onward FIFA demonstrated an interest in the development of professional soccer in the United States. The reasons for this went beyond its interest in employing the international spread of soccer to promote peace and goodwill among nations. The United States, which had undergone a decade of prosperity after the end of World War I and developed a considerable infrastructure of railroad networks and highways, was identified by FIFA as a promising spectator market for soccer. But we have seen that despite FIFA's certification of what would become the United States Soccer Foundation as the body controlling American professional soccer, several professional leagues not sanctioned by the USSF emerged in the United States, competed with one another, featured players from European clubs or from immigrant communities in particular cities and towns, and went in and out of existence.

By 1950 it had become clear that staging the World Cup, including denominating the host nation, had become big business for FIFA. In 1947 it awarded the 1950 World Cup to Brazil, and it would continue that pattern of naming World Cup hosts well in advance of tournaments. This practice was helpful not only to the host nation but also to FIFA. It gave host nations lead time to develop their infrastructure, building stadiums to host matches and improving transit and communication between sites. More stadiums, and better infrastructure, typically meant larger crowds at World Cup matches, and larger crowds brought more revenue to both the host nation and FIFA.[14]

By 1954, when the World Cup was held in Switzerland, changes in the staging of World Cups were taking place. The emergence of radio, and especially television, after World War II made it possible for supporters of World Cup teams to follow matches without attending them. That development would revolutionize the political economy and character of World Cup competitions. With television coverage, which made it possible for residents of Germany to watch all of the 1954 cup matches, there was no longer a need for gigantic stadiums, which had been a feature of World Cups since the initial 1930 tournament in Uruguay, and the emphasis on stadium building for cup competitions shifted from size to the convenience and comfort of spectators.[15] At the same time the opportunity for television networks to broadcast games meant dramatically increased revenue for those networks in the form of advertisements, and even greater revenue for FIFA, which controlled the media rights to World Cups.

FIFA responded to the growing importance of television rights to World Cup competitions along two parallel tracks. One was to partner with the Swiss sports marketing firm International Sports & Leisure (ISL), which would serve as a liaison between FIFA and companies interested in advertising on World Cup broadcasts. ISL's strategy was to approach major potential sponsors, sell them marketing packages to cup competitions at large sums, and reap the profits for FIFA.[16] At the same time FIFA opened bidding for television rights to cups among networks all over the globe. FIFA retained power to veto awards of broadcast rights on the ground that it wanted World Cup broadcasts to "remain accessible to viewers who do not possess expensive satellite or cable systems,"[17] but the primary effect of the arrangement was to funnel more revenues into FIFA and its marketing partners.

Although it had become clear by 1950 that staging the World Cup was enough to ensure financial solvency for FIFA, the advent of television and the broadcast and sponsoring rights associated with televising World Cup competitions ushered in a new stage in FIFA's history. What had begun as a modest effort by a group of European soccer devotees to promote the game by staging an international competition had evolved into an incredibly lucrative monopoly. In 1987 FIFA press officer Guido Tognoni noted that "FIFA has never had a problem finance wise" because "it's a monopoly enterprise" and thus "the money is always there," but that "FIFA is living from one event which is the World Cup and this event [was now] living from marketing and television receipts, television money, and marketing money." Tognoni recalled that in the 1970s, when television was becoming increasingly important in publicizing soccer internationally, Horst Dassler, the head of the Adidas sportswear firm in Germany, had "invented publicity on television" for soccer merchandising, including printing the names of merchandising companies on soccer uniforms and even the sponsorship of entire soccer leagues, such as the first-division English Premier League, by corporations such as Barclay's Bank.[18]

Although FIFA was initially conceived of as something like a nonprofit missionary organization promoting international soccer, it had from its origins insisted that it would be the only institution organizing an international tournament. Even when it was struggling to establish such a tournament, and dependent on the Olympic Games to help stage it, FIFA's founders insisted on the institution separating itself from the Olympics, eventually choosing to hold World Cups in a different four-year cycle, and at different locations, from that of the Olympics.[19] As FIFA emerged from World War I and moved toward staging the 1930 World Cup, its founders' dogged insistence that it alone would control the staging of an international soccer tournament came to be regarded as an established practice by the world soccer community. Once nations began to recognize hosting a World Cup as a way to boost their international reputation, FIFA stood to profit from this control. When the World Cup resumed in 1950 after a twelve-year hiatus resulting from World War II, that profit increased, and once television and sports marketing were added to the mix after 1954, the monopolistic position of FIFA became exceptionally lucrative. A private Swiss-based organization, not representing any nation, with a comparatively small staff and entirely internal controls on its budget and operations, was dispensing World Cups worth billions to television networks, sports marketing firms, and host nations.

It was in the years of television's growth that FIFA began to take a considerable interest in the development of soccer in the United States. There were several obstacles to that development, one of them organizational and another centering on the apparent lack of attraction of American audiences to the low-scoring character of most soccer games.

FIFA's practice in developing soccer around the globe was to establish associations, modeled on the English Football Association, that FIFA would sanction in exchange for modest dues fees and an understanding that all international matches engaged in by clubs identified with a particular association would also need to be sanctioned by FIFA. In European and some Latin American countries, FIFA permitted only one association per nation. But in other regions, notably Central America, the Caribbean, Mexico, and the United States, the FIFA-sanctioned association was CONCACAF, a federation created in 1961, headquartered in Guatemala, and dominated by Mexico.[20] During the Englishman Stanley Rous's 1961–74 FIFA presidency, CONCACAF operated largely independently from the larger body, in part because Rous encouraged independence among FIFA-affiliated associations. The result was corruption, poor management, and some apparent manipulation of World Cup qualifying matches. Rous, in an address to the CONCACAF congress in 1971, called for several reforms, including more effective and transparent use of financial resources, better appointments of delegates to the congress and referees, and greater accountability of officials to the congresses and ultimately to FIFA.[21] Little resulted from these calls for reform, and the United States Soccer Foundation continued to occupy a marginal role in FIFA.

Additional evidence of the USSF's marginal status would come in 1982. At that time the North American Soccer League was still in operation, and there was continuing optimism among its owners and FIFA that professional soccer would gain a foothold in America, though most of the NASL players were not US natives and the NASL had had little success in integrating American college players into the league. But in 1982 an apparent opportunity to expand the footprint of soccer in the United States emerged. FIFA had initially awarded the World Cup in 1986 to Colombia, but political unrest and violence in that nation had resulted in its dropping its bid for fear that it could neither build sufficient infrastructure for matches nor ensure adequate security for spectators..[22] The United States seemed a logical choice to replace Colombia. Los Angeles had been selected to host the 1984 Olympic Games, and as a result some additional stadiums would be built that might prove adequate for World Cup soccer matches. The only other credible candidate from the CONCACAF region, Mexico, had hosted the World Cup in 1970.

Yet FIFA, yielding to pressure within CONCACAF, decided to award the 1986 World Cup to Mexico.[23] The result was, according to one person familiar with the process,[24] that Warner Communications, a major backer of the NASL that was anticipating becoming a major sponsor of a 1986 World Cup tournament in the United States, decided that FIFA would never support professional soccer in America, and thus resolved to no longer support the NASL. By the time FIFA decided to award a World Cup to the United States in 1988, as we have seen, the NASL had folded.

The marginal status of the USSF in CONCACAF, and FIFA's perhaps myopic confidence in that association, was not the only barrier preventing FIFA from making a full-scale commitment to the development of American professional soccer for nearly all of the twentieth century. Another was the conflict arising from FIFA's insistence on developing and maintaining uniform rules for international soccer matches. This was one of FIFA's original goals on its founding: it selected the rules of the Football Association as a template for international matches and set out to participate in their refinement and to insist on their being followed in any FIFA-sponsored international matches, including the World Cup.

Occasionally FIFA sought to institute changes in the rules for international soccer. By the early 1960s, defensive play was beginning to overwhelm offensive play in European top-tier leagues, and concerns were raised that the resultant lack of scoring might adversely affect spectator interest.[25] Up to that point the only rule change initiated by FIFA and the International Football Association Board, which had been formed by the British in 1886 and had admitted four FIFA members in 1928, was to liberalize the offside rule.[26] But when the NASL began play in 1968, its founders proposed more sweeping rule changes: a further relaxation of the offside rule,; more liberal substitution rules; an increase in the width of the goals to facilitate scoring; and an opportunity for referees to stop play at intervals, or when balls were kicked out of bounds, so that broadcasters could insert commercial advertisements.[27] Of those proposed changes, all but the substitution rules represented substantial departures from existing international rules. As we saw in chapter 5, substitution rules had been modified over the course of the twentieth century from a rigid no-substitution rule (if players, even goalkeepers, were injured, teams had to continue play without them) to permit first the substitution of injured goalkeepers, and then of one player per match.[28]

By the time of the NASL's inauguration, the IFAB permitted two substitutes, but the NASL permitted three. When FIFA noticed the discrepancy and asked the NASL to correct it, the president of the NASL responded by lobbying to retain the change, citing the hot summer weather in the United States and the need for professional soccer to be a summer sport there. Unpersuaded, FIFA refused to permit three substitutions.[29] As for the other changes, the only one FIFA considered was a limited offside zone, drawn closer to the goal, which FIFA experimented with in 1978 in response to concerns about the decline of scoring in soccer. The NASL eagerly adopted the limited offside rule, and continued to employ it after FIFA had dropped the experiment after a year.

In December 1980, on realizing that the NASL was continuing to employ limited offside zones, FIFA threatened the USSF with suspension if the practice was not altered by January 15, 1981. The USSF protested, and a compromise was reached in which the NASL was permitted to use an "offside line" and three substitutions for the 1981 season, but thereafter revert to the official IFAB rules.[30] As for enlarged goals and the practice of shootouts to break ties, both of which NASL officials advocated, FIFA and the IFAB categorically refused to sanction those changes.[31]

The back-and-forth between FIFA and the NASL about rule changes was a product of the NASL team owners' conviction that American audiences would never fully accept the game of soccer unless it had higher scoring. That perception was still present a decade later. In 1993 a columnist for *USA Today* wrote, "The World Cup draw is Sunday and admit it, you don't care" because American sports spectators were only interested in "arms and hands, things that happen from the waist up." "Hating soccer," the columnist claimed, was "more American than mom's apple pie."[32] In his autobiography, written in 1978, four years after he was replaced as president of FIFA, Stanley Rous maintained that soccer in America "seemed doomed to remain a marginal activity . . . far from the mainstream of American sport."[33] A major reason for soccer's marginal status in the United States, Rous felt, was the inability of American professional soccer leagues to develop home-grown players. A media representative of the NASL agreed with him. In an interview in 1996, Jim Trecker attributed the failure of the NASL partially to its inability to "develop enough American players." "You just can't stack your team with all foreigners," Trecker believed: "There weren't any hometown heroes."[34]

But by 1988 FIFA was prepared to take a chance on staging a World Cup in the United States. Part of the reason was the noticeable financial and spectating success of the 1984 Summer Olympic Games, held in Los Angeles. Despite turbulent international relations connected to the later stages of the Cold War, which had resulted in the US team boycotting the 1980 Summer Olympics in Moscow and the Soviet Union's retaliating by refusing to participate in the 1984 games, the 1984 Olympics were held without any damaging incidents and made considerable profits for both the International Olympic Committee and the US Olympic Committee. The comparative efficiency with which the 1984 Olympics were staged confirmed, for FIFA, that the United States had the infrastructure and private resources capable of hosting a World Cup, notwithstanding the challenges posed by its vast territory.

Another reason was the continued belief among those who ran FIFA that the United States was one of the last undeveloped major markets for soccer. With careful planning, television exposure, and large stadiums that could be filled with foreign visitors as well as resident Americans, FIFA officials felt that a World Cup staged in the United States could be quite profitable. And they also felt that America's hosting the 1994 World Cup would create momentum for the launching of a new professional soccer league in the United States. As we will see in more detail in a subsequent chapter, FIFA actually sought to link the awarding of the World Cup to the United States to a pledge on the part of the USSF to commit to starting such a league on the heels of the 1994 Cup, and were disappointed when Major League Soccer, which had been awarded the league's franchise by the USSF, decided to postpone its opening to 1996 as it sought to locate sites for the ten clubs it had initially planned.[35]

Despite FIFA's confidence, a marked skepticism about the capacity of the United States to host a successful World Cup remained in place among both American and foreign commentators through 1993, when the draw for the cup was to be held. Weir's assumption that American audiences would be bored or alienated by soccer was shared by some other US commentators, and some British commentators were openly dismissive of the USSF's efforts to promote the cup, which included having celebrities obviously unfamiliar with soccer give canned speeches to welcome foreign visitors. A particularly vivid example of apparent American tackiness came when singer Diana Ross was enlisted to take a penalty kick in a ceremonial opening of the cup competition at Chicago on July 17, 1994. Ross's kick rolled slowly wide of the goal, and at the same time the "goal" created for the event collapsed.[36]

There were also rumors that the USSF would insist that goals be widened for the tournament to create more scoring; that matches would be divided into four quarters rather than two halves to allow more television advertising; that artificial turf fields would be substituted for grass ones, and that offside zones might be adopted.[37] None of those changes was made, but in the interval between the 1990 and 1994 World Cups, FIFA initiated some changes in its rules designed to favor offensive play and to limit the cynical fouling by defenders of offensive players who gained an advantage outside the goal's penalty area. Defenders were aware that when a player was fouled outside that area, his team was only awarded a free kick on goal, which could be guarded against by many opposing players. In contrast, a foul within the penalty area, a large rectangle extending out from the goal, resulted in a penalty shot for the offensive team, in which a player could take an unobstructed shot at the goal from only twelve yards away, with only the opposing goalkeeper defending.[38] FIFA's changes included waiving offsides unless offensive players gained a distinct advantage from them, subjecting defensive fouls to stricter penalties, including yellow cards (penalties that, if they accumulated over the course of a game, could result in a player's disqualification) and red cards (which warranted immediate disqualification). Yellow and even red cards were also given to players who feigned injury or "dove" after minimal contact to secure penalties against opponents.[39] The result was an improvement in the general pace and style of play from the 1990 to the 1994 cups, although defense continued to dominate, and the final matches, between international powerhouses Brazil and Italy, ended in a scoreless tie that required a penalty shootout.

In the end the 1994 World Cup surpassed expectations in spectator attendance, television ratings, merchandising, and economic impact. Approximately $4 billion in revenue flowed into the US economy, and the USSF made a profit of over $20 million, with FIFA garnering even more.[40] Two years after the 1994 tournament concluded, a USSF official recalled that when the United States was named as cup host, "it was considered a joke," with commentators predicting that "the United States could never pull off a successful World Cup, they would never get fans into the stadiums, they never sold sponsorships, they would cut the game into quarters, they have no passion, they have no idea of what is like to play." "Guess what?," he concluded. "All the European press had to eat crow."[41]

In FIFA's report on the 1994 cup, FIFA president João Havelange stated that its success "vindicated totally FIFA's decision to award the Finals to a

FIGURE 6. Jean-Marie Faustin Godefroid "Joao" de Havelange, president of FIFA from 1974 to 1998, photographed on April 19, 2010. After defeating Stanley Rous for the FIFA presidency in 1974, Havelange changed the culture of FIFA, inviting corruption in both presidential elections and FIFA's affiliated confederations. José Cruz/Abr, Agência Brasil.

country whose tireless efforts to promote our sport have long earned our respect." He added that the 1994 cup had featured "thrilling football, full stadia, fair play and a peaceful atmosphere."[42] The latter statement may have been accurate, but the former was far from candid. FIFA had long been apprehensive about the state of soccer in the United States, been inclined to believe that far from being tireless promoters of the sport, Americans had largely ignored it. But, as we have seen, FIFA's 1988 decision to award the men's World Cup to the United States, coupled with its subsequent decision to stage the 1999 women's World Cup in America, were major factors in gaining, at last, a substantial foothold for both professional and recreational soccer in the United States.

THE IMPACT OF FIFA ON US SOCCER

As we have just seen, despite its professed interest in developing soccer within the United States, FIFA remained reluctant to let that nation host a World Cup as late as the 1980s, this at a time when the NASL appeared to be on the brink of success. After the 1994 men's World Cup and the women's World Cup of 1999, however, the United States' ability to stage profitable cup tournaments with large attendance, decent television ratings, and worldwide attention was established. The current US men's professional soccer league, Major League Soccer, launched in 1996, expanded during the early years of the twenty-first century, began to attract visible international and U.S.-based players, and, as we will see in a later chapter, is now very possibly on the threshold of being a profitable enterprise. In addition, as we will also see, soccer as a recreational sport, one played by men and women and boys and girls, is thriving in the United States, expanding in high schools and colleges and creating new generations of informed American soccer fans. FIFA arguably launched that cycle of advancement when in 1988 it took a chance on holding the 1994 men's World Cup in the United States. Notwithstanding the largely unhappy history of soccer in America during the course of the twentieth century, especially in contrast to the remarkable growth and dominance of FIFA on the international scene, in the future FIFA may well be inclined to consider the United States as one of its most potentially valuable assets, and American soccer might be inclined to attribute at least part of its growth to FIFA.

One further example of FIFA's contribution to the growth of soccer in the United States, even if, again, in a halting fashion, bears mention. This was FIFA's sponsorship of a World Cup for women, held in China in 1991 and won by the US team. As we will see, after women's soccer began to be played in some nations after the 1970s, some national women's soccer organizations began to solicit FIFA for affiliation and sponsorship. Perhaps unsurprisingly in a world only starting to open up to feminism, most of the associations affiliated with FIFA resisted, primarily on the (preposterous) ground that women were most likely incapable of playing high-quality soccer, even going so far as to suggest that the sport was altogether unsuitable for women. Only after women's tournaments were staged successfully in several countries in the 1980s, and viable women's soccer leagues came into being, did FIFA realize that it was at risk of losing control over the worldwide administration of women's soccer. It eventually responded by staging an international women's tournament in China in 1988, in which twelve teams from six continents participated, and which was sufficiently successful to encourage FIFA to stage the 1991 women's World Cup.[43] That event, although it received comparatively little publicity in the United States, would launch the US women's World Cup team into the consciousness of American audiences, dovetailing nicely with the sharp rise in women's soccer in US high schools and colleges after the 1970s. The unusual history of women's soccer in America, culminating in the twenty-first century with the US women's World Cup team becoming a national cultural icon, is the subject of the next chapter.

Chapter Seven

The Unusual History of Women's Soccer in America

ANYONE SEEKING TO recount the history of women's soccer in the United States in the late twentieth and early twenty-first centuries confronts the fact that for the first six decades of that story, most American women and girls did not play soccer. They did not play the sport recreationally; they very rarely played it in in voluntary clubs and associations; with but one exception, they did not play it in private or public high schools, colleges, and universities; and, of course, there were no US professional or semiprofessional women's soccer leagues in which they might have played it.

WOMEN'S SOCCER IN THE EARLY TWENTIETH CENTURY

On initial consideration, the absence of women's soccer in the United States for most of the twentieth century might not seem surprising. When FIFA first sponsored an international women's soccer tournament—this in 1988—only twelve countries fielded teams.[1] It took pressure from women's soccer associations unaffiliated with FIFA to eventually convince that organization to stage a women's World Cup, and when FIFA polled its membership about the prospect of sponsoring women's soccer in 1970, only 90 of its 139 affiliated national associations bothered to respond, and only 12 of them voted in favor.[2] One might be inclined to believe that women's soccer was not played anywhere in the world until the late 1950s, and thus there was no particular reason, especially with the marginal status of early and mid-twentieth-century men's soccer in the United States, that women's soccer should have been played in America.

But in fact women's soccer was being played in other parts of the world as early as the first decades of the twentieth century.[3] In 1917, when the opposing sides in World War I had settled into a trench-war stalemate that promised to delete the ranks of young men in England, Dick, Kerr & Co., Ltd., a firm in Preston, Lancashire, created a soccer team as a recreational activity for its female munitions workers.[4] With so many men conscripted into the armed services, firms recruited women to work in factories connected to the war effort. Work in munitions factories was particularly demanding, with long hours and frequently dangerous conditions, and Dick, Kerr and other firms encouraged their female workers to engage in outdoor recreational activities as a contrast to their work environment.[5]

FIGURE 7. Dick, Kerr Ladies Football Club, photographed in 1921. The Dick, Kerr club, founded by an English munitions firm in World War I at a time when English men's football was disrupted by the war, was the most conspicuous and successful women's soccer team in the first two decades of the twentieth century. Courtesy of the Lizzy Ashcroft Collection.

The Dick, Kerr Ladies Football Club was specially created to raise funds toward the care of wounded soldiers in Preston, which was home to a military hospital. A number of other English munitions factories had offered soccer as a recreational activity for their female workers, so the Dick, Kerr club had no shortage of opponents. Preston hosted a founding member of the Football League, Preston North End, but it ceased play during the war, and the city's residents were hungry to watch soccer matches. On Christmas Day, 1917, 10,000 spectators watched a match between the Dick, Kerr club and that of another munitions factory, Arundel Coulthard. Dick, Kerr won the match 4–0, and raised over £600 for wounded soldier relief, the equivalent of almost £50,000 today.[6]

After the close of the war, while the FA was still reorganizing, Dick, Kerr continued to play against other female teams, and even in some exhibitions against male clubs, faring well enough to attract attention. The Dick, Kerr players received a stipend of 10 shillings per match to cover their expenses. Meanwhile, women had begun to play association football in France as well, and in 1920 a series of international matches was arranged between Dick, Kerr and a women's club based in Paris. The first four such contests were held in England, with Dick, Kerr winning matches at Preston and Stockport, drawing at Manchester, and losing to the French in London. This set was followed by four matches in France, with the teams drawing in matches in Paris, Roubaix, and Havre, and the Dick, Kerr club winning in Rouen. The last match in the series was held in Liverpool on Boxing Day, 1920, and drew 53,000 spectators, with the Dick, Kerr club winning 4–0.[7]

About a year later, the Football Association issued a resolution banning women's football from FA grounds, which made it difficult for women's teams to play before crowds of spectators in the UK. The FA cited two reasons for the ban. The first was in response to "complaints ... made as to football being played by women," the FA feeling "impelled to express the strong opinion that the game of football is unsuitable for females and should not be encouraged." The second was that "an excessive proportion of the receipts" from women's matches was "absorbed in expenses and an inadequate proportion devoted to charitable objects."[8] The first reason was patently bogus, since the Dick, Kerr club had demonstrated itself capable of competing with men's teams. The second, even if could have been substantiated, was nonetheless dubious, given that no one had ever expected clubs in the Football League or associations affiliated with it to donate most of their gate receipts to charity. If women's soccer was for some reason supposed to be primarily a charitable activity, the FA had not advanced a reason for that treatment. The far more likely reason for the ban was that the FA, noting that women's soccer matches could draw large crowds, potentially as large as or larger than those for many men's matches, simply wanted to eliminate organized women's soccer as a competitor. Whatever underlay it, the ban was to remain in effect until 1971. While it did not wholly prevent women's soccer from being played in the UK, it did serve to relegate matches to rugby fields with less capacity to host spectators, and some rugby authorities banned women's soccer from their grounds.[9]

In 1922 the Dick, Kerr club proposed a tour of North America. Its initial goal was to play a series of matches against Canadian and American semiprofessional men's teams. On learning of the proposed tour, the Dominion Football Association, Canada's FIFA-affiliated organization, took the position that it "objected to women football players" and refused to allow Canadian men's clubs to play against the Dick, Kerr Ladies FC. Consequently Dick, Kerr played nine American men's teams on its tour, winning three matches, losing three, and drawing three. The men's teams were largely composed of clubs in the American Soccer League or other eastern semiprofessional leagues, some of whose members would subsequently be on the 1930 US men's World Cup roster.[10] If there was any uncertainty about women's capacity of to play soccer competitively with men, the Dick, Kerr club's 1922 tour should have assuaged that.

While that US tour may have been a moderate success—the average attendance at its matches ranged between 4,000 and 10,000 spectators at a time when men's professional and semiprofessional matches were less well attended—it failed to generate anything like a groundswell fan base for women's soccer in the United States.[11] Indeed, it seems to have had no effect in terms of encouraging women to become fans and supporters of men's soccer or of encouraging a great many more women or girls to play soccer.

Still, the Dick, Kerr Ladies FC 1922 tour of the United States creates a puzzle. It was not the case that women's sports were affirmatively discouraged in early twentieth-century America. Many high schools and women's colleges offered basketball and volleyball, and some, mainly private ones, offered field hockey. Girls and women were also encouraged to play tennis and golf, and in the 1920s and 1930s some very successful women tennis players and golfers, such as Helen Wills, Alice Marble, and Babe Didrikson Zaharias, rose to national celebrity.

The entrenchment of field hockey in America—a governing body for the sport, the United States Field Hockey Association, was formed in 1922[12]—is particularly curious when paired with the nonexistence of women's soccer for much of the twentieth century. Field hockey, a sport played by both men and women in several countries in the nineteenth century, was introduced into the United States in 1901 by an Englishwoman, Constance Applebee.[13] The sport initially spread to some elite women's colleges in the Northeast and Middle Atlantic regions, such as Bryn Mawr, Mount

Holyoke, Radcliffe, Vassar, and Wellesley.[14] It has rarely been played by men in America, where it has never been offered as a boy's or men's high school or college sport. Yet field hockey is a sport with a fair amount of physical contact that emphasizes, as does soccer, the continuous movement of players around the field with comparatively few breaks in the action. In terms of conditioning, field hockey and soccer are similar, and they are also similar with respect to the style and pace of play, the object in both sports being to bring a ball down the field to a point where a player can take a shot on goal. Thus the argument that women are physically unsuited to play soccer would seem to apply equally to field hockey. But that argument did not gain traction when field hockey was first introduced in America, and although men played field hockey in other nations, field hockey has always been regarded as a women's sport in the United States.

EXPLANATIONS FOR THE ABSENCE OF WOMEN'S SOCCER IN THE UNITED STATES

The puzzle of the virtual nonexistence of women's soccer in early and mid-twentieth century America, in contrast to the growth of other women's team sports during the same period, requires further exploration. The literature on women's sports in the United States has advanced several explanations for the dearth of women's soccer in the early twentieth century.

The first of those explanations emphasizes a gender bias that takes two forms: a bias against women as physically unsuitable to play sports in general, or soccer in particular; and a bias in favor of sports, particularly team sports, as male preserves designed to encourage the physical (read "manly") development and prowess of boys and men. Evidence in support of both explanations exists.[15] In Victorian-era England, gender differences and stereotypes were emphasized, particularly when it came to physical exercise. Girls and women were thought to be "frail," "delicate" beings whose bodies were unsuited to hard physical labor or overly strenuous exercise. It was even believed in some quarters that vigorous exercise might damage female reproductive organs.[16] Part of the growth of gymnastics as a regular feature of physical education programs, which emerged in the UK and western Europe in the late nineteenth century, was that gymnastic exercises could be undertaken by women as well as men because they emphasized agility and grace rather than violence and physically taxing activities.[17]

On the other hand, "muscular Christianity," a movement that emerged in late nineteenth-century English and American high schools and colleges, emphasized the importance of physical activity, particularly in the form of games and sports, as a way of encouraging boys and young men to develop their "masculinity" in the form of competitive athletics, all the while learning the "Christian" virtues of fair competition and good sportsmanship. The movement valued physical prowess and athletic skills, even though it sought to cabin them in a "Christian" ethic, associating them with masculinity.[18]

One could argue, on the basis of those two gendered attitudes, that women's organized sports were being affirmatively discouraged as "unfeminine" at the same time that men's sports were being encouraged as "masculine." That argument might suggest that soccer, which was regularly played at the time at educational institutions that subscribed to the "muscular Christianity" ethos, would have been encouraged as a sport and recreational activity for men, but not for women. It might even serve to lend some credibility to the FA's 1921 claim that football was "unsuitable for females." An assumption that association football was a male preserve into which women ought not to enter might be said to have informed that claim. Since masculinity was associated with physical competition among men, it could not be served by men and women competing against one another in any sport, soccer included. Beyond that, however, competition in sports—at least team sports with some physical contact, such as soccer—was simply not something to which women were "suited."

Some scholarly works have sought to combine the late nineteenth-century ideas of "muscular Christianity" for men and limited physical activity for women in gender-based explanations for the absence of women participating in soccer in early twentieth-century England and the United States.[19] But the explanations swiftly run into difficulties. If gender stereotyping contributed to the view that the sport of soccer was "unsuitable" for women in England, that was inconsistent with the visibility and prowess of the Dick, Kerr Ladies FC, or of other women's clubs originally made up of English female factory workers during World War I and women's soccer teams in France, who were clearly capable of playing the sport at a high level. Indeed part of the spectator attraction for the Dick, Kerr club was its ability to provide strong competition to men's teams in exhibition matches.

And if gender stereotyping was responsible for soccer not being offered as a recreational or school sport in the early twentieth-century United States, it is hard to determine, then, precisely what the controlling gender stereotype was. It could not have been the belief that girls and women were unsuited to play sports at all, since a great many of them had been playing basketball and volleyball in high schools and colleges since the opening of the century, and girls and women were encouraged to play tennis and golf as well at the time.[20] Nor could it have been the belief that women were unsuited to play team sports, since basketball, volleyball, and field hockey are all team sports that feature the same sort of continuous action as does soccer. And in light of the success of the Dick, Kerr club in its 1922 American tour, it could hardly have been the belief that whatever ability women might have to play some sports, they simply couldn't play soccer at a competitive level, since on that tour the Dick, Kerr club beat men's soccer teams from semiprofessional leagues in the United States as much as they lost to them.[21]

So while one cannot fasten on gender bias as the sole, or even the principal, basis for inhibiting the growth or women's soccer in America, an element of gender consciousness was at play in the early twentieth-century history of women's sports. In no women's sport offered at American high schools or colleges, for the duration of the twentieth century, did female players compete directly with male players. Moreover, in those cases in which high schools and colleges fielded both male and female teams of the same sport, the rules of play were modified for women. In the case of volleyball, for example, the net has, from the outset of women's play, been lower for women than for men, and in basketball, until the 1970s, the number of players and pace of the women's game were different from that of the men's version.[22] In American field hockey, differences between the men's and women's versions never surfaced only because men did not play the sport competitively at the high school and college level.

When women's soccer was eventually introduced in American colleges in the 1960s, it adopted the same rules as those used for men's college soccer (which, as we have seen, differed from those of American professional soccer leagues with respect to the length of periods and substitutions). By adopting the same rules, women's soccer signaled that men and women soccer players in American colleges and universities were playing the same game. That had never before been the case with regard to any other women's team sport. So one might speculate that since there was no tradition of men and women playing a different game when women began to play soccer, having women in America play the sport might have threatened it as a male preserve, an issue that, as we have seen, arguably affected the FA's decision to bar women's soccer clubs from its grounds for fifty years.

But surely that speculation cannot furnish an adequate explanation for the nonexistence of women's soccer in America, for two reasons. First, there was virtually no history of women's soccer clubs in the United States, or of girls or women playing youth, high school, or college soccer, that might have threatened men's soccer as a male preserve.[23] Women soccer players were not banned from playing, as in the FA rules; there simply were not any female soccer players. Second, for most of the twentieth century there was no deeply entrenched tradition of soccer as a coveted sport in the United States. Until the 1960s soccer was played in a small number of private schools and colleges, in a cluster of communities with ethnic populations, and in professional and semiprofessional leagues that came and went, drew a very small number of fans and supporters, and received virtually no media coverage. The possibility that some prospective women's soccer club might have threatened men's soccer in America in a manner comparable to the apparent threat perceived by the long-established Football Association posed by women's soccer clubs in the 1920s seems a fanciful one.

Thus, even accounting for the role of gender bias in the development of women's sports in the United States in the early twentieth century, one is hard pressed to give it much weight as a factor retarding the growth of women's soccer in the nation. A more likely culprit is, as we have seen, the marginal status of men's soccer itself in the twentieth-century United States. In previous chapters we saw that when public comprehensive high schools came into being in the United States and began to include athletics as part of the experience of high school students, soccer was not one of the varsity sports offered.[24] The team sports offered were the "indigenous" ones, namely baseball, gridiron football, basketball, and volleyball, with only the latter two offered to female students. Comprehensive high schools never considered offering soccer, partly because so few colleges offered it and partly because of its "ethnic" image, which meant that most Americans were unfamiliar with the game, and few persons were able to teach it to high school students or coach high school teams.[25] Since soccer was not even offered to male high school students, there would have been no opportunity for female students to play the sport.

The significance of connections among professional soccer leagues, the growth of soccer in high schools and colleges, youth soccer activities, and the participation of girls and women in soccer can be gleaned from the posture of the North American Soccer League toward youth soccer, and the participation of girls in it, after the establishment of the NASL in the late 1960s. Title IX, requiring equal opportunities for female and male athletes in school-sponsored sports, was enacted in 1972, and in legal cases beginning in 1977, discussed further subsequently, the courts declined to conclude that soccer was a "contact" sport for the purposes of Title IX's exemption of such sports from its requirement that young women and men in high schools and colleges be afforded equal opportunities to participate in athletics. In light of those developments the NASL recognized that girls and women would be playing soccer in larger numbers, and that these female athletes, and quite possibly their parents, might well become fans of NASL clubs. The NASL thus began two initiatives to cultivate female and middle-class supporters of its teams. One was to encourage the communities in which its clubs were located to establish youth soccer programs for both girls and boys. The other was to portray soccer as a "family-friendly" sport, one that fans of NASL clubs could count on to be a safe, pleasant experience—unlike some European soccer contests in the 1970s, which were plagued by hooligan club supporters who engaged in coarse and sometimes violent behavior—and to which parents could comfortably bring children.[26] Although the NASL folded in 1984, the legacy of its youth soccer initiatives remained, and Major League Soccer, the professional men's league that came into existence in 1996, has continued to encourage youth soccer and stress the "family" atmosphere spectators can expect to enjoy at its matches.[27]

None of the connections between professional soccer leagues, the offering of soccer as a varsity sport in high schools and colleges, and youth soccer programs materialized in the United States. Not only was soccer not offered as a varsity sport for men in the vast majority of colleges and universities, and in nearly all public high schools, until the 1980s, but none of the NASL's predecessor soccer leagues made an effort to cultivate fans by supporting youth soccer or seeking to establish a family-friendly atmosphere at matches.[28] The NASL's predecessor leagues were fundamentally ethnic-based, both in terms of players and spectators. All of this helped assure that few if any American girls and women would have the opportunity to play soccer.[29]

Perhaps the best way to think about the effects of soccer itself on the nonparticipation of women in the sport is to recall the groups of persons who played, followed, or were otherwise engaged with soccer in early and mid-twentieth-century America. American soccer players in the late nineteenth and early twentieth centuries were overwhelmingly persons who had some experience with the sport before turning to it in the United States. They included citizens of other countries who came to American to play soccer full-time in professional leagues or, more commonly, to take jobs that gave them the opportunity to play part-time for their company teams or other clubs in the localities where they worked. They also included members of ethnic communities, many of whom were immigrants or the first-generation offspring of immigrant families. Some of those persons played soccer recreationally, and they may have been fans and supporters of local clubs as well. It does not seem much of a stretch to anticipate that virtually none of those persons had any experience with women's playing soccer or any particular reason for expecting women to do so.

Another group was composed of persons who, although they themselves did not play soccer recreationally, had become exposed to the sport as residents of communities that were home to professional or semiprofessional league clubs. This would have included many of the large number of spectators who attended the semifinals and finals of US Cup games in southern New England in the 1920s.[30] It would also have included journalists who covered soccer matches, local officials, and, typically, the owners and operators of league clubs, who sponsored clubs for financial and business reasons rather than because they were keen recreational players. Again, it seems safe to conclude that none of those persons gave any particular thought to the fact that women's soccer was not being played anywhere in America.

Finally, who else might have been engaged with soccer in the United States in the early and middle twentieth century? As we have seen, the sport was played in some men's private high schools and men's colleges, and there were aficionados of the sport who participated in its collegiate organization through the Intercollegiate Soccer Football League and Intercollegiate

Soccer Football Association from 1926 through the 1950s, as well as men who coached college and prep school soccer teams. There were also, of course, officials of the American Soccer League and other leagues, including persons such as Tom Cahill who were dedicated to furthering the growth of the sport in the United States. There is no evidence, in any of the sources I have consulted in connection with the history of American men's soccer in the first six decades of the twentieth century, that the people eager to promote the growth of men's soccer were interested in establishing women's soccer. So among the reasons for the absence of girls' and women's soccer in the United States in those decades, one certainly needs to include a combination of the marginal status of men's soccer and the lack of support for women's soccer among any of the groups of persons identified above.

THE OCCASIONAL EXCEPTIONS

Despite the various factors that combined to suppress the spread of women's soccer in the early and mid-twentieth century United States, it is worth taking a look at the few places in which women did play the game. In New York City, the St. George's Athletic Club created two teams from its women's auxiliary unit. They played against one another in December 1913, in a match covered by both the *New York Times* and the *Chicago Tribune*.[31] The players wore skirts and bloomers, and reporters commented on their hair and eye color. The *Tribune* characterized the match as "as free from injury as [croquet] and almost as gentle" and indicated that the players "apologized and forgave each other at once" when they collided.[32]

In Chicago, girls' soccer was introduced in park leagues and some ethnic clubs and high schools. Park leagues were affiliated with women's gymnasiums as part of the "playground movement," which included women's as well as men's athletics. Juvenile girls' teams were created in the park leagues, and both the Chicago Sparta—a club started by Czech immigrants—and the Western Electric Company, which had a large number of employees of Czech descent, sponsored women's teams.[33]

At least one women's college in the early twentieth century, Smith College in Northampton, Massachusetts, which had been founded in 1871, also offered soccer as a student sport. Smith quickly gained a reputation as a pioneering institution in furthering educational and professional aspirations for women. Its introduction of soccer as a recreational activity in 1924 was in keeping with that emphasis.[34] By the 1920s advocates of women's physical education had shifted their emphasis on exercises and gymnastics to activities that involved vigorous physical exercise and some competition among teams. The emergence of field hockey, established as a sport in some American women's colleges since 1901, illustrated the shift. Women's colleges began to institute "play days" featuring games, sports, and other outdoor pursuits.[35] And although soccer was not typically among the activities offered, women physical educators were aware of the sport. In 1923 Helen Frost and Hazel Cubberley emphasized the similarities between field hockey and soccer and suggested that "there could be no better training for a vigorous healthy girl than three years of soccer, followed by three years of field hockey in high school. Then she will be ready for any form of outdoor sport when she reaches college."[36] Another educator, writing in 1932, urged that soccer should "be compulsory in all of our physical education schools for women," emphasizing that soccer was relatively inexpensive in terms of required equipment, nonviolent and therefore safe, "a team game," that stressed "sportsmanship," and a useful preparation "for field hockey."[37]

Smith College went further, introducing soccer as a stand-alone activity on "play days." It established interhouse, interclass, and intramural soccer competitions and, in a publication called the *Smith Sports Book—Soccer*, set forth rules for engaging in the sport. In 1924 those rules required soccer players to wear leather shoes with a "light sole and flat heel" rather than "sneakers"; to dress in "middies and bloomers"; to run a "minimum of five minutes" each morning when not practicing; to get at least eight hours of sleep daily, beginning no later than eleven p.m.; to drink coffee "at breakfast" only, and to avoid tea at night; to drink six glasses of water daily between meals; to eat moderately, employing "discretion on game days"; and to avoid eating anything between meals other than "fruit, milk drinks, [and] plain ice cream."[38]

Smith's version of soccer featured matches held exclusively within the college. Those governing the institution, notably Dorothy Ainsworth, the director of physical education from 1929 to 1960, and Herbert Davis, who served in as college president from 1940 to 1949, believed that intercollegiate sports were "elitist," by which they meant too interested in raising revenue and promoting overt competition. During his tenure Davis issued a proclamation stating that Smith would not allow intercollegiate athletic contests in any of the college's facilities.[39] In their emphasis on intramural rather than intercollegiate sports, Ainsworth and Davis were reflecting the views of most female physical educators from the 1920s through the 1940s, who viewed men's intercollegiate sports as too focused on winning and raising revenue and felt female sports should be primarily for play and exercise and to further camaraderie and good sportsmanship. It was only in the early 1970s that Smith began to shift its emphasis to intercollegiate sports, fielding varsity teams in basketball, tennis, field hockey, and eventually soccer.[40]

Soccer at Smith was essentially a recreational activity, offered as a way for students to get exercise and engage in some appropriately conducted athletic competition. In that respect it was a contrast to field hockey played in the same time period, which featured intercollegiate competitions among the colleges who offered it and even some informal postcollege leagues in eastern cities. Soccer at Smith did not bear much resemblance to the soccer played in men's colleges in the early twentieth century, to say nothing of the soccer played in US professional or semiprofessional leagues. In the mid-1960s, however, three small private colleges in Vermont began playing a different version. Some Canadian universities, such as Bishop's University in Sherbrooke, Quebec, McGill University in Montreal, and Macdonald University, a branch of McGill located in Sainte-Anne-de-Bellevue, Quebec, had women's soccer teams as early as the 1950s, and in 1958 Johnson State College in Johnson, Vermont, established one, playing primarily against the Canadian colleges and possibly Lyndon State College in Lyndon, Vermont, approximately fifty miles away from Johnson.[41]

In 1937 Castleton College, also located in northern Vermont, hired Edith Ewald, a specialist in physical education, as the director of women's physical education. Ewald shared the view of Dorothy Ainsworth of Smith and other early twentieth-century women physical educators that "play days" were the appropriate forum for women's athletic events and that women's team sports should be conducted at the intramural rather than the intercollegiate level. Ewald remained at Castleton until 1963, resisting any efforts to establish a "varsity" intercollegiate women's soccer team. After Ewald's retirement, Richard Terry, who had joined the Castleton athletic department in 1958 and was an advocate of intercollegiate soccer for women, eventually organized a women's varsity soccer team in 1965 or 1966.[42] Beginning in the mid-1960s, Johnson State, Lyndon State, and Castleton

State women's soccer teams began consistently playing matches against one another as well as McGill, Macdonald, and Bishop's Universities.[43] The longest driving distance between any of those institutions was 207 miles, making it possible for teams to travel to and from each other's campuses comparatively easily. Roland Hess, the coach of the women's soccer team at Johnson State from 1958 on, recalled in 1994 that after the matches the host team would give a dinner for the visitors in the college dining hall, or, if a match was played early in the day, juice and cookies would be served, in the manner of a "play day." Hess also recalled that when the three Vermont colleges began playing one another in the 1960s, they used the field hockey rules for corner kicks, meaning that defensive players could stand behind the end line of the penalty area and offensive players were required to stand outside the penalty area until the ball was kicked. When the Vermont college teams played Canadian teams, players from both sides were permitted inside the penalty area.[44]

So while it would be erroneous to state that no women's soccer was played in the United States before the passage of Title IX, the soccer that was played barely resembled the sport played elsewhere in the United States and the rest of the world: it was either offered as part of the "play days" recreational activities endorsed by female physical educators, or it was one step from that conception of soccer.

THE IMPACT OF TITLE IX

The unusual history of women's soccer in the United States next took an unexpected turn. As women's college soccer seemed on the prospect of expanding in the 1970s, an unanticipated development occurred. Responding in part to the women's liberation movement, which, among other things, identified discriminatory practices and stereotypes affecting numerous areas in secondary and higher education, Congress passed Title IX of the Educational Amendments Act, which prohibited gender discrimination in any educational program or activity receiving federal aid. Although that legislation was apparently only incidentally directed toward athletic programs,[45] it came to be understood as requiring colleges and universities to establish sports teams in proportion to the ratio of men and women in the student body, and also to fund sports teams in proportion to the number of male and female athletes.

The Title IX mandates for American colleges—the legislation's effect on public high schools was delayed until 1978—were particularly advantageous for women's soccer. Unlike gridiron football, wrestling, boxing, and baseball, soccer is a sport that women can readily play, size and strength being less of a premium in soccer than in those other sports. So when colleges and high schools began to think seriously about expanding opportunities for women to play organized team sports to comply with Title IX, soccer seemed an obvious choice. As we will subsequently see, the effects of the new legislation on the growth of women's soccer in American colleges and high schools between 1972 and the present have been immense.

Two principal interpretations of Title IX have shaped its application to college and high school athletics over the five decades since the legislation was enacted. One is the 1979 "Policy Interpretation" of the provision by the Department of Health, Education, and Welfare, setting forth tests to ensure that colleges and high schools are complying with Title IX mandates. The first of those tests requires an institution to demonstrate that opportunities to participate in athletics for boys or young men and girls or young women are "provided in numbers substantially proportionate to [the] respective enrollments of males and females in a student body." The second requires institutions to "show a history and continuing practice of program expansion which is demonstrably responsive to developing interest and abilities of the members" of a sex that has been historically excluded from participation. The third asks institutions to show that "the interests and abilities of the members of that [historically excluded] sex have been fully and effectively accommodated."[46]

The "substantially proportionate" and "fully and effectively accommodated" requirements of Title IX have commonly been the bases on which challenges to institutions seeking to treat men's and women's sports teams differently have pivoted.[47] When colleges and schools can show a growing number of skilled female athletes in their student body populations, they can justify expenditures for the creation of separate women's teams. Conversely, the proportionality and full accommodation requirements prevent them from assigning a different status and different budgets to men's and women's athletic programs. These requirements have thus created strong incentives for institutions to provide women's teams and support them comparably to men's teams. Title IX applies to private as well as public schools, and most examples of noncompliance with its requirements have stemmed from the failure of private high schools to include girls on teams in sports in which they have sufficient skill to compete with boys.[48]

The second important interpretation of Title IX since its passage has been the contact sport exemption. That exemption, which first appeared in HEW regulations interpreting Title IX in 1974 and has been in place ever since, provides that "a recipient [of federal funding] may operate or sponsor separate teams for members of each sex where selection for such teams is based on competitive skill or the activity involved is a contact sport." It is unclear precisely why the contact sport exemption was formulated,[49] but it seems to have been based on a concern that Title IX's language, if read literally, would have required institutions to allow men to try out for female sports teams, and women to try out for male sports teams, potentially resulting in the demise of separate female teams because of the superior athletic skill sets of men. The "competitive skill" language of the 1974 regulation addressed that issue, but the "combat sport" language did not appear responsive to it. The "combat sport" language was apparently designed to ensure that women who sought to try out for male teams in some sports, notably gridiron football, basketball, ice hockey, boxing, and wrestling, would not be exposed to violent "combat."[50] This language has formed the basis of litigation against institutions that established separate teams for men and women and declined to allow members of one sex to try out for another sex's team, with lawsuits attempting to determine whether volleyball, field hockey, or baseball are "contact" sports.[51]

In the fall of 1976 Donna Hoover, a junior at Golden High School in Jefferson County, Colorado, was playing soccer on the boys' junior varsity team because the school had no girls' team. Several weeks into the season, the high school's principal ordered that Hoover be removed from the boys' junior varsity team because the Colorado High School Activities Association limited soccer to boys. Represented by the American Civil Liberties Union, Hoover sued the Jefferson County Board of Education and the Colorado High School Activities Association, claiming that the association's rule barring her from playing soccer violated the equal protection clause of the Fourteenth Amendment.

Technically speaking, Donna Hoover's case did not fall under Title IX, as that legislation would not apply to public high schools in the United States until 1978,[52] but the Colorado High School Activities Association's rules were modeled on Title IX regulations. One regulation, for example, required that the association "encourage the use of comparable athletic teams for members of each sex where selection for such teams is based on competitive skills." That tracked Title IX's regulation allowing educational institutions to "sponsor separate teams for members of each sex where selection for such teams is based on competitive skill."[53] There was also a parallel with Title IX's rule that institutions did not need to offer separate teams for members of each sex when the "activity involved is a contact sport." The Colorado High School Activities Association had also adopted the contact sport exemption, and concluding that "participation in [soccer] shall be limited to members of the male sex" because "inordinate injury risk jeopardizes the health and safety of the female athlete" playing soccer.[54] At Hoover's trial the association produced pediatricians and orthopedists who testified that soccer was physically dangerous to women because of the prospect of collisions.[55]

Although the posture of the *Hoover* case required the trial judge to emphasize its equal protection rather than its Title IX dimensions, he made it clear that although men and women differed physiologically, and men had a "natural advantage over females in the mechanics of running,"[56] size and strength differences between individual men and women might not be more marked than differences between individual men. He thus determined that the Colorado Association's conclusion that all women would be put at risk playing soccer because of their size and strength was overbroad, and consequently a violation of the equal protection clause.[57]

The judge then gave the association three options. First, since the only reason Donna Hoover had been allowed to play on the boys' team was that there was no separate girls' team, the association could establish such a team, although it would be required to give the team "substantially equal support" in the way of funding and facilities. Second, it could establish a mixed gender team and allow girls as well as boys to play on that team. Third, it could discontinue soccer as a high school sport in Colorado: it had no constitutional obligation to fund any particular sport. The one option it could not entertain, under the equal protection clause, was to continue to offer soccer as a boys-only sport.[58]

The judge's decision, along with the posture of the suit, allowed him to stop short of deciding whether soccer was a contact sport. But because the association's rationale for excluding girls from soccer was the physical risk to them due to collision, and because the judge had concluded that a mixed-gender high school soccer team would satisfy the equal protection clause, it seemed apparent that he did not think that the occasional "collisions" between soccer players made soccer eligible for a contact sport exemption under Title IX. Since the *Hoover* decision, whether soccer is a contact sport under Title IX has not been a prominent issue in litigation.[59]

The contact sport exemption may well be anachronistic where it functions to allow institutions to decline to provide separate teams for girls and women and at the same time prevent girls or women for trying out for contact sport teams. But if Title IX were understood to require institutions to establish separate teams for men and women in all sports, and to allow men to freely try out for women's teams, the result might well be, as one commentator has suggested, that men would come to dominate women's teams in certain sports, thus reducing athletic opportunities for women.[60] Thus, as we have seen, most courts, in the years since the contact sport exemption was established, have found ways to prevent men from trying out for female sports teams, even while declining to ground those outcomes squarely on finding that the sport in question is a contact sport. At present it is not clear whether soccer, whose rules about physical contact resemble those of field hockey but which has not historically been limited in America to one sex, qualifies for that designation, but it arguably should not.[61]

The cumulative result of the two major regulations interpreting Title IX, then, has been to create strong incentives for institutions to establish separate teams for girls and women in additional sports and to largely prevent those teams from being populated by boys or men. In that atmosphere women's high school and college sports have flourished, with soccer leading the way. Between 1972 and 2000, the number of women playing on college varsity athletic teams increased by 411 percent, compared with a 36 percent increase for men on such teams. The figures for high schools were even more startling: 847 percent for women and 6.9 percent for men. Between 1981 and 1999 the number of college female teams increased by 66 percent, as compared to a 0.4 percent increase for male teams. A dramatic growth in women's varsity college and high school soccer teams contributed significantly to that increase. Between 1991 and 2009 the number of NCAA-affiliated women's soccer teams grew from 318 to 959.[62] In 1972, 700 girls played high school soccer in the United States. By 1991 that number had reached 121,722, an increase of approximately 17,000 percent. By 2018 the number was 390,482.[63] Those figures reveal that the growth of women's and girls' soccer as a visible recreational, participatory, and spectator sport in late twentieth- and early twenty-first-century America has contributed significantly to the potential emergence of soccer as a "major" sport in the nation.

One needs to take two additional developments into account in a sketch of the unusual history of women's soccer in America. One is the participation (and nonparticipation) of FIFA in that history. The other is the emergence of the US women's World Cup teams as the dominant force in international soccer ever since the first women's World Cup was held in 1991. The latter development has had two distinct implications for women's soccer in the United States. One is that the style of soccer played by US women's teams has tended to reflect a particular brand of college soccer, originating at the University of North Carolina under women's coach Anson Dorrance and featuring an emphasis on aggressive offensive and defensive play and top-flight conditioning.[64] The other was the connection between the emergence of the US women's World Cup teams as cultural icons and the growth of female youth soccer in America, featuring the engagement not only of young girls as participants in and prospective fans of the sport but of their parents, "soccer moms and dads," in the latter capacity. The two developments will be taken up separately.

FIFA AND WOMEN'S SOCCER

For most of its history, FIFA's enthusiasm for promoting international soccer did not extend to the women's version of the sport. In fairness, there was virtually no women's soccer being played at high levels anywhere in the globe until the 1980s, and the rapid increase in girls' and women's soccer teams in the United States in the wake of Title IX had not been duplicated elsewhere. Developments in the 1970s, however, prompted FIFA's executives, and those of its affiliated confederations and associations, none of whom were women, to change their tune, as women's soccer leagues began to emerge in the Scandinavian countries, Germany, and Asia. Thereafter things moved quickly. By 1975 the Asian Ladies Football Confederation (ALFC) had affiliations with associations in Australia, Hong Kong, India, Malaysia, New Zealand, Singapore, and Thailand and proposed to evolve into a "Female Internationale de Football Federation" and organize a women's World Cup tournament. Finally getting the message, FIFA rebuffed the ALFC's effort to secure its sponsorship, encouraged women's associations in Asia to affiliate with FIFA and its associations rather than the ALFC, and eventually agreed to support an ALFC-staged international tournament in Taiwan in 1981, as well as to fold the ALFC into its own Asian Football Confederation.[65]

FIFA's next steps were to establish a committee on women's football in 1986 (with only one female member) and to organize two international tournaments in Asia the next two years, held in Taiwan in 1987 and in China in 1988. The latter was a conspicuous success, with twelve teams competing, 300,000 fans attending, and Chinese television broadcasting eight of the twenty-four games live. Immediately after that tournament was completed, FIFA announced plans to stage the first World Cup for women, also in China, in 1991.[66] As we have seen, throughout its history FIFA had insisted that it and its affiliated confederations and associations should have a monopoly on the staging of World Cups and the dispensing of all subsidiary rights connected to those events, and it reacted to the threat posed by the ASLC in characteristic fashion. This was despite the general lack of enthusiasm for women's soccer most of its members had displayed in 1970, and the continuing opposition to women playing soccer in one of FIFA's strongholds, Latin America.[67] Whatever FIFA executives might have thought about women playing soccer in the 1980s, they were not about to countenance any rival organization's administering a women's World Cup.

Thus by the late 1980s it was clear that a FIFA-sponsored women's World Cup was going to take place, although the somewhat tentative nature of FIFA's commitment to women's international soccer could be seen in the naming of its 1991 tournament, which was called not the Women's World Cup but the "1st FIFA World Championship for Women's Football for the M&M's Cup," the "M&M" reference indicating that the Mars candy manufacturing firm had sponsored the tournament rather than FIFA having awarded it to any particular nation.[68] In addition, FIFA insisted that the duration of tournament matches be eighty minutes rather than the standard ninety for men's international matches, prompting US team captain April Heinrichs to tell *Sports Illustrated*, "They were afraid that our ovaries were going to fall out if we played 90!"[69] FIFA was hedging its bets: if the 1991 tournament proved a distinct athletic and financial failure, it would not automatically be followed by additional World Cups every four years, the year after the men's World Cups. But the tournament was a success, averaging over 19,000 spectators per match, drawing 65,000 persons for the final, and being well covered by Chinese media.[70]

It was also clear that the US women's national team would be a strong contender as champions of the 1991 World Cup. In retrospect, two features of the US women's World Cup team's performance in the 1991 competition were noteworthy. The US women's national team won the competition, going undefeated in six matches over thirteen days between November 17 and November 30, in which they successively beat Sweden, Brazil, Japan, Taiwan, Germany, and, in the finals, Norway. They gave up a total of five goals in those matches, two to Sweden, two to Germany, and one to Norway, and scored twenty-six. Two of their wins, over Sweden and Norway, were decided by one goal; their other margins of victory were three, five, eight, and three goals.[71] They simultaneously demonstrated an ability to score and to keep opponents from scoring, and they dominated offensive possession in all of their matches. In short, the 1991 World Cup demonstrated that the American women's national team had reached a level of competence superior to that of other national teams.

The 1991 women's World Cup also revealed that American media, and the American public generally, were far from embracing women's international soccer, despite the dramatic growth of women's colleges and high school soccer teams since the passage of Title IX. None of the 1991 tournament games were televised in the United States, and media coverage was sparse at best. When the victorious women's team arrived at John F. Kennedy Airport in New York after traveling back from China, Michele Akers, who had scored the winning goal in the final against Norway, recalled, "Four people met our plane at the gate at JFK: two reporters, the coach of the Men's National Team, and a friend of mine."[72]

However, as Akers later told *Sports Illustrated*, "in reality, the 1991 World Cup was kind of like a silent trigger."[73] Silent, because very few Americans even knew that the tournament had been played, let alone that the US women's national team had won it; a trigger because the tournament's success convinced FIFA to take over its sponsorship and create a regular rotation of women's tournaments paralleling the men's World Cups. The next women's World Cup would be held in Sweden, a recognition of Scandinavia's prominence in developing women's soccer leagues,[74] and the 1999 cup, held in the United States, would be a pivotal event in the history of American women's soccer.

The 1995 cup revealed that Norway, which had barely lost to the US team in the 1991 final, had at least drawn even with the American squad in its level of competence. In the knockout round the Norwegian team scored seventeen goals and gave up none: it would only surrender one goal in the entire tournament. The tournament draw unfortunately called for the Norway and US teams to play each other in the semifinals rather than the finals, and Norway won, 1–0, in a game in which it dominated possession. Norway then went on to defeat Germany, 2–0, in the final. A Norwegian player was quoted in the *New York Times* as saying, "It's fun to beat the Americans because they get so upset and make so much noise when they lose."[75]

The fact that the *New York Times* ran an article on the 1995 women's World Cup was itself significant. Media coverage of the event had increased somewhat from the level of the 1991 tournament, with ESPN broadcasting the US team's games. ABC had an option to broadcast the final, but declined to exercise it after the US team was eliminated. Although attendance at tournament matches was far less than it had been in 1991, with an average 4,315 spectators in Sweden as opposed to 19,615 in China, that was partly a result of the relatively small stadiums chosen to house matches and the far-flung locations of the cities hosting matches.[76] Even so, women's international soccer received a large boost from the event: in 1996 the Summer Olympics, the first games since women's soccer had been made an official Olympic sport in 1993, were held in Atlanta. But because of the timing of the 1995 women's World Cup, there was no opportunity to hold an elimination tournament for the Olympics, so the eight best teams in the 1995 cup automatically received Olympic bids.[77]

The athletic and financial success of the 1994 men's World Cup, hosted by the United States, had convinced FIFA that staging a women's cup competition in the United States might be commercially feasible. But neither FIFA officials nor anyone else anticipated the attraction of spectators to the 1999 women's World Cup. When the tournament was launched, USSF officials planned for the sale of 312,000 tickets for the matches; a week before it opened, 500,000 had been sold.[78] Nearly 194,000 fans watched the US team's group matches against Denmark, North Korea, and Nigeria, which the American women swept, scoring thirteen goals and surrendering just one. In the quarterfinals, 54,642 fans witnessed the US team beat Germany; in the semifinals, 73,123 saw it beat Brazil; and in the finals, in which the United States and China played to a 0–0 draw before the Americans won on penalty kicks, 90,185 spectators attended the event.[79] Moreover, the smallest attendance for any of the matches was 14,873 fans in Foxboro, Massachusetts, to watch a Group C match between Norway and Russia and a Group D match between Australia and Ghana on June 20, 1999. When the US team played North Korea and Italy played Mexico in Foxboro a week later, they did so to 50,484 spectators.[80]

The undefeated passage of the US women's team through the 1999 tournament, coupled with the spectacular way in which it won the final game against China on penalty kicks, made the players on the team instant celebrities. Brandie Chastain, who scored the winning shootout goal in the final, Mia Hamm, Christine Lilly, and April Heinrichs from the University of North Carolina, Julie Fowdy from Stanford, and Michele Akers were featured in cover stories in *Time* and *Newsweek* magazines the week after the tournaments, appeared on television talk shows, and modeled sportswear in advertisements. Christine Brennan, a columnist for *USA Today*, wrote that the women's national team players "looked so wholesome and all-American, they almost didn't seem real. I had heard that they were all college-educated. None, I believe, has a police record."[81] Although Brennan's comments were tongue in cheek, the coverage of the team tended to emphasize the gender of the players.

Part of the attractiveness of the members of the US women's national team to American audiences was their obvious commitment to emphasizing team solidarity over individual accomplishments. But another element of their iconic status came from their style of play. Americans watching the 1999 World Cup, many of whom still had little appreciation for the subtleties of defensive soccer and a tendency to focus on goal scoring, warmed to the US women's team's aggressive style, which featured double-teaming of opposing players who ventured into the US team's end of the field, constant efforts to secure and keep possession of the ball, and frequent shots on goal.

In all those respects the US team mirrored the style of Anson Dorrance, their coach in the 1991 tournament. Dorrance was succeeded as head coach in the 1995 and 1999 World Cups by Tony DiCicco, one of his assistants in 1991, who continued to emphasize Dorrance's aggressive, offensive-minded approach. Dorrance first became the coach of the North Carolina men's soccer team in 1977, and coached that team until 1989. In 1979 North Carolina instituted a women's soccer program, and Dorrance became the coach of the women's team as well. He is now entering his forty-third season as the North Carolina women's team coach. It was for that reason that Dorrance decided to step down from coaching the US women's national team after 1991: he did not believe the job would leave him enough time to coach the North Carolina women.[82]

Under Dorrance's tenure the North Carolina women became one of the dominant teams in the history of sports, winning twenty-two national championships between 1981 and 2012 and compiling an 847–74–40 record for the first forty years of Dorrance's tenure.[83] It achieved that position through a combination of successful recruiting and fine coaching. Because Dorrance had played college soccer at a high level, as well as coached the North Carolina men's and women's soccer teams together for a decade, he managed to inject some of the styles and tactics of men's soccer into the women's version. As noted, the most representative of those tactics was pressing opponents in possession of the ball everywhere on the field, sometimes through double-teaming. North Carolina's tenacious style required that its players be in superb condition, so Dorrance instituted demanding practices, during which players stayed active throughout, seamlessly moving from one drill to another for the duration of each session.[84] Dorrance also quickly recognized that although some styles and tactics could successfully be adapted from men's play to women's play, others worked less well because of gender differences.[85]

Whatever underlay the success of Dorrance's players, his influence carried over to the US national women's team, which from its first international tournament in 1991 on was dominated by players from North Carolina.

FIGURE 8. Mia Hamm as a member of the North Carolina women's soccer team, for whom she played from 1989 to 1993. Hamm was one of a number of stars on the North Carolina roster who would go on to play for the successful US women's national soccer team in the 1990s. Courtesy of University of North Carolina Athletics.

Nine of the eighteen players on the 1991 team had played for Dorrance; five on the 1995 team; and eight on the 1999 roster.[86] Two additional coaches of the team, Lauren Gregg (1997–2000) and April Heinrichs (2000–2005), also had played for Dorrance at North Carolina. In that respect the very positive reaction of American audiences to the 1999 women's national team could be said to have been partly a product of an appreciation of North Carolina–style women's soccer.

THE RISE OF YOUTH SOCCER

The other dramatic effect of the success and elan of the US women's World Cup team on American culture came in the form of stimulating interest in and the growth of girls' youth soccer in the United States and helping to create a legion of new American soccer fans who, for the first time, included a great many girls and women. We have seen that as early as the formation of the North American Soccer League (NASL) in 1968, marketers of US professional leagues adopted a strategy of combining efforts to recruit American families as fans of the sport with developing youth soccer as a way of creating a more knowledgeable fan base in the United States.

At its founding in Torrance, California, in 1964, the American Youth Soccer Organization registered about a hundred boys to play on nine teams.[87] At its founding four years later, the NASL required its players to sponsor or attend youth soccer camps or clinics in the regions in which their teams were located. It also encouraged team management to create "family nights" for matches for which reduced-price tickets for children would be offered. The league publicized the family-friendly atmosphere at its games, seeking to highlight a contrast between US matches and those hosted elsewhere in the world,.[88] Some of the NASL clubs opened their fields to youth soccer teams to play before the start of games, charging the opposing groups discounted rates for the pro game to come if they purchased a sufficient number of tickets (ideally one for every member of each team) for the designated youth games. The New York Cosmos also allowed spectators who had purchased a pregame youth-match ticket to stay to watch the Cosmos play at no extra charge, as well as allowing fans who had purchased a full-price Cosmos ticket to show up early and take in the youth match while it was still in progress, thereby swelling the attendance for those games as well as cleverly adding to the prospective fan base in two ways.[89]

By 1977 youth soccer was growing rapidly in the United States, with approximately half a million boys and girls playing the sport, and the NASL had reached the peak of its success.[90] A year earlier the Cosmos had signed Pelé, and would add the West German star Franz Beckenbauer that year;

the club averaged an impressive 40,814 for its home games in the 1977 season.[91] Attendance among nearly all NASL clubs grew so rapidly in 1976 and 1977 that in 1978 the league resolved to expand from eighteen to twenty-four clubs.[92]

The combined growth of youth soccer and the success of the NASL set off a flurry of newspaper and magazine articles about soccer in the United States, most of which highlighted the bright future of the sport. *Time* announced that "Soccer Soars."[93] An article in the *Christian Science Monitor* was entitled "Soccer's U.S. Success Story."[94] One in the *New York Times* referred to "The Selling of Soccer Mania."[95] A report on the *CBS Evening News* noted the "Rising Popularity of Soccer."[96] Several of the articles and reports suggested that one of the great appeals of soccer was that children of any size and gender could play the sport. The Consumer Products Safety Commission was reported in 1977 to have determined that the injury rate among youth soccer players was only about 2 percent, comparable to tennis or squash, whereas the injury rate among young men playing football was nearly 16 percent.[97] Other articles pointed out that soccer was inexpensive to play, about one-third of the cost of football to a parent or a school.[98] Finally, an article claimed that the stereotype that male soccer players tended to be those young men who could not make football teams was erroneous, quoting a high school soccer coach who said that in 1963 he had asked the school's football coach to refer boys cut from the football team to him as potential soccer players, but by 1977 he was being asked by the football coach to refer soccer players who didn't make the team to the football program.[99]

Many media accounts of the rise of soccer included references to the growth in the number of young women playing the sport, some emphasizing that not only were women well suited to the game but they could also compete with men in matches. The author of one such account stated that soccer "can be played by girls, who are happy to discover that soccer is not, like baseball and football, a long-established bastion of masculinity, a male secret society where machismo reigns."[100] NASL commissioner Phil Woosnam was quoted in one article on the rise of soccer as saying that women could develop the skills and endurance necessary to play "on the same field" as men at any level. That same article claimed that 45 percent of the spectators at NASL games were women.[101]

WOMEN'S SOCCER AS AN "AMERICAN" SPORT

Perhaps the most arresting sidelight of the greater attention on the part of American media to soccer, and to women's soccer, in the late 1970s was the implication that because women had not traditionally played soccer in the rest of the world, their doing so in the United States served to transform the women's version of soccer from a "foreign" to an "American" sport. Two paired articles in the *Chicago Tribune* in 1977 implicitly communicated that message. One, entitled "Soccer Resolving an Identity Crisis in Chicago," emphasized the soccer heritage of some recent immigrant groups and the different cultural status of the sport in America.[102] The other focused on the growth of women playing soccer in the United States.[103] Taken together, the articles seemed to suggest that the "identity crisis" pertaining to soccer in the United States was not one affecting women, who were welcomed as participants in and fans of the sport, but one still hanging over certain ethnic populations, who needed to reassess what their playing soccer in America signified.

With the 1999 women's World Cup hosted in the United States, those themes seemed to converge to boost the cultural stature of American women's soccer. When MLS came into existence in 1999, it followed the NASL's strategies of marketing soccer as a family-friendly sport, emphasizing connections between the league of youth soccer programs, by this time being offered to girls as well as boys, and seeking to recruit female fans for the league's clubs. Merchandizing of the 1999 World Cup included the sale of jerseys with the names and numbers of the (very popular) players to fans, particularly young female ones. Media attention to the cup increased spectacularly, with nearly 2,500 outlets covering the tournament, all of the thirty-two matches being broadcast live on American national television, and an estimated 40 million viewers in the United States alone.[104]

On the heels of the World Cup's success a woman's professional soccer league, the Women's United Soccer Association (WUSA), was launched in 2001, with sponsorship by John Hendricks of the Discovery Channel, approval by the USSF in 2000, and an understanding with MLS to cooperate on marketing. Composed of eight teams, the league survived for three seasons, but it never attracted enough fans or media coverage to fully establish itself and folded after the 2003 season.[105]

The collapse of the WUSA set off a decade of chaos, in which unsuccessful efforts were first made to relaunch that league, then a new one; Women's

FIGURE 9. The US women's national soccer team celebrates after winning the World Cup in 2015. © Andrew Chin/ZUMA Wire/ZUMAPRESS.com/Alamy Live News.

Professional Soccer (WPS) was started with seven teams in 2009, only to fold three years later. WPS had sought to emphasize a more local, modest approach, with some clubs located in smaller cities and incurring reduced expenses.[106] But despite closer cooperation with MLS and an upsurge of attendance after the US women's World Cup victory in 2011, league teams consistently lost money, and eventually the WPS, too, ceased operations in 2012.[107] Yet almost immediately steps were taken to revive women's professional soccer once again, this time with MLS franchises being even more closely affiliated with, and sometimes the owners of, women's league clubs. A new league, the National Women's Soccer League (NWSL), was formed in 2013[108] and is still in operation, having signed a three-year television contract with the A&E network that provides for the twenty-two regular-season NWSL games as well as the playoffs to be broadcast on a national cable outlet.[109] After A&E declined to renew its contract, on March 11, 2010, the league announced it had signed a three-year contract with CBS Sports and the streaming service Twitch to broadcast and livestream most of the league's matches.[110] A number of players on the successful 2015 and

2019 women's World Cup teams have since joined NWSL franchises.[111] Although the NWSL has not yet become profitable, it is currently the longest-tenured women's professional soccer league in the United States.

Meanwhile women's soccer continues to grow in American colleges and high schools, and even though the 2019 women's World Cup was held in France rather than in the United States, fan interest and media coverage in the United States rivaled that of the 1999 tournament.[112] When one adds to that the continuing growth of girls participating in youth soccer, the mixing of girls and boys on coed soccer up to the average age of nine, and the enhanced participation of the parents of boys and girls in their children's youth soccer activities, the importance of the growth of women's and girls' soccer in general and the twenty-first-century resurgence of the sport in America seems indisputable. Women's soccer in America has evolved from virtual nonexistence to a central place in the recent history of the sport, leaving one to wonder whether the advocates for soccer as a healthful activity for intramural "play days" at women's colleges could have imagined such an outcome.

Chapter Eight

The Emergence of Major League Soccer

IN THE DISCUSSIONS held in 1988 that led to its selection of the host nation for the 1994 men's World Cup, FIFA, as we have seen, expressed to those associated with the US entry its strong desire to see a men's professional soccer league established in connection with the US bid. The United States was the clear favorite to host the 1994 cup, nations from Europe and South America, as well as Mexico, having previously hosted, and Asian and African nations not yet having the infrastructure in place to make competitive bids.

In the course of negotiations FIFA pressed the United States Soccer Federation (USSF) to launch a new league before the 1994 World Cup started. When the announcement of the winning US bid came, Werner Fricker, the head of the USSF at the time, appeared to acquiesce to FIFA's request. The day after the announcement, he was quoted in the *New York Times* as saying that the USSF was committed to establishing a new national soccer league, which, he predicted, "will encompass in some way teams from existing semiprofessional indoor and outdoor leagues."[1] Since the USSF not only controlled the process by which a US bid for the 1994 cup would be generated but also nominally controlled the organization of men's professional soccer in America, Fricker's prediction carried considerable weight.

But neither Fricker nor his promise would survive for long. In 1990 a new election was held for the presidency of the USSF, with foundation treasurer Paul Stiehl, who had been a member of the team that made the 1988 bid, opposing Fricker's reelection. In the lead-up to the election, Stiehl suggested that the USSF's lack of progress on preparations to host the World Cup in the last two years was Fricker's responsibility. Neither candidate seemed to have a clear majority, and ten days before the election a third candidate emerged: Alan Rothenberg, a Los Angeles lawyer who had been part of the very successful hosting of the 1984 Olympics and subsequently was briefly involved in the operations of both the Los Angeles Wolves and the Los Angeles Aztecs in the NASL. Rothenberg's candidacy was supported by Peter Uberroth, the chair of the 1984 Olympic Committee, and allegedly by international star Pelé and the American NASL star Kyle Rote Jr. as well.[2]

On the morning of election day, Stiehl announced to the members of the USSF that he had received a call from a FIFA representative asking him to step down in favor of Rothenberg. Stiehl declined to do so, describing the call as an attempt at a "hostile takeover" of the USSF by FIFA. Nevertheless, his plea to the delegates was largely rejected, and Rothenberg won the election by a wide margin.[3] Among the first things Rothenberg did after taking office was to "go back to FIFA and indicate to them that their expectation that there would be a pro league created before the World Cup was not going to work."[4] His approach was to first stage a successful and entertaining World Cup, and then to build on the momentum generated by that event to encourage investors in the new league.

Rothenberg's strategy to draw attention to the 1994 World Cup combined three ventures. One was to launch a series of pre–World Cup tournaments in which the US team would play matches against other nations. Between 1991 and 1994 the American squad entered in three such tournaments: the CONCACAF[5] Gold Cup, first staged in 1991; the US Cup, first staged in 1992; and the Copa America, a much older South American competition, first offered in 1916 and in which the US team was first invited to play in 1993. The US team won the 1991 Gold Cup and the 1992 US Cup, beating Ireland, Italy, and Portugal in the latter competition. It then hosted Brazil, England, and Germany in the 1993 US Cup, upsetting England while losing to both Brazil and Germany.[6] All the matches were televised, and the competition drew around 286,000 fans.[7] The US team fared less well in the 1993 Copa America competition, losing to Ecuador, Uruguay, and Venezuela, as several of its starters remained at home.[8]

The second venture was identifying American stadiums in which to play World Cup matches. Although the nation had an abundance of sports stadiums, this proved a difficult task; some of the venues did not have fields that met FIFA's requirements, in most cases because they were too narrow. FIFA initially balked at staging World Cup matches on synthetic turf or in indoor stadiums but eventually relented, so that the New York Giants football stadium in New Jersey, which had synthetic turf, and the Detroit Lions football stadium, an indoor facility, made the list of locations chosen for the 1994 World Cup matches. Another issue had to do with the very large seating capacity of a number of the stadiums. Rothenberg and others believed that if the matches held in these giant stadiums drew comparatively small crowds, this would give the impression that they were poorly attended, a perception that television might well accentuate. In the end, however, big stadiums such as the Rose Bowl, Robert F. Kennedy Stadium in Washington, DC, Soldier Field in Chicago, the New York Giants' facility in New Jersey, and the New England Patriots football team's facility in Foxboro, Massachusetts, were among the selected stadiums and drew quite large crowds, even when the US team was not playing.[9]

The third venture involved publicity. A year before the World Cup competition started, *Sports Illustrated* reported that Rothenberg had sent several memos to his staff "bemoaning the Cup's low profile in the press."[10] American sports journalists remained largely uninformed about and unenthusiastic about soccer, but by the early summer of 1994 Rothenberg had succeeded in getting regular mentions of the forthcoming World Cup in the sporting press. Some of those were snide—an *Orlando Sentinel* columnist quipped that soccer "may be the world's most-beloved sport, but the world has always been overrated"[11]—but the combination of ABC and ESPN televising all the World Cup matches and a drumroll of publicity calling attention to the great teams and players participating in the competition eventually produced large crowds, bolstered by the good performance of the US team, which, after tying Switzerland, defeating Columbia, and losing to Romania, advanced out of its group to the quarterfinals. It then lost 1–0 to Brazil, the team that would eventually capture the cup on penalty kicks after a scoreless draw with Italy in the final match.[12]

The United States' experience with the 1994 World Cup, which secured a large amount of money for the USSF and produced no ugly instances of hooliganism or serious injuries to players or spectators, seemed ideal for the launching of a new professional soccer league.[13] Prior to the start of the World Cup, in December 1993, the USSF entertained proposals from groups of investors interested in starting a league; it had indicated as early as 1988 that it would only seek to establish one top-tier league, fearing that multiple leagues might produce ruinous competition. Rothenberg himself headed one of the investor groups submitting proposals. The other two were League One America, led by Chicago real estate developer Jim Paglia, whose group planned to buy land, build soccer-specific stadiums, and associate them with new commercial developments; and the American Professional Soccer League, a lower-tier league in operation that wanted to use the bidding process to upgrade itself. Although the dual capacity of Rothenberg as chair of the USSF and one of the bidders raised eyebrows, his group, which would come to be called Major League Soccer, was awarded the backing of the USSF.[14] On December 17, 1993, Rothenberg announced that a twelve-team league would be created and hoped that play would begin in 1995.[15]

When he was named president of the USSF in 1990, Rothenberg had not expected to be the organizer of a new soccer league. But as he was preparing for the hosting of the 1994 World Cup, no prospective investors in a new league emerged, so Rothenberg decided to move forward himself. He hired one of the associates at his law firm, Mark Abbott, to develop a business plan.[16] The plan that would emerge represented a singular departure from those of earlier professional soccer leagues in America, indeed from that of any existing professional sports league in the United States. As we will see, it more resembled the English Football Association and Football League models of organization, but went beyond them in its emphasis on command-and-control.

In developing a business plan, Rothenberg and his associates drew upon the failings of previous American soccer leagues, identifying three reasons why the NASL and its predecessors had failed to thrive. The first was the uneven performance of league clubs. Some clubs, in part because their owners had more money to spend and in part because they were located in cities with populations capable of attracting large crowds to games, were better able to pay the high salaries of and therefore recruit top-level foreign players, while other clubs were not. In an interview Abbott contrasted the situation of the New York Cosmos in the NASL with that of his hometown club, the Minnesota Kicks. "The Kicks," he noted, "had basically gotten into a million-dollar-a-year business, whereas the Cosmos were in a ten-million-dollar-a-year business, and there was such a weak set of common business principles, that ultimately when the weak teams failed, the strong ones had nobody to play, so the league collapsed."[17]

The second reason was connected to the first. In previous American soccer leagues the owners of clubs linked together in a league had been competitors, not business partners. The structure of those leagues created incentives for individual franchise owners to field successful teams that attracted fans and consequently made money, and maybe even turned a profit. Owners were not expected to be interested in the success or financial health of the clubs with which they competed. A league functioned only as a collective entity organized for the purpose of playing soccer matches and establishing competitive rivalries. The model was a traditionally American approach to entrepreneurship, the competition of enterprises in a "free market" in which success was linked to profits, and in which success stemmed from the ability to place a product on the market that was superior to that of one's competitors. In soccer that meant a club that won most of its matches.

Abbott noted that the founders of MLS found that model of league organization flawed. "We needed to have successful teams," he said, "but we needed to have a strong league, because even strong teams need to be part of a common enterprise." The "simple idea" driving the league structure of MLS, Abbott maintained, was "that we [all of the team owners] were business partners, while competitors on the field, and that as a business partnership" the league needed to operate in an active business environment, one in which all its clubs thrived regardless of their on-the-field success. "We did not think there was a market," Abbott said, "for people who wanted to own teams or fans who wanted to follow teams that had absolutely no chance of being successful. . . . We did not believe that an old NASL-style league, with one or two dominant teams, would allow us to grow."[18] Thus from the outset the MLS founders searched for an organizational model in which the owners of clubs would simultaneously act as competitors on the field and business partners dedicated to fostering the financial health of the league as a whole.

The third reason identified by the founders of MLS for the failure of previous soccer leagues was the long-standing difficulty of attracting American sports fans to soccer. Part of that might be traced to the inability of fans who had not played the game to appreciate its subtleties, which resulted in observers who witnessed long stretches of play without goals being scored concluding that soccer was boring, or that rules such as those preventing offensive players from being offside or allowing goalkeepers to receive backward passes from defenders with their hands[19] robbed the game of much of its goal-scoring opportunities. But an important reason for soccer's marginality remained the lack of coverage it received in the American sporting press.[20]

The founders of MLS were determined to capitalize on the interest generated by the 1994 World Cup by launching a postcup marketing campaign to publicize soccer and the forthcoming new league. They believed that if the World Cup could draw large numbers of American spectators to matches involving foreign teams and players, of whom they had little previous awareness, a professional soccer league featuring American-based clubs and players could also draw crowds. But American audiences needed regular reminders that a Division I professional league was coming into being. In addition, MLS needed to take advantage of the growing participation of American youth in soccer by supporting that participation and cultivating youthful fans. With those goals in mind, MLS created a publicity and marketing apparatus, Soccer United Marketing, which from the 1990s on would have a hand in a variety of ventures, from publicizing matches to selling merchandise associated with MLS clubs.[21]

Another dimension of marketing, which would emerge as MLS was being launched, was the cultivation of supporter fan clubs by teams. The initial model for that strategy was the DC United team. Washington, DC, had been awarded one of the first MLS franchises, and DC United was an immediate success on the field, winning three of the first four MLS championships. Washington had been chosen as a location for a franchise in part because of the expectation that its large ethnic populations would be a source of strong fan support. That turned out to be the case, and even before MLS started play in 1996, Kevin Payne, one of the investors in the DC United franchise, was approached by two fans representing different "supporters' groups" of the team. One, known as the Screaming Eagles, was composed of fans that had followed professional soccer in Washington since the advent of the NASL's Washington Diplomats in 1974. The other, called Barra Brava, was modeled on South American supporter groups and was composed largely of Latino fans.[22]

Both groups proposed being allowed to buy blocks of tickets in particular sections in Robert F. Kennedy Stadium, possibly at discounted rates, and being permitted to bring flags, banners, drums, and other instruments into the stadium. They also proposed being allowed to bring in portable metal stands that could be moved around the stadium to suit configurations for soccer or gridiron football. The combination of supporters' groups being seated together, making noise, displaying banners, and jumping up and down, which caused the seats in the metal stands to vibrate as well, created the sort of atmosphere familiar to first-tier league matches in Europe and Latin America, where bands of fans of particular clubs cheer, sing, and are in constant motion during the play of matches.[23]

Supporters' groups would become a fixture of several MLS clubs in their early years, most particularly, in addition to DC United, the New York MetroStars and the Chicago Fire. Rather than resisting the overtures of supporter groups, MLS franchises encouraged stadium officials to allow them to bring paraphernalia to games and make a lot of noise. They also enlisted the groups' participation in publicizing matches and encouraging local fans to follow the fortunes of their home clubs.[24] The embrace of such groups by MLS franchises, at a time when the hooliganism and violence of soccer fans in Europe and Latin America had threatened to tarnish the sport, was a considered decision to attract fans to matches, potentially unruly or not.[25]

MLS's encouragement of supporters' groups and their "foreign" style of reacting to soccer matches was designed to address one of the longtime obstacles professional soccer has faced as a spectator sport in the United States. That obstacle resulted from a combination of the low scoring in soccer matches and the general unfamiliarity of American audiences with high-level soccer, with its emphasis on long possessions of the ball by one team, featuring intricate runs and passes among that team's players as the ball is moved down the field. In many of those possessions the offensive team is not directing shots toward its opponent's goal, and sometimes not even seeking to advance the ball forward. Meanwhile the defensive team seems to be making little effort to wrest the ball away from the team on offense, except on those occasions in which offensive players mishandle passes, resulting in the ball's being "loose" on the field and defensive players having an opportunity to possess it.

It is not at all uncommon for certain teams who believe that they are inferior to their opponent in offensive capabilities to employ a defensive strategy called "packing it in," in which they station most of their players, including offensive players, in their own end of the field and seek to prevent their opponents from getting the ball into a position from which shots can be taken on goal. That strategy tends to produce long intervals of play during which an offensive team controls the ball, passing it among its players and hoping to free an offensive player from the tight guarding that results from a packed defense. Much of the action on the field during those intervals resembles an elaborate chess game in which the pieces on both sides are moved strategically, but little offensive action in the form of shots on goal or passes close to goals occurs. That style of play is the quintessence of what uninformed American audiences have found "boring" about watching soccer, and it was that very reaction that made many overseas commentators believe that soccer would never establish itself as a spectator sport in the United States.[26]

In contrast, soccer spectators elsewhere in the world have for many years reacted to the chess-game quality of high-level versions of the sport by occupying themselves during long offensive possessions with songs, chants, and cheers, sometimes led by habitual supporters of a club and sometimes erupting spontaneously. Club supporters typically have favorite songs and cheers they associate with their clubs, and often create satiric chants they can direct toward opposing teams or their players. While action takes place on the field, singing and chanting in the stands goes on nearly continuously, punctuated by bursts of cheers when the club being supported does something of which its fans approve.

Rarely do the fans and supporters of major sports teams in the United States react in a comparable fashion during games. In baseball, when there are gaps between action on the field, fans are largely silent, or talking to one another in the stands. Baseball spectators will often react to action taking place on the field by cheering or groaning, and occasionally music will be played in intervals in the action, with fans sometimes encouraged by a public address announcer to cheer. But there is rarely any continuous singing, cheering, or chanting while action is going on; cheering or groaning is reserved for actions in progress on the field, which take place in bursts.

Although the pace of American gridiron football, basketball, and ice hockey varies, and differs from that of baseball, in none of those games do spectators sing or chant continuously during the flow of the action. Gridiron football has long intervals between plays, and spectators react as baseball fans do in those intervals, talking with one another about what has just transpired or what might come next. Occasionally fans cheer loudly as a play is about to begin, typically when an opponent has the ball and they hope to disrupt the forthcoming play with noise. Gridiron football fans cheer or groan loudly when plays are run in the manner of baseball fans, but then revert to murmuring among themselves. Basketball and ice hockey differ from baseball and gridiron football in having a more continuous flow of action, which is punctuated by regular cheers and groans, but never by continuous singing or chanting. Sometimes chants, usually derisive, are directed at individual opposing players, and sometimes gridiron football or basketball fans attempt to distract field-goal kickers or free-throw shooters by cheering or waving objects from the stands, but in general cheering for teams tends to take place during time-outs, and there is no singing and little chanting.

In short, there is an etiquette of watching major American professional sports that does not typically include continuous singing, chanting, or cheering as games are being played. Were spectators to engage in such behavior at professional baseball, gridiron football, basketball, or hockey games in the United States, that behavior might be resented, and efforts by other spectators to silence them might occur (putting aside periodic outbursts by intoxicated individuals, which are typically tolerated up to the point where an individual is ejected). In encouraging fan supporter organizations to attend soccer matches en masse, to stand during the action, and to sing, chant, and cheer as much as they pleased, MLS was self-consciously deviating from American sports spectator etiquette and adopting the nearly universal etiquette of soccer fans in the rest of the world.

A final concern of the MLS founders was another traditional obstacle to the success of professional soccer leagues in America: stadiums inappropriately designed for soccer matches. That problem was evident in the United States during the staging of the 1994 World Cup. None of the stadiums chosen by the USSF to stage matches had been built with soccer in mind; all were designed to host gridiron football. As such they were too large to allow the majority of spectators to sit close to the action, which created yet another obstacle for the average uninformed American observer of soccer to appreciate the flow of play. Many of the big stadiums were particularly unsuited for soccer, in some instances having a great deal of space between the playing field and the stands. Although the choice of stadiums that could host large crowds contributed to the high attendance at the 1994 World Cup matches, it deprived many spectators of opportunities to watch soccer up close.

But although the MLS founders had an aspiration to build soccer-friendly stadiums that would seat 20,000 to 30,000 and allow spectators to sit close to the action, as in European soccer arenas, there were few sports stadiums of that size in the United States at all when MLS was launched, and none built for soccer. The MLS founders resolved to concentrate on cities with potentially lucrative markets that also happened to have gridiron football stadiums in place, and to cover up large sections of empty seats with colored tarpaulins that gave the impression that there were no seats beneath them. If more than the expected number of spectators turned up, the tarpaulins could be lifted.[27] But MLS resolved to defer the question of building soccer-specific stadiums, such stadiums would be an important part of the successful expansion of the league, although that would not take place for several years.

MLS SINGLE-ENTITY ORGANIZATIONAL STRUCTURE

As Rothenberg, Abbott, and the others involved in developing a business plan for MLS sought to respond to the problems they had associated with the failure of earlier leagues, they hit upon a model of league structure that borrowed heavily from, but modified, the model developed by the Football Association and the Football League in England. The founders of MLS established Major League Soccer as a single-entity organization. As such, it was a limited liability company, incorporated in Delaware in 1995, owned by a number of independent investors (corporations, partnerships, and one individual) and operated by a board of governors. MLS retained a significant amount of centralized control over the operations of both the league and individual teams. It owned all the teams that played in the league (initially ten in number) as well as all intellectual property rights, broadcast rights, tickets, and equipment it supplied. It set the teams' schedules, negotiated stadium leases, including assuming all related liabilities, paid the salaries of league employees and officials, and agreed to supply a good deal of the equipment required to put on soccer matches.[28]

MLS also had the sole responsibility of negotiating and entering into agreements with players, as well as determining their compensation. It recruited players, fixed their salaries, paid them from league funds, and determined with which teams they would play. In order to balance talent among clubs in the league, MLS designated certain players as "marquee" players and then decided where to place them. Those decisions were made by the MLS board of governors, with input from team operators, but that input was treated as nonbinding.[29]

Initially MLS operated two of the first franchises it assigned, the Dallas Burn and Tampa Bay Mutiny, as well as owning them. It delegated some control of the remaining franchises to "operator/investors," who signed contracts with MLS that gave them the exclusive right and obligation to provide management services for clubs within their home territories. Those services included hiring team staff, including general managers and coaches; licensing local broadcast rights and selling tickets; and conducting local marketing and promotion. The operator/investors did not need approval from MLS to conduct those tasks. They were responsible for paying half of the stadium rent, with MLS absorbing the other half. They also had some discretion to select and trade players, although they needed to do so under strict league rules and were not permitted to exceed the maximum player budget established by the MLS board of directors (operator/investors were in a majority on that board.)[30]

In exchange for those services, MLS paid each operator/investor a management fee, calibrated by the performance of their clubs. This fee consisted of half the revenues from local tickets and concessions; the first $1,124,000 of local broadcast revenues, plus 30 percent of any amount over that base; half the net revenues from the MLS championship game; and a share of revenues from exhibition games.[31] Although all the remaining revenues of MLS were divided equally among all of its investors, the worth of the operator/investors' shares would vary with the performance of their teams. The more tickets and concessions they sold and the more broadcast rights they were able to license, the more money they would receive, and revenues from those operations were likely to be affected by how well a team was doing.

MLS retained legal title to all its teams, but operator/investors were permitted to transfer their ownership stakes and operating rights to other current investors, retaining the fair market value of those rights and their ownership interests. They could also seek to transfer ownership to investors not currently associated with MLS, although such transfers required consent of two-thirds of the board of directors. MLS could terminate an operating agreement with an owner/investor if a two-thirds majority of the board of directors concluded that the owner/investor had failed to act in the best interests of the league. In that instance MLS was required to pay the owner/investor the fair market value of his operating rights and ownership interest.[32]

In February 1997, after MLS had concluded its first season, eight MLS players filed a federal antitrust suit against the league, naming MLS, eight owner/investors, and the United States Soccer Federation as defendants.[33] The suit was entitled *Fraser v. Major League Soccer*.[34] Of the various claims the players advanced, three were eventually considered by the federal district court in which the suit was originally brought.[35] All were claims under the two principal federal antitrust statutes, the Sherman Antitrust Act of 1890[36] and an amendment to that act, the Clayton Act of 1914.[37] One was that MLS and its operator/investors had violated section 1 of the Sherman Antitrust Act, which seeks to restrain "combinations of capital tending to retard competition" by agreeing not to compete for player services. A second, brought under section 2 of the act, which prohibits agreements "creating or tending to create monopolies in markets in interstate commerce," was that MLS had sought to monopolize the market for the services of Division I professional soccer players in the United States by preventing, in combination with the USSF, any other entity in the nation from being sanctioned as a Division I professional soccer league. The third claim was that MLS's single-entity organizational structure, which combined assets of MLS's operator/investors with those of the league itself, amounted to a merger of competitors in the same market that substantially lessened competition and tended to create monopoly, in violation of section 7 of the Clayton Act.[38]

At the district court, both sides made motions for summary judgment.[39] The plaintiffs pointed to the requirement stating that when an MLS club signed an out-of-contract player—one not currently a member of another team—the signing club had to pay a transfer fee to any club that had previously employed the player, citing this as a per se violation of the antitrust laws because it had the effect of reducing competition for players. The plaintiffs consequently moved for summary judgment on the invalidity of that requirement.[40] George O'Toole, the district court judge, denied the motion. He concluded that of the two existing categories of agreements potentially illegal under the antitrust laws, agreements that were per se illegal because they were so "plainly anticompetitive that no elaborate study of the industry is needed to establish their illegality" and agreements whose competitive effect could only be determined by an analysis of the "facts peculiar to the business" and "the reasons why [the restraint] was imposed," the transfer-fee requirement fell into the second category, which was to be evaluated by means of a "rule of reason."[41] Under that method of evaluation, Judge O'Toole concluded, the transfer fees, which had the effect of lowering the prices of player services, might be shown to have not just anticompetitive effects but some that fostered competition, such as lowering the price consumers paid to watch MLS matches, or helping to create competitive balance among MLS clubs by creating disincentives for them to outbid other clubs for player services.[42]

The defendants in *Fraser* also moved for summary judgment on the transfer-fee issue, first on the ground that the issue was not ripe for adjudication (meaning that it had been raised prematurely) because MLS had yet to pay or request a transfer fee; and next on the ground that the issue was moot (meaning that as a practical matter it had already been decided) because the commissioner of MLS had declared that the league would never pay such a fee. Judge O'Toole concluded that the defendants were "wrong in both respects."[43] The issue remained ripe for adjudication because, although MLS had not yet paid or requested a transfer fee, there remained a threat that it would; and it was not moot because the commissioner's declaration, since it was not accompanied by a formal stipulation that MLS would never pay a transfer fee, was not legally binding.[44]

With both of those motions for summary judgment denied, the case was allowed to go forward on the plaintiffs' antitrust claims. The defendants argued that MLS was a single-entity LLC corporation, not a merger of competitors, and thus it could neither be said to have violated section 1 of the Sherman Act nor section 7 of the Clayton Act. They made a motion for summary judgment to dismiss the claims, and Judge O'Toole agreed, concluding that under existing precedent MLS was in fact a single entity, despite its affiliated clubs being competitors for some purposes, and that there was no "existing market" in which MLS's creation reduced competition, as MLS was entering into an entirely new venture. Thus, the district court reasoned, there was no conspiracy among participants in a market to suppress competition in that market or to establish a monopoly, since MLS was not a collection of individual entrepreneurs but a single entity, and there was no current market for what was termed Division I—that is, in the top-tier leagues in the UK and Europe—professional soccer players in the United States.[45]

That left the alleged violation of section 2 of the Sherman Act, in which MLS, together with the USSF, had purportedly sought to monopolize the market for Division I professional soccer players in the United States by preventing any other entity from being sanctioned as a Division I league. At trial, after the close of evidence,[46] Judge O'Toole submitted a fifteen-question special verdict form to the jury. The jury responded by answering only the first two questions, which they treated as dispositive of the remaining ones. Their first answer was that the plaintiffs had failed to prove that the relevant geographic market affected by MLS's actions was the United States. Their second answer was that they had failed to prove that the relevant product market was limited to Division I soccer players. Accordingly, Judge O'Toole dismissed the section 2 claim.[47] The plaintiffs appealed to the US Court of Appeals for the First Circuit.

There were no particular surprises in the First Circuit's decision: it affirmed all of the conclusions of the district court. But the court did intimate that the district court's conclusion that MLS was a single entity might have been erroneous, although the error was harmless in light of the jury's conclusions about relevant markets.[48] It further pointed out that "MLS and its operator/investors have separate contractual relations giving the operator/investors rights that take them part way along the path to ordinary sports team owners."[49] They could do some independent hiring and make investments in their own teams without the consent of MLS. They retained a large share of the assets of their teams, and they had limited sale rights to those assets. Moreover, the operator/investors constituted a majority of MLS's managing board, and MLS served as a corporate entity that commonly made collaborative decisions through individual entrepreneurs. This suggested that if those individuals found certain collective decisions, such as the fixing of above-market prices for sellers, mutually beneficial, they might be able to achieve those decisions through the aegis of the MLS, whereas they would not be able to do so, under the antitrust laws, by individual price-fixing agreements.

Thus the First Circuit's opinion in *Fraser* stopped short of declaring MLS a single entity for antitrust purposes, finding it instead to be a "hybrid arrangement, somewhere between a single company. . . . and a cooperative agreement between existing competitors."[50] But, again, the distinction did not matter, because the creation of MLS was clearly not a per se violation of section 1 of the Sherman Act—the decision to launch a new Division I American soccer league had pro- as well as anticompetitive effects—and the jury verdict under section 2 rendered any confusion over MLS's status irrelevant, because the plaintiffs had not shown that the relevant market affected by MLS's actions was limited to Division I professional soccer players in the United States.[51] Accordingly, the district court decision, which rendered a complete victory to MLS, was affirmed.

MLS'S ROCKY START

Despite its victory in *Fraser*, MLS was far from being out of the woods as a viable sports venture. After averaging over 17,000 fans per game in its initial season, the league's attendance fell to less than 15,000 in its second year,[52] a development accentuated by MLS commissioner Doug Logan's prediction that in its second year attendance would average 20,000.[53] Kevin Payne said of Logan's comment, "It ended up being a millstone around our necks. . . . For years, every MLS game story started out, in the first paragraph, [with a] mention of the attendance," even though some professional sports teams in other leagues, such as the Washington Capitals in the National Hockey League, were at the time only drawing around 6,000 people a game.[54] Rick Lawes, who covered MLS for *USA Today* in the 1990s, felt that Logan's comment had invited the media to use attendance as a proxy for assessing the league's success.[55]

One way to bolster attendance and the visibility of the league was thought to be through expansion. In 1998, MLS's third season, clubs in Chicago and Miami were added. The reasons for expansion were threefold. First, adding new franchises in large cities increased the league's exposure and created new television markets, which hopefully would secure additional income not only to operator/investors but to the league as a whole. Second, the entry fee for new operator/investors added to the league's assets. Third, the more clubs the league could accommodate, the more established professional soccer would become in communities across America, hopefully stimulating not only fan interest but participation in youth soccer programs in those communities.

MLS's choice of Chicago was an obvious one: it was among the nation's largest cities and media markets; it was a transportation and communications hub; and its midwestern location gave MLS a foothold in a region where the only other established franchises were in Columbus, Ohio, and Kansas City, Missouri, and in which there was rapidly growing youth participation in soccer. On coming into MLS as an operator/investor when the league started, Philip Anschutz had been given an option to purchase a second franchise should MLS expand, and he elected to run the Chicago team. The launching process for the Chicago Fire, which included enlisting supporters' groups in the fashion of DC United, was a success: the Fire drew over 36,000 people to its first home game, held in Soldier Field, home of the Chicago Bears.[56]

Miami turned out to be a different story. MLS had chosen Miami as a base for an expansion team because of the large Latino population in the city and because Ken Horowitz, the founder of the Cellular One wireless network, had made a bid for a team. Horowitz paid a $20 million entry fee, a price considerably inflated from those paid by the founders of MLS two years earlier. Almost immediately the Miami franchise, named the Fusion to reflect the ethnic diversity of the city, ran into difficulties because Miami's mayor balked at the terms of a lease for the club to play in the Orange Bowl, which was city-owned. Horowitz had wanted a three-to-five-year lease, with an out clause if average attendance fell below 16,000, whereas the mayor demanded a ten-year lease.[57] The prospective arrangement collapsed, leaving the Fusion with no stadium, since other area stadiums did not meet MLS's minimum capacity. Moreover, the franchise couldn't be moved from south Florida without league approval.

At this point Horowitz hit upon an ingenious solution. There was a municipal stadium at Fort Lauderdale, Lockhart Stadium, operated by the Broward County Public Schools, which could seat 7,800 people. Horowitz proposed to renovate the stadium, enlarging its capacity to 20,000. He also anticipated putting in new lighting, an electronic scoreboard, and offices for the Fusion's daily operations. MLS approved the renovations, which were also acceptable to Broward County officials because they would result in a much nicer stadium, one capable of accommodating Florida high school gridiron football championship games.

In terms of the atmosphere it generated for soccer matches, the renovated Lockhart Stadium was a conspicuous success: years later a writer in the *Miami Sun-Sentinel* recalled the "intimate, almost claustrophobic . . . pulse" created by "20,450 people packed into" the Fusion's opening game against DC United in 1998.[58] Lockhart was the precursor of the soccer-specific stadiums to which many clubs in MLS eventually committed, beginning with the Columbus Crew's stadium in 1999. But even Horowitz's successful rebound from his initial difficulties in finding a site for the Fusion would not result in his franchise's survival.

In some respects Miami had seemed an ideal location for an MLS franchise. At the time the Fusion came into being, there were nearly 5 million people in the greater Miami area, many of them Latinos, and it was also home to a community of expatriates from Europe.[59] The greater Miami area had had two teams in the NASL, one of which, the Fort Lauderdale Strikers, had regularly been successful in terms of results and attendance. But professional soccer in Florida, both in Miami and in Tampa Bay, would face the same obstacles that all professional sports teams, from baseball to basketball to hockey, had encountered in the Sunshine State. The problems centered in two areas: the deep commitment of native Floridians to high school and college gridiron football games, by far the most regularly attended sport events in the state;[60] and the state's climate, which made outdoor attendance at athletic contests either uncomfortable because of the heat and humidity or risky because of the constant threat of lightning-producing thunderstorms.[61] Because of the uncertainty of the summer weather, fans were not inclined to buy tickets to games in advance, making it difficult for the Fusion, or the Tampa Bay Mutiny, to sell a great many season tickets. On numerous occasions fans inclined to attend a game would end up not going because of the weather, even though the Fusion and Mutiny both played matches under adverse conditions, stopping them only when there was a risk of severe thunderstorms. Whatever the reason, the Fusion sold only 939 season tickets in 1999.[62]

The initial seasons for the Fusion were not successful in terms of the team's performance, and attendance remained low, averaging only 7,460 in 2000.[63] Beginning in 2001, however, the team's play dramatically improved under new coach Ray Hudson, reaching the MLS championship game in 2001. Its average attendance that year also improved, to 11,777.[64]

But Horowitz was already becoming discouraged. He had tried playing some games in the Orange Bowl, and was heartened when the Miami City Council arranged for downtown buildings to be lit up in the Fusion's colors on game nights. The Fusion received considerable coverage in the Miami media, outdistancing many other MLS clubs in that respect.[65] But, as Horowitz would note in 2015, "people still didn't come" to the Fusion's matches. Eventually, at the end of 2001, he approached the other operator/investors of MLS to inform them that he was considering "saying this is enough" and closing the team. "Unless somebody has an answer to this," he recalled saying, "this can't go on. We're bleeding [money]."[66]

The founders of MLS resolved to have a meeting to consider the effects of the Miami franchise ceasing to operate. Under the agreements associated with the formation of MLS, the league itself did not have the right to close a team. But every time a franchise lost money, it affected all of the other owners as well as the team's operator/investor, and when a team owned by the league itself lost money, as in the case of the Tampa Bay Mutiny, all the losses were incurred by the league, which meant they fell directly on the founding owners. When the MLS board of governors met in Columbus in the wake of Horowitz's announcement, "that was a very, very difficult meeting," Payne recalled. "The business model was broken. There was not much consensus about how to go forward."[67] After the Columbus meeting there was a conference call among the owners and a subsequent meeting in New York, in which the owners resolved to take MLS into bankruptcy.

Then, just forty-eight hours later, things turned around. Anschutz said that he would take responsibility for six teams;[68] Lamar Hunt said that he would continue to support the two teams with which he was affiliated, Columbus and Kansas City, and become an operator/investor in Dallas as well; and Robert Kraft agreed to continue in his operator/investor role with the New England Revolution. A "very strict five-year spending plan" was initiated, with the hope of "get[ting] the losses under control" and "build[ing] up commercial revenues."[69] At the same time, the remaining MLS operator/investors agreed to contract the franchises in Miami and Tampa Bay. The latter franchise, which played its games in Raymond James Stadium, home of the Tampa Bay Buccaneers, had never thrived: the stadium was cavernous and poorly configured for soccer, the Mutiny was plagued by some of the same weather problems that often affected the

Fusion, the quality of soccer played by the Mutiny was not high, and the low attendance was felt directly by all the MLS owners because the league itself owned the franchise.

At the same time MLS began Soccer United Marketing to generate revenue from "other aspects of the soccer business," such as television rights and merchandising, and announced a multiyear deal with ABC and ESPN to televise the 2002 and 2006 men's World Cups, the 2003 women's World Cup, and some MLS matches each year. The remaining operator/investors also resolved to move in the direction of building soccer-specific stadiums immediately, and to seek to attract star players to the league in the hope of bolstering attendance.[70]

The first major venture of Soccer United Marketing (SUM) was televising the 2002 men's World Cup, hosted jointly by South Korea and Japan. It was a distinctly risky step. The US men's team had not met with success in the 1998 World Cup, losing all of its first-round matches,[71] and although it had qualified for the 2002 competition, there was no assurance it would fare better. Moreover, the time differences between the United States and Japan or South Korea meant that live matches would be broadcast very early in the morning in the United States. The US team's match against South Korea would come on at 2:25 a.m. Eastern Standard Time; that against Portugal at 4:45 a.m. EST; and that against Poland at 7:25 a.m. EST.[72]

The US team did far better than anticipated, beating Portugal, tying South Korea, and losing to Poland to advance to the second round, where it then beat Mexico to advance to the quarterfinals, losing by 1–0 to Germany, which would go to the finals.[73] But the television attendance was down from 1998. The network rating dropped from 2.6 to 1.4, although the cable rating (not including Spanish broadcasts) actually increased slightly, from 0.5 to 0.7. In 1998, 8.6 million Americans had watched the World Cup finals; 6 million watched in 2002, when the finals were aired at 6:30 a.m. EST, as compared to midafternoon for the 1998 finals.[74]

Despite the low television attendance and ratings, the 2002 World Cup gave MLS a boost because of the US team's success and visibility. Some of the men's World Cup team players were already playing in MLS, and others were expected to join clubs. Having contracted to ten clubs for the 2002 season, the operator/investors of MLS were cautious about spending, but SUM's inspired decision to combine television coverage of the men's and women's World Cups with commitments from networks to broadcast some MLS games in World Cup cycles was likely to result in increased revenue for the league. Buoyed by those developments, the MLS board directors began focusing on soccer-specific stadiums and future expansion.

MOVING TOWARD SOCCER-SPECIFIC STADIUMS

Although Ken Horowitz's renovation of Lockhart Stadium in 1998 had actually produced the first MLS soccer-specific facility, most commentators associate the league's move to such facilities with the opening of Columbus Crew Stadium in May 1999.[75] That stadium, which seated 22,500, was configured similarly to soccer stadiums in Europe, featuring sloping stands placed close to the field, giving spectators a good view of the action and making their reactions to play on the field an integral part of the atmosphere of a match. The choice of Columbus as the first MLS city to have a soccer-specific stadium was partly fortuitous and partly made out of necessity. The building of soccer-specific stadiums in MLS cities had been delayed since the league opened because of a combination of reluctance on the part of operator/investors to spend a great deal of money on construction and indifference or hostility toward the facilities by host municipalities, whose approval was often required. Existing stadiums in MLS cities were typically unsuited for soccer, so new ones needed to be constructed from scratch, a prospect at which municipal authorities often balked.

In Columbus, however, both the city and the Crew franchise had incentives for the building of a soccer-specific facility. In 1998 Ohio State University announced that its football stadium, in which the Crew had been playing, would be renovated over the course of several years.[76] Ohio Stadium was already an inadequate facility for housing soccer matches, seating over 100,000 spectators and with a field only sixty-two yards wide and surrounded by a running track, placing fans far from the action and making it difficult for players to keep the ball within the sidelines. When crowds were under 20,000, the cavernous dimensions of the stadium became starkly apparent.[77] But although Ohio Stadium was far from a desirable home field for the Crew, its anticipated renovations suggested that the Crew would be displaced.

Initially the Crew approached Franklin County and the city of Dublin, Ohio, both located near Columbus, as potential sites for a new stadium.

In both instances a public referendum or a positive vote from the city was a necessary step in gaining approval for the stadium, and in both cases the approval failed. At that point Lamar Hunt, who since joining MLS had been an advocate of soccer-specific stadiums, resolved to finance a stadium in Columbus himself. City officials supported the effort because they saw it as a way for Columbus to detach itself somewhat from the influence of Ohio State, the city's dominant entity, and identify itself as a city capable of hosting professional sports.[78] Construction began on the stadium in August 1998, and MLS scheduled the Crew for road games in the early part of the 1999 season. The stadium was an instant success, with the Crew leading MLS in attendance in the structure's inaugural season. The Crew's official historian commented that it "completely changed the way the game looked, played, and felt to those in the stands and watching on TV." More than forty media publications wrote articles about the opening of the stadium. It "was an incalculably better experience than the Horseshoe over at Ohio State," one writer maintained. "Fans were seated just a few feet from the corner flags. You were right on top of the action."[79]

The next soccer-specific stadium to open was the Home Depot Center in Carson, California. Play began there in June 2003, with the Los Angeles Galaxy as hosts. The stadium seated 27,000 and was part of a multi-sport complex that included tennis courts and a track. A Teflon-coated roof covered some of the seats, and the facility included a grass berm at one end to accommodate overflow crowds. MLS immediately staged both the 2003 All-Star game and the 2003 MLS Cup finals in the Home Depot Center.[80] MLS commissioner Don Garber called the Home Depot Center "the Cathedral of American Soccer," declaring that "it really celebrated the game for the first time that rivaled the rest of the world," and that it "wasn't just a building" but "a statement about what the future holds for us if we're able to build [soccer-specific stadiums] for all our teams."[81]

Over the first two decades of the twenty-first century, MLS has made a determined effort to establish soccer-specific stadiums in its cities, with partial success. As the league has expanded, several franchises, such as those in Philadelphia, Toronto, Montreal, Los Angeles, Minneapolis–St. Paul, Orlando, and Houston, either debuted with new soccer-specific stadiums or built them after joining the league, and the established franchises in Dallas, Chicago, Kansas City, New York, Salt Lake City, and Washington have built new soccer-specific facilities. One such new stadium is currently under construction in Cincinnati, home to the most recently awarded MLS franchise. But the New England Revolution, the New York City Football Club, the Portland Timbers, the Seattle Sounders, and the Vancouver Whitecaps still play in "multipurpose" gridiron football stadiums, and have encountered resistance from municipalities in seeking to move to new soccer-specific facilities.[82]

It seems incontrovertible that the construction of soccer-specific stadiums for MLS clubs has been an important ingredient in the league's growth. Consider the comparative experiences of watching a soccer match in a gridiron football stadium and watching one in a soccer-specific facility. Football stadiums in America were built with the purpose of providing maximum attendance for a game typically played only once a week. Whether the stadiums were designed for college or professional football, they tended to be massive, not conducive to an intimate experience for spectators. The spectacle of watching a gridiron football game included pregame rituals, cheers orchestrated by cheerleaders, and comparatively long periods between plays during which fans' attention did not need to be focused squarely on the field. In that setting, being close to the field and its players might have been desirable for some fans, but those spectating from a distance could follow the action as well.

The experience of watching soccer is dramatically different. Action on the field is virtually continuous. Most of it consists of efforts by clubs to move the ball up and down the field, sometimes in patterns and sometimes in spontaneous, improvised dribbling or passing. The players on opposing teams are in close proximity, and there is an ongoing drama centering on which team can retain possession and whether it can advance toward an opponent's goal. In short, there is a great deal on the field for soccer fans to see, much of it involves close contact between players, and being close to the field, or having an unobstructed view of the action, greatly enhances the experience of spectators.

In sum, spectators at a soccer match need to be in a position to understand what is happening on the field at every moment. When one considers that in the early years of American professional soccer leagues, even those fans of clubs that aspired to "major" status—none of which, of course, played in soccer-specific stadiums—were often denied clear lines of sight, and that many of them had not yet developed a good understanding of the intricacies of the game, one can understand how fans easily became bored. To a large extent, then, the configuration of stadiums in which NASL and early MLS games were played prevented American fans from becoming excited about the game or well acquainted with it.

When MLS resolved to build soccer-specific stadiums that could hold around 20,000 spectators, that choice was not a random one. By the time the league came into being, its founders were well aware of attendance numbers at Division I matches in Europe. They also knew that some repeatedly successful European clubs, such as Barcelona, Real Madrid, Manchester United, and Bayern Munich, were capable of drawing very large crowds, and nevertheless chose not to build new large stadiums. It appeared that 20,000 spectators, seated closely together and continuously engaged with a match, created an ideal atmosphere for watching soccer. Thus by limiting the seating capacity of soccer-specific stadiums, MLS implicitly suggested not only that their attendance figures ought to be compared to those at professional basketball or hockey games but also that soccer fans would have a better experience in smaller stadiums.[83]

The last feature of MLS's decision to build soccer-specific stadiums in as many of its cities as possible was the connection between the emergence of those facilities and the league's expansion. In 2002, when MLS nearly folded, the league had contracted to ten clubs. By 2019 it had expanded to twenty-four, having added new clubs in 2005 (Salt Lake City), 2007 (Toronto), 2008 (San Jose), 2009 (Seattle), 2010 (Philadelphia), 2011 (Portland and Vancouver), 2012 (Montreal), 2015 (Orlando and New York), 2017 (Atlanta and Minneapolis–St. Paul), 2018 (Los Angeles), and 2019 (Cincinnati).[84] Of those new clubs, only Montreal and Los Angeles had built a new soccer-specific stadium before their clubs began MLS play, but Salt Lake City, Toronto, San Jose, Orlando, Minneapolis–St. Paul, and Cincinnati began building soccer-specific facilities shortly after entering the league. It was clear that as MLS sought to expand, cities that had built or were prepared to build soccer-specific stadiums held a distinct advantage as potential entrants.

MLS took two additional steps in its effort to achieve major status. The first of those, undertaken after the 1999 season, was the initiation of two rule changes designed to make MLS conform to European leagues. As was noted in a prior chapter, when the league first startedits founders resolved to count down time in the manner of American basketball or hockey games, from the beginning of a half to zero. This was in direct contrast to the European leagues' system of counting up from zero to forty-five minutes, then adding stoppage time, which was also counted up from zero to whatever minutes had been allocated. When Don Garber replaced Doug Logan as MLS commissioner in 1999, he immediately took a survey of persons who had identified themselves as fans and supporters of the league, and the results revealed that they strongly disliked the existing countdown clock and thought it should be changed to conform with international practice. Beginning with its 2000 season, MLS began to count up.[85]

The second rule change involved the shootout as a way of resolving matches that had ended in draws. The practice of European leagues was not to resolve drawn matches but to award a point to both clubs, in contrast to the three points a club received for a win. Both the NASL and MLS believed that American audiences would be disenchanted with tie games, pointing out that all of the other professional sports in the United States had mechanisms for resolving ties. MLS initiated a practice known as the shootout, which consisted of a designated player dribbling the ball from midfield in the direction of his opponent's goal, with the goalie poised to encounter him, either in the penalty area or elsewhere on the field. A time limit of five seconds was established for the player to shoot at the goal. If a player failed to score, one from the other team would repeat the shootout until one team scored and the other did not match it, when the match would end.

Several players in the MLS did not like shootouts. One of them, Eric Wynalda, described the system as "odd," noting that on one occasion he failed to get off a shot in the required five seconds. He attempted to get pointers on shootouts from goalkeepers. "It really came down," he was advised, "to hitting it hard, slotting it to one side or another, or chipping it . . . those three options."[86] Although the shootout virtually eliminated dribbling around the goalkeeper, already an extremely difficult task in soccer because goalkeepers may use their hands, the "options" goalkeepers presented to Wynalda were ones that he and his MLS contemporaries already would have been aware of. In short, the shootout was unlikely to result in many goals, and Garber's survey also revealed strong hostility toward it among fans. It was also discontinued in 2000.

The next step was more radical. In 2006 MLS had conducted a consumer research survey, initiated after the World Cup that year, which asked American soccer fans their reaction to the current state of the league. That survey was comparable to the one undertaken in 1999. It produced a strong preference on the part of MLS supporters to "see more star players—more world-class players—and . . . to see more American players who they watched compete for their country in the World Cup."[87] It was still the case, ten years after MLS had come into being, that the best American college players were seeking to play in European leagues rather than MLS, and that the foreign players in the league either did not have top-draw international reputations or were reaching the end of their careers in overseas leagues. MLS still lacked the reputation of being a Division I soccer league comparable to such leagues in Europe or South America, and because of that perception it still had difficulty attracting star foreign players.

And there was an additional, even more formidable obstacle. MLS had come into being against the backdrop of the NASL's collapse, which the founders of MLS had attributed to excess spending on the part of some clubs, largely directed at signing foreign players, that served to create a competitive imbalance, eventually resulting in the league's weaker clubs folding and the stronger ones subsequently having too few opponents to play. MLS' single-entity structure was designed to force operator/investors to consider the effects on the league as whole, and all of its franchises, on their financial decisions. Moreover, MLS, particularly after its retrenchment in 2002, had adopted a policy of exercising tight controls on spending by clubs, limiting each franchise's budget for player salaries, with only a few exceptions, to no more than $2 million a year.[88] How was MLS, given those budgetary constraints, going to attract star players?

The answer would come from connections the Los Angeles Galaxy franchise had with David Beckham, perhaps the best-known international soccer star of the 1990s and 2000s and, along with his wife Victoria ("Posh Spice" of the Spice Girls), a worldwide celebrity. Highly interested in "branding" himself since becoming a visible star, Beckham had established soccer camps in Los Angeles in 2005, and in the process had made contacts with persons in Anschutz's Anschutz Entertainment Group (AEG) organization, which managed the Galaxy.[89] Galaxy representatives initiated talks with Beckham that they hoped would result in Beckham's joining the

FIGURE 10. David Beckham after signing with the Los Angeles Galaxy of Major League Soccer in 2007. The acquisition of Beckham, at that time the world's best known soccer player, by an American professional soccer league franchise was arguably a turning point in the emergence of MLS as a viable and potentially profitable organization. REUTERS/ Alamy Stock Photo.

club, and MLS, for the 2006 season, by which time Beckham would be thirty-two years old.

Beckham had played Division I professional soccer in England since he was eighteen, becoming part of Manchester United's roster in 1994. After being loaned to Preston North End for the next season to get experience as a starter, he returned to Manchester United in 1995, beginning a series of years in which he and his club thrived, winning several Premier League titles and, in the 1998–99 season, the FA Cup and the Champions Cup in addition to the Premier League, the first English club to have done so. After 2000, however, Beckham's relationship with Alex Ferguson, Manchester United's longtime manager, began to deteriorate; Ferguson believed that after his marriage to Victoria, Beckham had become more interested in celebrity life than in playing soccer. Despite having his best season statistically in 2001–2, Beckham was replaced as a starter in the 2002–3 season after sustaining an injury. In the summer transfer window of 2003, Manchester United placed Beckham on their designated transfer list, and clubs outside England began bidding for his services, most conspicuously Barcelona and Real Madrid, perennial powers and rivals in Spain's La Liga.

Beckham signed with Real Madrid, beginning in the middle of the 2003 season. Although he played well, the club did not meet expectations in La Liga play that season nor the next, and chaos descended, with Real Madrid going through a succession of managers and, after the summer of 2006, a new club president. On January 10, 2007, Real Madrid first announced that Beckham would not remain with the club after the end of the league season, then changed its statement to say simply that his contract had not been renewed. The next day Beckham announced that he had signed a five-year contract with the Galaxy, to begin on July 1, 2007.[90]

How was the Galaxy able to sign Beckham? It was by virtue of MLS's new Designated Player rule. Under that rule, each club in MLS was allowed to exceed its $2 million salary budget restriction to sign one "designated" player for an amount that could exceed the restriction to any limit and to which the league would contribute $400,000.[91] The rule allowed MLS finally to compete with Division I overseas leagues for star players, so long as the operator/investors of franchises were willing to pay those players large salaries out of their own pockets. But it also restricted clubs' capacity to sign such players, thus avoiding the sort of widespread spending engaged in by the New York Cosmos of the NASL. And MLS anticipated that along with star players such as Beckham would come opportunities for endorsements and other merchandising, in addition to a projected growth in attendance. In Beckham's case the Galaxy paid him a $9 million salary, covering five years, but he also received endorsements and other marketing opportunities, eventually earning about $250 million for the five-year period. Meanwhile the Galaxy allegedly received $5 to $6 million a year from Adidas for the right to sponsor the club's jerseys.[92]

Beckham's career with the Galaxy was, in retrospect, a clear success for MLS and moderately successful for the club, which won the MLS Cup in the 2011 and 2012 seasons. It was less of a success for Beckham, in part because he negotiated a loan to AC Milan for the Italian league Serie A's 2008 and 2009 seasons, returning to the Galaxy in the middle of the summers and completing the MLS season. His absence for part of the Galaxy's season angered supporters of the club in LA, who held up signs calling Beckham a "part-time player," and advising him to "Go home, fraud."[93] While playing for Milan in its 2010 season, Beckham tore his Achilles tendon, causing him to miss the World Cup and most of the MLS season that year. For his 2011 season with the Galaxy, however, Beckham trained with, but did not play for, Tottenham in the Premier League, and in 2012, although linked to the French Ligue 1 club Paris Saint-Germain, signed a new two-year contract with the Galaxy. He would eventually retire from MLS after the cup final that year and sign with Paris Saint-Germain for the 2013 season, donating his salary to a children's charity in Paris. In May 2013 he announced that he would retire from professional soccer altogether after the conclusion of the Ligue 1 season.[94]

Although Beckham's playing association with MLS was mixed, his acquisition, and the Designated Player rule that accompanied it, were incomparable benefits to the league. The Designated Player rule allowed MLS to maintain its single-entity restrictions on signing players and player salaries while giving the operator/investors of clubs, many of whom had considerable assets, flexibility to bring star players into the league. Beginning with Beckham's signing, such players began coming on a regular basis. They included not only the visible American World Cup players Michael Bradley, Clint Dempsey, Omar Gonzalez, Jermaine Jones, and Claudio Reyna, but also Guillermo Schelotto from Argentina, Kaka from Brazil, Juan Pablo Ángel and Fredy Montero from Colombia, Thierry Henry from France, Rafa Marquez and Giovani dos Santos from Mexico, Freddie Ljungberg from Sweden, Robbie Keane, Frank Lampard, and Steven Gerrard from England, Didier Drogba from the Ivory Coast, Sebastian Giovinco from Italy, and David Villa from Spain.[95]

In addition, MLS tweaked the Designated Player rule since Beckham's signing to allow even more star players to be brought in from overseas. When Beckham signed with the Galaxy, clubs were limited to one designated player; by 2014 the limit had been increased to three per team. Then, in 2015, the league announced a change in its salary cap rules, the caps having risen from approximately $2 million when Beckham signed to $3.49 million that year. Under the change, clubs were permitted to spend an additional $500,000 above the $3.49 million salary cap, and could also use "targeted allocation money" to "convert a Designated Player to a non-Designated Player by buying down his salary budget charge to below the maximum salary budget charge." When clubs did that, they were required to "simultaneously sign a new Designated Player at an investment equal to or greater than the player he is replacing."[96] Although the rule changes might favor wealthier clubs over time, they made it possible for MLS to sign more visible international players, arguably contributing to the increased visibility and prestige of the league as a whole.[97]

The Designated Player rule and MLS's subsequent tweaking of it clearly resulted in the influx of visible overseas players that came into the league on the heels of Beckham's signing, but other factors contributed to the increased international visibility of MLS and eventually to the upgrading of league play to the point where it could aspire to become the equivalent of a high-tier overseas league.

One was the increased interchange not only between overseas league players and MLS, but between American players and high-level European leagues. The US men's performance in the 1994 World Cup demonstrated to Premier League clubs in the UK that there were some quite competent American players who might be signed by those clubs at salaries far below those expected by players from European leagues, and that playing in the more demanding competition of the Premier League would be attractive to some Americans. Cobi Jones, a longtime member of the US national men's team, was signed by Coventry City of the Premier League shortly after the 1994 tournament. Coventry City was among the Premier League's less wealthy franchises: it paid a £2.6 million transfer fee for Jones, but paid him far less for a one-year contract.[98] Other Premier League clubs followed suit, resulting in some of the most gifted American players of the late twentieth and early twenty-first centuries, such as Clint Dempsey (Fulham and

Tottenham Hotspur), Claudio Reyna (Sunderland and Manchester City), the goalkeeper Tim Howard (Everton), and Landon Donovan (brief intervals at Everton) joining Premier League clubs. The paths of such players from the United States to overseas leagues and, in some instances, eventually back to MLS—Jones to the Los Angeles Galaxy, Dempsey from the New England Revolution to the Premier League to the Seattle Sounders, Reyna from the Premier League to the New York Red Bulls, Howard from Everton to the Colorado Rapids, Donovan from Everton to the Galaxy—served to further contacts between that league and the top-flight European leagues, thereby increasing MLS's visibility. It has even been suggested that some Premier League clubs have "feeder" relationships with some MLS clubs, in which they shuttle younger players to MLS to gain experience or older, now marginal, but well-known players to MLS to enhance the league's visibility.[99]

In addition, American cable broadcast networks began televising Premier League games and some La Liga and Bundesliga games as well, and broadcasts of MLS games began to be made available to some UK and western European audiences, furthering the impression that the stars of both MLS and top-division overseas leagues were part of some interchanging global pool. That trend has become particular noticeable in recent years with the influx of players from Mexico's first-division league, Liga MX, into MLS, accompanied by the increased television exposure of MLS matches in Mexico and Latin America through Spanish-speaking networks such as Univision.[100]

THE FUTURE OF MLS

By the twentieth anniversary of MLS, in 2016, several developments had occurred that, taken together, augured the possibility of a bright future for professional men's soccer in America. The league's attendance, for the first time since its creation, averaged over 20,000.[101] One club, the Seattle Sounders, still playing in a "multipurpose" stadium it shared with the Seahawks, averaged 44,247 spectators, a higher figure than the perennially successful English Premier League franchise Liverpool and more than all but one other club in the western hemisphere. No club in the league averaged fewer than approximately 16,000 spectators.[102]

Another intriguing, and hopeful, development was the expansion of MLS's "digital space" as a way of increasing its fan base. Through the league's website, social media platforms, an online channel broadcasting

MLS games, "gamecasts" featuring comments from fans watching games in progress, and videos covering the activities of fans as well as players, MLS Digital sought not only to make it easier for American and overseas audiences to follow its matches but also to encourage connections among soccer fans. As such platforms enhanced the opportunities of fans to communicate their support for particular clubs, the model of passionate club supporters, long a common feature of UK, European, and Latin American soccer, had a greater capacity to take root.[103] A passionate fan base for MLS clubs arguably makes it more likely that those clubs will maintain good attendance and visible media coverage, even if their performance on the field fails to consistently reach high levels. Expanding the digital space for MLS and its clubs also encourages youthful soccer enthusiasts in a community to grow up supporting their local teams, and continue that support as adults.

Two other positive developments had occurred by MLS's twentieth anniversary in 2016. One was a startling decision on the part of the television network ESPN. The network had planned to follow its broadcast of the August 23 finals of the Junior League World Series, featuring international youth baseball teams with players between the ages of twelve and fourteen, with an MLS match between the Los Angeles Galaxy and NYCFC, in which recently signed designated players Steven Gerrard and Frank Lampard, both former stars in the English Premier League, would compete against one another. The MLS match was expected to start slightly after noon Pacific time, and ESPN intended to begin airing it at 3:00 p.m. eastern time, when it assumed the Junior League game would have concluded.

The Junior League finals, however, were still going on at 3:15, with a team from Chinese Taipei leading one from Virginia 10–0 in the seventh inning of a nine-inning game. At that point ESPN broke off its coverage of the Junior League game and switched to Los Angeles, where the MLS soccer match was about to start. That decision represented virtually the first time in ESPN's programming history that it had ended coverage of a live sports event before it had concluded, and it was a clear signal that the network believed that the audience for an MLS game would be sufficiently larger than that for the finals of the Junior League.[104] A soccer commentator from Philadelphia described ESPN's switch from covering youth baseball to soccer as "a moment in which people could say here is an event within MLS that ESPN will draw a large-enough audience to be bigger than a little league baseball game," and thus "among the most stunning moments in MLS history."[105] That was not much of an overstatement; ESPN's decision confirmed not only that the network was committed to televising MLS games but that it believed an ordinary regular-season match between two MLS clubs, with a fair amount of the season still to be played, might well attract a significant television audience because the clubs in question were from large cities, and highly visible international players were now on the rosters of MLS teams.

The second development in MLS's anniversary year involved the structure of its single-entity franchise ownership. When the league was tottering on the brink of extinction in 2001, Philip Anschutz, through his Anschutz Entertainment Group, had assumed responsibility for six of the league's remaining ten clubs. Although that was an emergency measure, and MLS would subsequently expand again, it revealed how dependent the league was, in its early years, on the largesse and commitment of a few operator/investors. In 2016, by contrast, the Houston Dynamo announced that one of its minority owners, Gabriel Brener, had bought a controlling interest in a club from Anschutz Entertainment Group.[106] The San Jose Earthquakes franchise, controlled by Anschutz since 2002, had moved to Houston in 2005 to become the Dynamo. Brener's purchase meant that AEG owned only the Los Angeles Galaxy, so that each of the then twenty club franchises in MLS had separate operator/investors. Over twenty years the league had shown itself capable of attracting more individual franchise owners without dissolving its command-and-control structure, and its organization now resembled that of the English Premier League.

But there remained one feature of the operation of Division I soccer leagues outside the United States that MLS still refused to adopt. This was the formal "tiering" of leagues in a nation and the use of promotion and relegation to move clubs up and down in those leagues. Although the process of promotion and relegation has been discussed in preceding chapters, one feature of it has not hitherto been emphasized. For clubs to be promoted at the end of a season to a higher-tiered league or relegated to a lower-tier one based on their season-long records, two additional dimensions of playing professional soccer in a particular nation need to exist. One is a general recognition, not just among owners and administrators of soccer clubs but also among their supporters, that a status hierarchy of soccer leagues exists in a nation, with Division I leagues clearly distinguished from Division II leagues, and so on up and down the hierarchy. The other is that despite differences among tiers, the quality of play of clubs at the bottom of a higher status league is close enough to that of clubs at the top of the league directly below it that promoting the top three clubs of a Division II league to a Division I league and relegating the bottom three clubs of the higher-status league to the league below it will not unduly affect the competitive balance of play in either league.

Not only had promotion and relegation never been a feature of professional soccer leagues in the United States, but no established hierarchy of leagues had ever existed at the time MLS was formed.[107] As we have seen, multiple professional and semiprofessional soccer leagues coexisted at several times in twentieth-century America; there was sometimes competition among such leagues, particularly in the form of cup events; and at times, such as when the NASL came into being while the ASL remained in existence, there seems to have been an understood hierarchy of leagues. But no such hierarchy was ever formally established by the USSF, nor was there ever anything like a general understanding as to the comparative quality of play in leagues. So even had promotion and relegation seemed attractive to American professional soccer leagues as they formed, there would have been no easy way to put it into practice. Consequently American men's professional soccer leagues came and went, rose and fell, on their own, without any effort at coordination.

By 2015 three men's professional soccer leagues existed in the United States: MLS; a new version of the NASL, launched in 2011; and the United Soccer League, an entity composed of twenty-nine teams loosely arranged in various divisions, many with ties to particular MLS clubs, having players on their rosters who were signed by MLS teams and delegated to the USL. Many of the teams were located in or near the cities housing MLS clubs, some employing versions of the clubs' names, such as the LA Galaxy II and Orlando City B. The USL was "considered the third-tier league in [a] hierarchy" by the USSF, but nothing particularly followed from that. Nor did anything significant follow from USSF's designation of the twenty-first century version of the NASL as a second-tier league. Although both the USL and the NASL signed contracts with cable networks to televise games, there was little expectation of the broadcasts getting beyond niche markets.

Moreover, neither the NASL or USL franchises have proven profitable: they exist largely for player development.[108]

Nonetheless by 2015 a group of American soccer fans had become strident advocates for promotion and relegation in MLS.[109] They sought to convince the USSF to mandate it in all of the existing men's professional soccer leagues in the United States, arguing that MLS was "suffocating" the development of American professional soccer by not adopting it. Promotion and relegation, they argued, would create opportunities for every club in a US league to aspire to compete with MLS clubs, which would result in lower-tier clubs making serious efforts to attract good players, and result in soccer "exploding" in America.[110]

In an interview with the journalist Phil West on September 15, 2015, MLS commissioner Don Garber responded at some length to advocates of promotion and relegation for that league and the other US professional leagues. After suggesting that the advocates didn't understand "that the economics of . . . MLS differ vastly from the economics of a Football Association hierarchy,"[111] Garber went on to say:

> I get asked a lot and read a lot about soccer promotion and relegation. It is coming from a handful of media people and a very small set of fans who are very active on social media. It is not something that is resonating in our fan base. It is not something I get asked about by the traditional soccer press or sports media. . . . All the pro leagues here in the U.S. don't have promotion/relegation. Their playoffs rate anywhere from two times to five times their regular season. Their championship events are some of the biggest events on television that year. . . . And every team is fighting hard to win every game and to win a championship. . . . There's no reason American soccer can't be defined by what makes our leagues great. . . . So I dismiss entirely this view that just because it works in the rest of the world in football means that needs to work here in the United States.
>
> We have a system of a player draft. We have union agreements. We have investors that have committed billions. They are partners in Soccer United Marketing. They have agreed to certain rules . . . commitments that they make to others as partners. To think that somebody can come in or out of that partnership just because of the

> [team's] performance, just because it exists in international football, is a structural and legal impossibility.[112]

Garber's remarks made it clear that the commissioner of Major League Soccer was unalterably opposed to the institution of promotion and regulation. He characterized the economics of MLS and the "Football Association hierarchy" as vastly different, asserting that the prospect of instituting promotion and relegation did not resonate with MLS's fan base and was only being urged by a small minority of persons on social media. He seemed to be claiming that the playoffs culminating league seasons in MLS and all the other American professional sports leagues generated from two to five times the amount of television viewers as regular-season matches, whereas overseas leagues with promotion and relegation only had playoff games on the rare occasions when the records of two clubs seeking to become the third promoted club in a league or seeking to avoid becoming the third relegated club were identical. Should MLS adopt promotion and relegation, he implied, opportunities for high television ratings as the league's season culminated would be lost.[113]

Those were not, however, Garber's most fundamental objections to promotion and relegation. He called it a "structural and legal" impossibility because of the way MLS had been organized as a single-entity corporation. MLS was an organization in which the operator/investors of clubs had "committed billions" of dollars and were partners with one another in league commercial ventures, such as Soccer United Marketing, while at the same time being competitors in league matches. They had "bound themselves" to rules about signing players, bidding against one another for players, and establishing limits on players' salaries. They had agreed to form that particular ownership structure, and make those financial and legal commitments, because they believed that doing so would help the league grow and flourish, eventually resulting in their making money from investing in and operating the clubs with which they were associated. They wanted, in short, a closed-league model of operation, analogous to that of Major League Baseball or the National Football League, where the owners of clubs make collective decisions about salaries, revenue sharing, and other operational costs free from interference by any regulatory body or by other clubs in other leagues, either within the United States or overseas.[114]

Promotion and relegation, in Garber's view, substituted that closed-league model for one in which other clubs, with different operator/investors, could "come in or out of" MLS "just because of [their teams'] performances." If that were the case, the "partnership" of MLS owners would no longer turn on their agreement to be bound by certain obligations and to lay out large sums of money in exchange for achieving a collective command-and-control structure, but on whether the clubs with which they were associated remained in MLS after the conclusion of a league season. Should DC United, for example, be among the three bottom clubs in MLS at the end of a season, it and its operator/investor group would no longer be in MLS the next season, but find themselves in whatever league the USSF had designated as Division II. Or, say, if the Rochester Rhinos, an American Professional Soccer League club that had defeated several MLS teams to win the US Open Cup in 1999,[115] should hypothetically finish first in the APSL after promotion and relegation were introduced, that club, with its operator/investors, would suddenly become part of MLS's single-entity corporate structure. When Garber called that "a structural and legal impossibility," he was defending the investments of the owners and operators of existing MLS clubs, some of which stretched back to the original formation of the league.

For all of his passion, Garber was not quite accurate in asserting that the economics of MLS were vastly different from those of the hierarchy of clubs in the Football League. The principal difference was that American men's professional soccer had not become sufficiently established to permit a designation of tiers of leagues that roughly tracked levels of play, as in the UK. If anything, the tendency of clubs in the current USL to have affiliations with MLS clubs, resembling the affiliations between major- and minor-league baseball teams, serves to make the task of hierarchically classifying American pro soccer leagues even more difficult. But beyond that quite important difference, the economics of the Football Association leagues and MLS have similarities. Both are command-and-control rather than free market operations. Both have revenue sharing and self-imposed controls on bidding for players' salaries.[116] Both have moved to build soccer-specific stadiums. Both receive, or hope to receive, an important amount of their revenue from contracts with television networks. And both are seeking increased presences on digital media and attempting to build overseas fan bases. In many respects Major League Soccer is seeking to replicate the growth and flourishing of association football in the UK.

But for all those similarities, the economic future of MLS will remain connected to its being a professional soccer league in the United States, with all of the historical and cultural dimensions of that status. We thus turn back, in a concluding chapter, to what playing soccer in America, not only at the men's and women's professional levels but for colleges, high schools, youth groups, and recreational teams, has meant and may mean in the future.

Chapter Nine

Summary and Conclusions

ON FEBRUARY 26, 2020, MLS held a kickoff event in New York, three days ahead of the start of its 2020 soccer season, commemorating the league's twenty-fifth season. Several of the league's owner/investors as well as MLS commissioner Don Garber spoke at a press conference in connection with the event. The owner of the Los Angeles Football Club, Larry Berg, predicted that major-league soccer would surpass major-league baseball in popularity during the next ten years, and become "the No. 3 [spectator] sport in the U.S. behind football and basketball." The co-owner of the Inter Miami franchise, Jorge Mas, said on the same occasion that "MLS will be one of the top sports leagues in the United States . . . on par or exceed[ing] the best leagues in the world," including the English Premier League, Spain's La Liga, and Italy's Serie A. Yet another owner/investor, Clark Hunt of the Dallas franchise, said that MLS had sufficient "momentum . . . to take us to where the [National Football League] is today."[1] Although those comments may be exaggerated, it seems plain at this writing that both MLS in particular and American soccer in general are on an upsurge. The arc of the history of association football in twentieth- and twenty-first century America appears to be moving toward its establishment as a major recreational and spectator sport.

AN OVERVIEW OF THE BOOK'S NARRATIVE

This book began by posing two questions. The first was why, when association football, having flourished in the UK, began to spread around the globe in the late nineteenth and early twentieth centuries, it did not take root in the United States, either as a participatory or a spectator sport. The second was why, after several decades of existing as a marginal men's participatory and spectator sport and a virtually nonexistent women's participatory and spectator sport, soccer dramatically emerged in each of those capacities after the 1970s. As a result, it is now the fourth largest participatory sport in American high schools, trailing only track and field, gridiron football, and basketball;[2] in 2018, Americans listed it as their fourth most favorite sport, behind gridiron football, basketball, and baseball; interest in MLS rose 27 percent between 2012 and 2018; MLS's average attendance between 2013 and 2018 ranked it eighth in the world among men's professional soccer leagues; and the expansion fee for new MLS clubs is now $200 million.[3]

This book has traced the global success of association football, from its English origins through its growth and transformation in the UK in the late nineteenth and early twentieth centuries to its spread across most regions of the globe, from western and ultimately eastern Europe to Latin America, Africa, and Oceania, so that it is now by far the world's most played and most watched sport.[4] We have seen how a Swiss-based private amateur organization with a French name, FIFA, piggybacked on soccer's global spread to become a very wealthy, very powerful, and essentially unregulated institution, primarily by controlling the staging of a worldwide soccer tournament every four years.

We have also followed, in more detail, an anomalous episode in soccer's global spread: the failure of association football to become significantly established in the world's richest and one of its most sports-obsessed twentieth-century markets, the United States. We have seen how English amateur football clubs traveled to America in the first decade of the twentieth century, yet experienced little athletic or financial satisfaction. We have noted Americans' limited participation in soccer through most of the twentieth century, a period when the sport was unable to establish itself beyond a few communities with ethnic populations, was played at the high school level in only a few private schools, and had a very limited presence at early twentieth-century colleges and universities. We have further noted the early twentieth-century transfer of high school and college extracurricular activities, including athletics, from voluntary clubs and associations to the schools and colleges themselves, a development that served to inhibit the development of soccer because, for the most part, those institutions ignored the sport.

We have traced the efforts of early- and mid-twentieth-century professional and semiprofessional soccer leagues to establish themselves in the United States, identifying the obstacles those leagues encountered. One obstacle was the clubs' lack of fan bases, and their reliance for sponsorship on businesses whose support was sometimes profit-driven and sometimes whimsical, causing them to pass in and out of existence. Another was the difficulty that clubs in the American Soccer League and the North American Soccer League had in recruiting homegrown players. Still another was professional soccer's struggle to function as a winter sport in the harsh conditions over much of the North American continent. Accentuating all those obstacles was the lack of any command-and-control structure for US soccer leagues, which were thus dependent on the financial health of their individual clubs, but at the same time incapable of exercising control over those clubs' fiscal operations. We have seen how this pattern culminated in the failure of the North American Soccer League, an organization launched at a time when television revenues and a vibrant American economy seemed to ensure its success, due to its clubs' inability to staff club rosters with American-born players or to control their quite uneven outlays for overseas player salaries.

And we have investigated two other developments that initially served to obstruct the growth of soccer as a participatory and spectator sport in the United States. One was the unfortunate relationship between FIFA and the United States Soccer Foundation for much of the twentieth century. FIFA officials, who were highly interested in promoting the growth of soccer, especially youth soccer, across the globe, for decades assumed that soccer was simply not a good fit for the United States, partly because of competition from indigenous American team sports and partly because America did not seem capable of producing an adequate pool of gifted young soccer players. Instead of working to develop youth programs in the United States, as it did in many other nations, FIFA devoted much of its attention to soccer in America to fussing about the NASL's efforts to deviate from established international rules for the sport. It was not until, with an eye on the American market, FIFA decided in 1988 to award the 1994 World Cup to the United States that anything resembling FIFA sponsorship of American professional soccer existed. And even then FIFA officials expressed doubt that American audiences would come to watch World Cup matches, or that a new American professional soccer league could get off the ground.

The other factor delaying the growth of soccer in the United States—the nearly complete absence of women playing soccer at any level in America, or as an important part of the sport's spectator audience—might at first seem counterintuitive. One might think that the absence of women's soccer in America had no causal significance because, with rare exceptions, women had not played soccer across the rest of the globe until the last quarter of the twentieth century, either, or traditionally formed a large part of the supporter audience for football clubs anywhere in the world.

But in the United States there were no obvious reasons why soccer was not suited to women. Strictures were imposed in some circles in the early twentieth century against women engaging in overly strenuous physical exercise, but on the other hand, girls and young women regularly played basketball, volleyball, and field hockey in American high schools and colleges, and in the 1920s accomplished women tennis players and golfers had come to be widely celebrated. Nonetheless, soccer was simply not offered to girls or women as a high school or college sport, or as a recreational youth activity, until the advent of Title IX in 1972.

One can readily see how the implicit exclusion of women from soccer for most of the twentieth century in the United States would have affected the sport's growth. The tremendous increase in girls' participation in youth soccer in the twenty-first century demonstrates that women can play the sport with competence and enthusiasm. But of equal significance, if perhaps less apparent, were the negative effects of excluding women on American soccer's growth as a spectator sport. If their daughters are implicitly not permitted to play a sport, whether in community youth leagues or at high schools or colleges, parents are less likely to become interested in the sport as spectators, or to become "soccer moms" (or dads), supporting their daughters' recreational activities. Thus more than one generation of American women, and some American men, were lost as prospective soccer fans. The very close correlation between the US women's World Cup teams' success and the growth of women's soccer in high schools and youth leagues demonstrates that if American women are to learn to appreciate soccer, at least some of them need to be playing it. Thus the dramatic growth of women's soccer at all levels after the passage of Title IX in 1972 is an important element in the twenty-first-century resurgence of soccer as a participatory and spectator sport in the United States, just as the absence of women's soccer was a factor in the sport's earlier marginality.

Finally, we have reviewed the emergence of Major League Soccer as the principal American professional soccer league in 1996, and the history of that league in the subsequent two decades. From its launching, Major League Soccer represented a self-conscious effort to avoid some of the difficulties encountered by previous professional soccer leagues in the United States. It initially adopted a command-and-control structure that made it resemble professional leagues in the UK and western Europe more closely than had its predecessor American leagues, even if it did not duplicate their organization precisely.

MLS also made a conscious decision to staff its club rosters primarily with players from US college teams or youthful players from other nations, notably those in Latin America. At present each club is limited to eight foreign players out of a roster of up to thirty, but international players with green cards are not counted as foreigners, and those cards are comparatively easy to secure. For the 2020 season, only seven of the Los Angeles Football Club's twenty-three roster players, and only ten of DC United's, were born in the United States.[5] Nonetheless, most of the players on most MLS club rosters are American-born, not only because of the league's desire to hold down the costs of player salaries but also because of its wish to establish a wider base of fans familiar with players, and to foster a rapport between players and the localities in which their clubs operate. Although over time MLS has modified its constraints on salaries to allow clubs to sign a limited number of "designated players," typically highly visible stars from leagues outside the United States who are late in their careers, it also has taken pains to prevent league clubs from competing for players. Players can be traded between clubs, and frequently are, but these trades do not affect the players' salaries. Over time the number of clubs owned by MLS itself has dwindled, but MLS has permitted investor/operators to own more than one franchise. In general, the MLS in structure more closely resembles a collective entity than an aggregation of autonomous clubs.

Also, as soon as it began to expand, MLS placed a premium on soccer-specific stadiums, similar in size and configuration to those used by first-division European leagues. The entrepreneurs who launched MLS recognized from the start that building soccer-specific stadiums, with an emphasis on good visibility, shelter from the elements, and closeness of spectators to the field, would greatly enhance spectators' experience, as well as reducing the significant numbers of vacant seats that were one of the unfortunate features of NASL matches played in large baseball or gridiron football stadiums. It would be nearly two decades before a majority of MLS franchises could make the move from large football or multisport stadiums to those built expressly for soccer, with a capacity of from 20,000 to 30,000 spectators, but by the middle of the twenty-first century's second decade that transition was well under way.

At present MLS plans to expand to thirty clubs from its original ten, which was expanded to twelve in 1998 but then cut back to ten in 2000, when the league nearly folded because of weak attendance. Some of its clubs appear to be on the verge of making profits, and attendance for MLS matches grew steadily in the second decade of the twentieth century. MLS has been increasingly successful in recruiting players from Mexico's top professional league, Liga MX, as its clubs have become more able to afford transfer fees and more expensive signings.[6] One could argue that all the elements are in place for a qualitative leap in the level of play in MLS, with greater fan and spectator support for its clubs, local rights to broadcast MLS games, and the interest from national US television networks in regularly broadcasting MLS matches throughout the season.[7]

THE SOURCES OF AMERICAN SOCCER'S MARGINAL STATUS

Turning to the questions posed at the outset, I have identified several factors that, taken in combination, resulted in the long-term failure of association football to take root in America. Much space has been devoted to those factors in the course of the book's narrative, so they need only be briefly summarized here.

First, gridiron football and baseball were established sports in the United States by the early twentieth century, when some American communities began to play soccer. Association football competed with those sports, particularly as a spectator sport, and was not a successful competitor. Americans associated soccer with ethnic immigrant groups who had learned the sport in other countries and thought it less compelling to watch than gridiron football. The result was that in the early twentieth century, when American spectator sports witnessed a golden age of expansion, soccer failed to grow in colleges or high schools, and its professional and semiprofessional leagues were confined to a few communities with ethnic populations who had a history of playing association football.

Second, important institutional factors stimulating the growth of association football in the UK were not present in the United States. The Football Association and the Football League had a command-and-control administrative structure that not only set the rules for football but invited town and county associations to join its membership and established nationwide competitions, such as the FA Cup, that served to enhance spectator interest and garner revenues. The Football League cemented enduring club alliances that resulted in club teams being supported by their fans regardless of their competitive success. And when league clubs became registered corporations, the directors and shareholders of the clubs agreed to plow revenues back into the development of club franchises rather than to seek profits. Thus the league ensured that fan alliance rather than profit-making would motivate clubs, and that club allegiances would remain stable over time.

None of those institutional factors was present in US semiprofessional and professional soccer. The earliest American professional leagues were simply clusters of clubs in particular localities organized by businesses that had a high percentage of immigrant workers from countries where association football had been played recreationally. The clubs amounted to vehicles to allow workers to play soccer and to garner some revenues and create publicity for the businesses that sponsored them. When clubs did not perform well or amass what their owners regarded as a sufficient amount of revenue, they were moved to different locations or disbanded. The result was that none of the early twentieth-century American professional or semiprofessional soccer leagues had any stability of membership over time. In addition, no effort was made to impose a command-and-control administrative structure on those leagues; they were controlled by the owners of clubs.

Third, in the UK association football, as a recreational sport, was played at voluntary clubs and associations as distinguished from schools and universities. The one exception to that was some English public schools, which offered football as a recreational activity but did not establish school teams or competitions with other schools. Otherwise football was centered in clubs or associations, which anyone interested in playing the sport could join. It was thus not a sport whose participation was limited by wealth, education, or class. Persons who ended up playing for clubs in the Football League were gifted players who had been recruited by their clubs and were, in effect, professionals, whose salaries and expenses, beginning in the late nineteenth century, were paid by their clubs or by local businesses who hired them.

In the early twentieth-century United States, in contrast, recreational sports were taken out of the hands of voluntary clubs by schools and colleges, and soccer was very rarely even offered as a varsity sport. As a result no significant pool of gifted players was created that could potentially staff American professional soccer leagues, and, equally importantly, no large class of enthusiasts for soccer, as participants or spectators, emerged among American communities, ensuring that sports media in the United States would pay little attention to the sport.

Fourth, the virtually complete absence of soccer as a recreational activity or high school or college team sport for women throughout the first six decades of the twentieth century inhibited the sport's growth in America. Women as well as men attended public high schools, and several private women's colleges and some coeducational public colleges and universities existed from the early twentieth century into the 1960s, but apparently only one of them, Smith College, offered soccer in any form, and that was as an intramural activity associated with the "play days" favored by female physical education instructors at the time. Women did not play college soccer until a cluster of colleges in northern Vermont began to stage soccer matches among themselves and with three Canadian universities in the 1960s.

The result of the virtual nonparticipation of American girls and women in soccer through the 1960s meant that the female population of the United States did not view the sport as a prospective recreational activity. Not only was a sport eminently suited to girls and women implicitly not made available to them, its absence meant that American women had no particular reason to learn to play the sport, or to follow it as spectators.

Finally, FIFA had been an active force in encouraging the spread of association football throughout the world. It had done so by standardizing the rules of the game and by creating associations and federations in various nations that were sanctioned by FIFA, had the exclusive right to stage international competitions, and served as centers for the development of youth soccer across the globe, often with FIFA's financial support. In the United States FIFA had followed its usual model by designating, in 1913, the institution eventually named the United States Soccer Foundation as its affiliated entity. But for most of the twentieth century FIFA took comparatively little interest in the USSF or in the development of soccer in the United States.

In sum, a number of factors combined to ensure that soccer would remain a distinctly marginal sport in the United States, both as a recreational activity and an object of spectator and fan attention, for nearly all of the twentieth century.

SOCCER'S RECENT RESURGENCE IN AMERICA

I have also sought to determine the reasons for soccer's dramatic growth as a participatory and spectator sport in the late twentieth and twenty-first centuries. Why did soccer emerge, beginning in the 1970s, as a growing youth sport, one increasingly played in public high schools, colleges, and universities? And why did soccer become, in the twenty-first century, a spectator sport attractive enough to American audiences that a new professional men's soccer league, MLS, could establish itself in 1996 and, after a rocky start, expand and flourish in the second decade of the twenty-first century?

Certain factors combined to accelerate the emergence of soccer as a youth activity after the 1970s. Perhaps the most important of those was Title IX, which mandated equal opportunities for girls and women to participate on school and college athletic teams. After high schools and colleges realized that they were *required* to offer athletic opportunities for girls and women, they identified soccer as an appropriate sport for them. That was in contrast to the almost complete absence of soccer as an option for high school and college women prior to Title IX's passage. A handful of colleges had introduced soccer in the late 1960s, but the NCAA had not taken steps to administer the sport. After Title IX the situation dramatically changed, with women's soccer teams proliferating in both colleges and high schools. The result was that soccer became identified as a youth sport for pre-high-school girls. The dramatic increase in soccer as a youth activity was partly a function of the growing number of girls who participated in the sport.

Meanwhile boys' and men's soccer was also growing in high schools and colleges after the 1970s. The NCAA did not even administer a national team soccer championship until 1959, and in the early years of that tournament only a few colleges entered.[8] But that number grew significantly in the 1960s and has continued to do so. More opportunities for men to play soccer in colleges and universities begat more opportunities to play on high school teams, and educators and administrators came to realize that soccer was a comparatively inexpensive, relatively safe sport for boys and young men to play. The increase in men's soccer teams at colleges and universities had the same effect on youth soccer as the increase in female teams: more American communities began offering soccer as a youth recreational activity.

Finally, FIFA's late twentieth-century engagement with both men's and women's World Cup tournaments in the United States served to enhance the visibility of the sport, not only for participants but for spectators. The 1994 men's World Cup in the United States was a decided financial and athletic success, with the US men's team performing unexpectedly well and cup matches drawing large crowds. This success was a decisive factor in generating interest and publicity for American men's professional soccer, both domestically and internationally, helping MLS to get off the ground in 1996. The 1999 women's World Cup was, if anything, even more successful; the US team won the competition, its players became celebrities, and numerous fans and potential youth players were generated for women's soccer.

The advent of a new men's professional soccer league, MLS, was a logical consequence of those developments. As soccer became a more visible sport in the US high schools and colleges in the late twentieth century, and women's soccer emerged in those institutions, interest in community youth soccer grew, creating a larger constituency of prospective soccer fans. Meanwhile FIFA made the creation of a new men's professional soccer league a condition of awarding the 1994 men's World Cup to the United States, and a group of solvent investors, committed to a version of command-and-control organization, founded Major League Soccer.

Perhaps most important to the future of MLS, a coterie of truly gifted American-born soccer players has emerged, some having bypassed college soccer to join overseas leagues, others having joined MLS rosters after high school or after less than four years in college. Although the preferred route for the most coveted of those players appears to be joining European rather than MLS clubs after high school, MLS clubs have recruited some players with experience in overseas leagues later in their careers. Moreover, MLS clubs are successfully recruiting some top players from overseas leagues, notably but not exclusively in the western hemisphere. And as American television networks increasingly broadcast matches from European leagues, the players in those leagues become more well known to American audiences, so their potential recruitment by MLS becomes a way of increasing that league's stature and visibility.

All of these recent developments suggest a bright future for soccer in America, both as a recreational activity and as a high school, college, and professional sport that may one day achieve major-sport status. Several of the difficulties that soccer faced in establishing itself as an attractive recreational and spectator sport to Americans for most of the twentieth century appear to have been overcome, or minimized, in the twenty-first. Young men and women are playing soccer recreationally much more in than the past. Most public and private high schools in the United States, and a great many colleges, offer it as a varsity sport for both men and women, and several universities with highly competitive varsity soccer teams offer club soccer programs to their students as well.

MLS appears poised on the threshold of both profitability and international visibility. A signal of the league's current status is the growth of its income from broadcast rights as its matches are increasingly televised or streamed in domestic and international markets. Although MLS has not instituted promotion and relegation, it retains tight internal controls on the financial outlays of its clubs, seeking to avoid the competitive imbalance due to unrestricted spending that doomed the NASL.

While the shift of the locus of athletic activities in the United States from voluntary clubs and associations to high schools and colleges may have inhibited the growth of soccer in the twentieth century, that shift now seems to be distinctly benefiting soccer in the States, both as a participatory and spectator sport. However well established and financially solvent an American voluntary club or association engaged in organizing athletics might be, its social and economic reach cannot compare with that of most public high schools, colleges, or universities. So long as those institutions are dedicated to offering soccer as a participatory sport, their impact on the game's attractiveness to American youth and their family members will be considerable.

FIFA, after many years of inattentiveness, has apparently recognized the great potential of US markets for international soccer. So have broadcast networks. The result is that after many years of struggling for revenues from networks, advertisers, sports merchandizers, and domestic tournament competitions, both the USSF and MLS are poised to reap major financial rewards. MLS has apparently learned, as some of its predecessor leagues did not, that on the American continent soccer needs to be played in the spring, summer, and fall. Its commitment to creating soccer-specific stadiums can be seen as a tacit recognition of that fact.

It remains to contrast the explanations advanced in this book for soccer's longtime marginality in America, and for its late twentieth- and early twenty-first-century emergence, with those put forward in the existing historiography of the sport. There has been little scholarly treatment of the dramatic resurgence since the turn of the twenty-first century of men's and women's soccer in the United States, the phenomenon being comparatively recent. This book represents the first scholarly effort to explain soccer's remarkable recent growth as a participatory sport for both sexes in the United States, the great interest generated by the US women's national team in World Cup competitions since the 1990s, and the prospective long-term success of Major League Soccer, with its emphasis on two strategies new to American professional soccer leagues: a modified command-and-control administrative structure and a commitment to building soccer-specific stadiums for its franchises. American professional soccer has begun to thrive as it has adopted structural features that have for many years characterized soccer leagues in the rest of the world.

Earlier in this book I identified four established explanations for association football's failure to become a major sport in twentieth-century America, and suggested that each of these explanations, standing alone, is insufficient. The interpretation I have advanced does, however, draw upon each of them and combine them in modified form.

The first of these explanations is that in the late nineteenth- and early twentieth-century history of western nations, there was a critical period, roughly from 1880 to 1930, when advanced industrialization and urbanization made possible the establishment of spectator sports as leisure-time activities. If a sport did not develop in that period, this explanation posits, it was too late for it to become established, in part because the space for sports in particular nations was finite, preventing new sports from competing with those that were already entrenched.

That explanation can be said to complement a second one, resting on the nature and content of the sports that were occupying major "spaces." According to that argument, gridiron football occupied the principal space for sports played in America after the conclusion of the baseball season in October, preventing soccer, which was understood as a competitor for that space, from becoming established. And then, since soccer failed to entrench itself as a participatory or spectator sport in the critical period, it was subsequently unable to do so. One might employ those two explanations to account for soccer's failure to become a major sport during the first two decades of the twentieth century, the United States' golden age of sport.

I agree that in the early twentieth century, gridiron football was perceived as competitive with soccer in American colleges and universities, and the commitment made by many universities to building football stadiums and investing in football teams was deleterious to soccer's growth. But since college sports were not seen as competing with professional sports in the golden age—professional baseball was played as well as baseball in colleges, and a professional football league was formed in the 1920s—it is hard to understand why professional soccer leagues could not have come into being during that time as well, and in fact, as we have seen, one did. The puzzle is thus not why gridiron college football prevented professional soccer from emerging—it didn't—but why professional soccer largely failed to thrive as a spectator or, for that matter, participatory sport. Neither the critical period nor the sports space explanation can fully explain that failure.

A third explanation for the difficulty American professional soccer leagues had in establishing themselves is competitive balance. All sports leagues, according to this hypothesis, require roughly equal competition among their teams to generate spectator interest. One-sided contests are unattractive to fans, and over the course of a league's season, the dominance of some teams or the consistent futility of others also discourages spectator attendance. The English Football League, through devices such as promotion and relegation and the retain-and-transfer system, made a particular effort to foster competitive balance, but American professional soccer leagues did not, resulting in club franchises regularly disbanding or moving to different locations. The eventual folding of the North American Soccer League after its prominent start because some of its clubs could spend far more on players than others, resulting in competitive imbalance, is prominently mentioned as part of this explanation.

The difficulty here is twofold. First, some American professional sports leagues, notably Major League Baseball, internalized restraints on unbridled competition through such devices as the reserve clause, which prevented clubs from bidding against one for players, and territoriality, which until 1953 had the effect of freezing the location of major-league franchises, thereby preventing clubs from being moved to other cities if they fared poorly. Second, other American professional sports leagues did not formally prevent franchises from being moved, or clubs from bidding against one another for players, yet three of those leagues—the National Football League, the National Basketball Association, and the National Hockey League—began to flourish in the years after World War II, even though their administrative structures were largely of the free market, individual-entrepreneur variety. In fact collective agreements restraining competition in those leagues, such as the reserve clause, were held to be violations of the antitrust laws by courts. So the prospect of competitive imbalance in professional sports leagues did not serve to affect the viability of those leagues in the latter years of the twentieth century.

The last explanation centers on the "ethnic" or "foreign" status of soccer in the United States, as a sport primarily played in communities with sizable ethnic populations of immigrants from nations familiar with the game. According to this explanation, when colleges and high schools assumed control of athletics as part of the comprehensive high school movement and the emergence of the National Collegiate Athletic Association in the early twentieth century, educators involved in athletic programs exhibited a preference for "indigenous" American sports such as baseball, gridiron football, basketball, and volleyball. Soccer, which was largely played by ethnic minorities, was perceived as a "foreign" sport, and thus not typically included among the offerings of public high schools, nor treated as a varsity sport in many colleges. As a result, few Americans grew up developing much familiarity with the sport, contributing to its marginality.

I agree that soccer's perceived foreignness likely contributed to its not being included among public high school athletic offerings for much of the early and mid-twentieth century. I also agree that this lack of inclusion contributed to Americans' general unfamiliarity with soccer, reducing its attractiveness as a participatory or spectator pursuit. But the presence or absence of "foreign" players in other sports has not, over time, affected the visibility or economic success of those sports. Only the National Football League, over the course of the late twentieth and twenty-first centuries, has generally not included many foreign-born players on its rosters, while the number of foreign-born players in Major League Baseball, the National Basketball Association, and the National Hockey League has consistently grown over time.[9] Moreover, as we have seen, a contributing factor to Major League Soccer's success in the twenty-first century was its introduction of the Designated Player rule, which allowed its clubs to sign foreign-born players on terms that exceeded the league's salary limits.

In sum, my explanation for soccer's long-term marginality in America rests not solely on any one of the previous hypotheses advanced in the scholarly literature of that topic but on a particular combination of those hypotheses, each modified to take into account some distinctive cultural features of twentieth- and twenty-first-century American history.

Although much of the narrative of this book has been about various instances of failure in the history of soccer in America, its twenty-first-century chapters are largely about the sport's success, and the prospect of even more success in the future. In that sense the beautiful game, both as a participatory and spectator sport, may have arrived in America. But the puzzles with which this study began persist. Why do some sports migrate well from one nation, and one culture, to another, while others do not? Why, for example, is rugby played all over the world, but gridiron football essentially played only in the United States? Why is basketball, which for decades was played almost exclusively in the United States, now played so widely that the US Olympic men's basketball team is no longer a clear favorite to win the gold medal in every Olympic Games? Why has baseball been successfully exported to Japan and several Caribbean and Latin American nations, but not to much of the rest of the world?

This study has advanced a variety of reasons why association football flourished around much of the globe, but not the United States, for most of the twentieth century, and why, after a long interval in which soccer was a distinctly marginal sport at every level in America, it may now finally be on the road to major-sport status. But these reasons seem to be unique features of the sport itself and of the economic, social, and educational environment of the United States for much of the twentieth century, not easily generalizable across a range of sports. Sports history seems appropriately lacking in grand explanatory theories. We might well conclude that the attractiveness of particular sports to cultures around the world remains largely mysterious, as mysterious as why athletes perform well on some occasions and poorly on others. That mystery is part of the enticement of athletics, and perhaps we should simply respect it.

Notes

INTRODUCTION

1. "Top 10 Most Popular Participation Sports in the World," http://www.realbuzz.com/articles-interests/sports-activities/article/top-1-most-popular-participation-sports-in-the-world/; "Top 10 List of the World's Most Popular Sports," http://www.topendsports.com/world/lists/popular-sport/fans.htm.

2. Alison Baker, "The Most Watched Sporting Events in the World," http://www.roadtrips.com/blog/the-most-watched-sporting-events-in-the-world/.

3. The term *soccer*, as we will see in more detail, is a contraction of "association football," the name for the sport that distinguished itself from rugby in England in the middle of the nineteenth century, established its own rules, and spread throughout the United Kingdom in the late nineteenth century under the aegis of an organization called the Football Association.

4. Nearly every work on the history of international sports has emphasized the failure of soccer, when it spread from the United Kingdom around the rest of the world in the late nineteenth and early twentieth centuries, to take root in the United States. The following are only some examples: James Walvin, *The People's Game: A Social History of British Football* (London: Allen Lane, 1975); Allen Guttmann, *A Whole New Ball Game: A Reinterpretation of American Sports* (Chapel Hill: University of North Carolina Press, 1988); Andrei S. Markovits, "The Other American Exceptionalism—Why There Is No Soccer in the United States," *Praxis International* 8, no. 2 (1988): 125–50; Andrei S. Markovits and Steven L. Hellerman, *Offside: Soccer and American Exceptionalism* (Princeton, NJ: Princeton University Press, 1991); John Sugden, "USA and the World Cup: American Nativism and the Rejection of the People's Game," in *Hosts and Champions: Soccer Cultures, National Identities, and the USA World Cup*, ed. John Sugden and Alan Tomlinson (Aldershot, England: Ashgate, 1994), 219–52; David Wangerin, *Soccer in a Football World: The Story of America's Forgotten Game* (Philadelphia: Temple University Press, 2006); Simon Kuper and Stefan Syzmanski, *Soccernomics: Why England Loses, Why Germany and Brazil Win, and Why the U.S., Japan, Australia, Turkey and Even India Are Destined to Become the Kings of the World's Most Popular Sport* (New York: Nation Books, 2009); and Maarten van Bottenburg, "Why Are the European and American Sports Worlds So Different?," in *Sport and the Transformation of Modern Europe: States, Media, and Markets, 1950–2010*, ed. Alan Tomlinson, Christopher Young, and Richard Holt (London: Routledge, 2011), 205–25.

5. This argument is advanced in Andrei Markovits, "The Other 'American Exceptionalism': Why Is There No Soccer in the United States?" *International Journal of the*

History of Sport 7, no 2 (1990): 230–64; Markovits and Hellerman, *Offside*, 13–28; Michael Veseth, "The Beautiful Game and the American Exception," *International Review of Modern Society* 32, no. 2 (2006): 181.

6. Markovits and Hellerman, *Offside*, 52–98.

7. See Daniel H. Cole and Peter Z. Grossman, "When Is Command-and-Control Efficient: Institutions, Technology, and the Comparative Efficiency of Alternative Regulatory Regimes for Environmental Protection," *Wisconsin Law Review* 888 (1999), defining "command-and-control" as "essentially a regulatory approach whereby the government 'commands'" certain responses from particular industries.

8. Kuper and Szymanski, *Soccernomics*, 75–95; Markovits and Hellerman, *Offside*, 44–46. That description may be accurate for the early years of each of those professional leagues, but today each of them operate with restraints on the activities of clubs, notably in the area of salaries, where Major League Baseball, the National Football League, the National Basketball Association, and the National Hockey League each have imposed salary caps on clubs, or the equivalent, which have the effect of taxing clubs whose salary budgets exceed prescribed amounts.

9. See Guttmann, *Whole New Ball Game*, 56; Benjamin G. Rader, "The Quest for Sub Communities and the Rise of American Sport," in *The Sporting Image: Readings in American Sport*, ed. Paul J. Zingg (Lanham, MD: Rowman and Littlefield, 1988), 139–51; Guy Oliver, *The Guinness Record of World Soccer: The History of the Game in 150 Countries* (London: Guinness, 1992), 789; and Sugden, "USA and the World Cup," 236–40. For evidence of the "ethnic" character of late nineteenth- and early-twentieth-century soccer in Chicago, see Gabe Logan, *The Early Years of Chicago Soccer, 1887–1939* (Lanham, MD: Lexington, 2019).

10. http://www.sportytell.com/sports/top-10-most-popular-sports-in-america/

CHAPTER ONE

1. The status of "professional" soccer player was understood in late nineteenth-century England to refer not only to persons who were paid to play soccer full-time but also to those who, in addition to playing soccer, held jobs in the cities and towns where their soccer clubs were housed. Initially the number of full-time paid players was small. For more detail, see Dave Russell, "From Evil to Expedient: The Legalization of Professionalism in English Football," in *Myths and Milestones in the History of Sports, 1884–85*, ed. Stephen Wagg (New York: Palgrave MacMillan, 2011), 32–56.

2. Thus an "amateur ethos" consisted of adherence to the principle that one should not receive remuneration of any kind for playing soccer. For more detail, see Tony Collins, *How Football Began: A Global History of How the World's Football Codes Were Born* (New York: Routledge, 2018), 53–63.

3. On the differences between what came to be called soccer (association football) and what came to be called rugby in the early history of those sports, see Collins, *How Football Began*, 6–8.

4. For an overview of the controversy over professionalism within the Football Association in the last two decades of the nineteenth century, see Tony Mason, *Association*

Football and English Society, 1863–1915 (Highlands, NJ: Humanities Press, 1980), 69–81.

5. For more detail see Mason, *Association Football*, 9–13.

6. For more detail see Mason, *Association Football*, 44–49.

7. The official historian of the Football Association described its posture toward profit-making by clubs as follows: "As for the ample income and property of the Association, it is applied solely towards the objects set out in its Memorandum of Association, which in a word means that all money returns into the game for the improvement of the game, so that no holder of any share in the capital of the Football Association Limited receives, or indeed is entitled to receive, any dividend, bonus, or other payment by way of profit or income." Geoffrey Green, *The History of the Football Association* (London: Naldrett, 1953), 40.

8. For more detail, see Matthew Taylor, *The Leaguers: The Making of Professional Football in England, 1900–1939* (Liverpool, England: Liverpool University Press, 2005), 39–43.

9. Taylor, *The Leaguers*, 44.

10. For more detail, see Richard Holt, *Sport and the British: A Modern History* (Oxford, England: Oxford University Press, 1989), 203–61.

11. B. O. Corbett, *Annals of the Corinthian Football Club* (London: Longmans, Green, 1906), vi–vii.

12. Green, *History*, 19. Green's *History* is the most authoritative source for the origins and development of association football in late nineteenth- and early twentieth-century England, virtually a primary source because Green had access to the minutes of the Football Association and quotes liberally from them. Green's *History*, as a primary source, should be supplemented by Alfred Gibson and William Pickford, *Association Football and the Men Who Made It*, 4 vols. (London: Caxton, 1906), which contains largely anecdotal accounts of clubs and individuals, as well as brief synopses of events that Green describes in greater detail. Gibson and Pickford's collection is undocumented, and, where its coverage overlaps with Green, rarely differs from it.

A work in the vein of Gibson and Pickford's *Association Football* is Simon Inglis, *League Football and the Men Who Made It: The Official History of the Football League, 1888–1988* (London: Collins Willow, 1988), an anecdotal account of the emergence of the English Football League in 1888 and its subsequent history for the next century. As with Gibson and Pickford's volumes, Inglis provides some rich detail about events and personalities connected with the league, and in addition contains a bibliography, but is otherwise undocumented.

An additional effort to describe the state of association football in the late nineteenth century by a contemporary is J. A. H. Catton, *The Real Football: A Sketch of the Development of the Association Game* (London: Sands, 1900).

Several secondary works have studied the origins and early development of association football in England. One is Mason, *Association Football*, "an attempt to write a social history of association football in the late Victorian and Edwardian periods" (9). Mason's attempt is conspicuously successful: the work is impressively documented from primary and secondary sources. An earlier work, James Walvin's *The People's Game: A Social History of British Football* (London: Allen Lane, 1975), represents another attempt to write a social history of English football, in this instance extending coverage into the 1960s. Walvin's book contains a bibliography and some thoughtful observations, but its conclusions are undocumented and, on the whole, do not differ significantly from Mason's.

More recent sources on the history of English soccer are Dave Russell, *Football and the English* (London: Carnegie, 1997); Taylor, *The Leaguers*; Matthew Taylor, *The Association Game: A History of British Football* (Harlow, England: Pearson Education, 2008); Collins, *How Football Began*; Russell, "From Evil to Expedient"; and Robert Collins, *This Sporting Life: Sport and Liberty in England, 1760–1960*, 235–77 (Oxford, England: Oxford University Press, 2020). The Russell and Collins works are particularly helpful on the relationship between the Football Association and the English Football League after the latter came into being in 1888.

13. Green, *History*, 19–33, chronicles the six meetings between October 26, 1863, and December 8 of that year in which the rules of soccer were discussed and debated. The dates of the meetings given by Green are each seven days apart, suggesting accuracy, and Green had access to the "Minute Book" of the Football Association, in which many of the discussions that took place at those meetings were recorded. See Green, *History*, 28.

14. In Sam Foulds and Paul Harris, *America's Soccer Heritage: A History of the Game* 4 (Manhattan Beach, California: Soccer for Americans, 1979), 4, a meeting to form the Football Association is said to have taken place on October 23, 1863, with no indication that there were subsequent meetings. In Stefan Szymanski and Andrew Zimbalist, *National Pastime: How Americans Play Baseball and the Rest of the World Plays Soccer* (Washington, DC: Brookings Institution Press, 2005), 35, the correct date of October 26 for the first meeting of those who would form the Football Association is given, but there is no mention of any subsequent meetings having taken place.

15. Szymanski and Zimbalist, *National Pastime*, 20–22.

16. Mason, *Association Football*, 12–13.

17. See Mason, *Association Football*, 13. The authoritative source on Thomas Arnold's life and career is Arthur Penrhyn Stanley, *The Life and Correspondence of Thomas Arnold, D.D., Master of Rugby* (London: B. Fellows, 1844).

18. Catton, *The Real Football*, 9–10, gives a description of the effect of physical surroundings on the way football was played at various public schools:

> The size of the playing area, and the character of the ground and buildings, would have their effect [on the game]. . . . At Rugby battalions of boys could disport themselves on an arena which measured 130 yards long and 80 yards wide; while at Winchester they found six-a-side very convenient on an enclosure 80 yards in length and 25 yards in breadth . . . Whereas it would not be a serious casualty for a boy to be collared and hurled upon well-knit and luxuriant turf, it would be positively dangerous to throw an opponent on gravel ground, or adamantine pavement, or against the pillars of cloisters. Thus the use of the hands in tackling

> and playing became resisted, and the employment of the feet encouraged. In the circumscribed area of Westminster and Charterhouse it was not lawful to carry the ball; while in the field game at Eton the use of the hands was prohibited in every way. . . . At Eton, Winchester, Charterhouse and Harrow every precaution was taken to prevent any undue advantage without honest work. The boys had to be careful to keep in play, and not to get, as it was expressively and technically termed, "offside."

See also Green, *History*, 11–12.

19. H. C. Malden, quoted in Green, *History*, 15–16.

20. Quoted in Green, *History*, 17. See also Catton, *The Real Football*, 14, stating that the Cambridge rules provided that "the ball must not be held or hit by the hands, arms, or shoulders; that all charging was fair; and that holding, pushing, tripping, and shinning (or hacking) were illegal." He added that "when a player has kicked the ball, anyone on the same side nearer the opponent's goal line was out of play" (an "onside" rule) that "touch-downs were allowed, and a free kick at goal given at a point which was twenty-five yards distant in a straight line from the spot where the ball was touched by the attacking side." For more on touchdowns, see note 31.

21. Green, *History*, 25–26. Green lists the date of the fourth meeting as November 14, but the sequence of the meetings reveals that 14 is a typographical error, and that November 24 was the date.

22. Green, *History*, 26.

23. Green, *History*, 26.

24. *See* Green, *History*, 38.

25. Green, *History*, 26.

26. Green, *History*, 28.

27. Green, *History*, 28.

28. Green, *History*, 28.

29. Green, *History*, 35.

30. The differences between the London and Sheffield rules did not involve running or hacking. Sheffield had a more liberal offside rule, allowing offensive players to remain onside if at least one opponent was between them and the goal, in contrast to the 1863 London rule, which required three opponents. Green, *History*, 17, 41. As subsequently noted, there were also different treatments of touchdowns under the London and Sheffield rules. For more detail on the Sheffield rules and their divergence from the London rules, see Percy M. Young, *Football in Sheffield*, 19–22 (1964).

31. Green, *History*, 42; Young, *Football in Sheffield*, 23. The reference to "four touchdowns" requires explanation. The 1863 association rules provided that when a ball went beyond the goal line and a player on the opposite side from the team defending the goal touched the ball first, one of his side was entitled to a free kick at the opponent's goal from a point fifteen yards from the goal line, opposite the place where the ball was touched. All players from the opposing side, including the goalkeeper, were required to "stand behind their goal line" when the kick was taken. They also provided that a goal "shall be won when the ball passes between the goal posts or over the space between the

goal posts at whatever height." Goals were defined as "two upright posts 8 yards apart, without any tape or bar across them." Green, *History*, 37.

32. Alcock wrote a letter to a Glasgow newspaper proposing such a match sometime after the Queen's Park club was founded in 1867, and an informal match was played in London in 1870. Green, *History*, 47–48.

33. Green, *History*, 49–51. See also Catton, *The Real Football*, 25–26, listing the clubs.

34. Green, *History*, 51.

35. Green, *History*, 48.

36. Green, *History*, 49.

37. Green, *History*, 49.

38. Between 1867 and 1885 the number of county and district associations affiliated with the Football Association grew to 39, those associations typically being composed of several clubs. Green, *History*, 53. This meant that by the latter date hundreds of clubs were playing association football in England, and there were additional clubs in Scotland, Wales, and Ireland: one source listed 1,000 clubs affiliated with the Football Association in 1888. See W. Pickford's introduction to C. E. Sutcliffe, J. A. Brierly, and F. Howarth, *The Story of the Football League, 1888–1938* (Preston, England: Football League, 1938).

39. The association received £54 from cup "ties" in the period, £144 from "takings" (gate receipts) for the match between England and Scotland, £15 from receipts for the London–Lancashire match, nearly £11 from the London-Sheffield match, and £8, 10 shillings from the London-Birmingham match. Green, *History*, 65.

40. Green, *History*, 65. Receipts for London-Birmingham match, £8, 10 shillings; expenses £21, 4 shillings.

41. Quoted in Green, *History*, 65.

42. Green, *History*, 65.

43. Green, *History*, 66.

44. Green, *History*, 70.

45. Green, *History*, 57.

46. Green, *History*, 57.

47. Green, *History*, 57–58. In 1880 the *Athletic News* and in 1883 the *Sheffield Daily Telegraph* reported that some particularly coveted players were appearing for several different clubs in the FA competition in those years. *Athletic News*, January 14, 1880, and Sheffield *Daily Telegraph*, February 27, 1883, quoted in Mason, *Association Football and English Society*, 71.

48. Green, *History*, 58.

49. For more detail, see Mason, *Association Football*, 70–72.

50. Green, *History*, 66.

51. Green, *History*, 57. FIFA's formation and history are discussed in Chapter Six.

52. Green, *History*, 59.

53. Green, *History*, 59.That game, and events that led up to it, is the subject of Julian Fellowes' recent Netflix series *The English Game*, which focuses on the hiring of two Scottish players, Fergus Suter and Jimmy Love, to play for the Darwen football club

in Lancashire and then subsequently to play with the "simple tradesmen" of Blackburn Olympic. Receiving payments for playing association football was strongly resisted by the Football Association, which in the series is portrayed, incorrectly, as being dominated by members of the Old Etonians. At one point in *The English Game*, the Football Association resolves to suspend Blackburn Olympic for "professionalism," eliminating them from the FA Cup competition in 1883, but then reconsiders, enabling Blackburn to defeat the Old Etonians in the final.

54. For an overview of the rise of professionalism in English soccer in the 1880s, see Russell, "From Evil to Expedient," 32–56.

55. Green, *History*, 61.

56. Green, *History*, 80.

57. See Green, *History*, 90.

58. Green, *History*, 91.

59. Between 1871 and 1883 one of those three clubs was a finalist in the Challenge Cup competition every year except three. Green, *History*, 593–94.

60. D. D. Molyneux, *The Development of Physical Recreation in the Birmingham District from 1871 to 1892* (MA thesis, University of Birmingham, 1957), 39–40, quoted in Green, *History*, 26.

61. See generally Brian Harrison, *Drink and the Victorians: The Temperance Question in England, 1815–1872* (Pittsburgh: University of Pittsburgh Press, 1971).

62. On the origins of the Arsenal football club, see Bernard Joy, *Forward Arsenal!* (London: Sportsman's Book Club, 1952), 2–4; on West Ham, see Alfred Gibson and William Pickford, *Association Football and the Men Who Made It*, 4 vols. (London: Caxton, 1905), 3:87–89.

63. Collins, *How Football Began*, 61–62; Taylor, *The Leaguers*, 53–55.

64. For more detail on the origins of promotion and relegation in the Football League, see Taylor, *The Leaguers*, 7–8.

65. Gabe Logan, *The Early Years of Chicago Soccer, 1887–1939* (Lanham, MD: Lexington, 2019), 13–15.

66. Logan, *The Early Years*, 48–49.

67. Roger Allaway, Colin Jose, and David Litterer, *The Encyclopedia of American Soccer History* (Lanham, MD: Scarecrow, 2001), 5–6.

68. Allaway, Jose, and Litterer, *Encyclopedia*, 5.

69. See Green, *History*, 86, 87, 90.

70. An account of the Pilgrims' 1905 tour of North America is given in David Wangerin, *Distant Corners: American Soccer's History of Missed Opportunities and Lost Causes* (Philadelphia: Temple University Press, 2011), 5–15.

71. Fred Milnes, "A Football Tour with the Pilgrims in America," 1905, Box 3/18, Hap Meyer Soccer Collection, 1898–1963, Louisa H. Bowen University Archives and Special Collections, Southern Illinois University Edwardsville. Details of the Pilgrims' 1905 tour are taken from Milnes, and the attendance figures for matches and their results are impressionistic.

72. Wangerin, *Distant Corners*, 9–11, reports the alleged attendance figures for Pilgrims games at St. Louis and Philadelphia but does not identify the sources of those estimates. This

book and Wangerin's *Soccer in a Football World: The Story of America's Forgotten Game* (Philadelphia: Temple University Press, 2006) represent the most astute treatments of the early history of American soccer, but are unfortunately undocumented and lack bibliographies.

73. See Wangerin, *Distant Corners*, 10–15, quoting undocumented comments.

74. Details of the Corinthians' 1906 tour are taken from Wangerin, *Distant Corners*, 21–24, which relies on magazine and newspaper accounts and some player reminiscences cataloged in Robert Cavallini, *Play Up Corinth: A History of the Corinthian Football Club* (Stroud, England: Stadia, 2007).

75. Wangerin, *Distant Corners*, 14.

76. Wangerin, *Distant Corners*, 27, 33.

77. Wangerin, *Distant Corners*, 27.

78. The relationship of American gridiron football to the status of soccer in the United States in the early twentieth century is explored in more detail in the next two chapters.

79. For more detail, see John Sayle Watterson, *College Football: History, Spectacle, Controversy* (Baltimore: Johns Hopkins University Press, 2000), 9–39.

80. Quoted in Wangerin, *Distant Corners*, 14.

81. Wangerin, *Distant Corners*, 17.

82. Wangerin, *Distant Corners*, 26–27.

83. Quoted in Wangerin, *Distant Corners*, 27.

CHAPTER TWO

1. James Walvin, *The People's Game: A Social History of British Football* (London: Allen Lane, 1975), 109, describes the state of association football in the United States in the early twentieth century:

> Football had taken root and rapidly established itself as a mass spectator sport in the cities of Europe and South America. . . . Outside Europe and South America, the U.S.A., with its great cities housing social groups similar to those which monopolized football in Europe, appeared to be the most likely society to adopt the game. But . . . where indigenous sports evolved from the distinctive cultural roots of a region, it proved impossible to dislodge them by more artificial importations of games from abroad. . . . Soccer did take root in certain American cities, though never to compete with local American football.

As will become evident, I don't fully accept Walvin's explanation that soccer failed to take root in the United States because "it proved impossible to dislodge" indigenous sports that had developed in America. For more detail on the spread of association football around the globe in the late nineteenth and early twentieth centuries, see David Goldblatt, *The Ball Is Round* (2006), 50–226.

2. The term *gridiron football* to characterize the sport initiated in American colleges beginning in the 1860s was coined after, in the 1880s, the rules of the sport were changed to allow a team in possession of the ball to retain possession if, in the course of a designated number of downs (signifying the ball being put into play from a "down,"

or motionless, stance by the players on the team possessing the ball), the team was able to advance the ball toward the opponent's goal line a certain number of yards. Eventually that number of yards became fixed at ten, and the number of downs in which ten yards needed to be advanced fixed at four. In order to facilitate the measurement of yards, American football fields were divided into five-yard intervals marked by parallel chalk lines on the field. The appearance of a field, with those yard markers superimposed upon it, resembled a grid.

3. By the 1890s gridiron football had become so dangerous that in 1894 one of its principal plays, the flying wedge, in which offensive players would link arms and race toward defenders, followed by a player running with the ball, was abolished. For more detail, see Scott A. McQuilkin and Ronald A. Smith, "The Rise and Fall of the Flying Wedge," *Journal of Sports History* 20 (1993): 57.

The most complete treatment of American gridiron football in the early twentieth century, when it faced a crisis connected to a high rate of injuries and even some deaths, is John Sayle Watterson, *College Football: History, Spectacle, Controversy* (Baltimore: Johns Hopkins University Press, 2000), 64–99. This chapter is primarily concerned with the relationship of gridiron football to soccer on American college campuses at the time of gridiron football's crisis.

4. Quoted in David Wangerin, *Distant Corners: American Soccer's History of Missed Opportunities and Lost Causes* (Philadelphia: Temple University Press, 2011), 14.

5. "English 'Socker' Team Won Football Match," *New York Times*, October 22, 1905.

6. James Sullivan, quoted in "Rapid Growth of Soccer Football," *Chicago Daily Tribune*, September 22, 1907.

7. Wangerin, *Distant Corners*, 27.

8. *New York Sun*, November 22, 1913.

9. Julian Curtiss, quoted in "Thinks Rules All Right," *Minneapolis Journal*, January 6, 1903.

10. Julian Curtiss, 1903 comment, quoted in "Thinks Rules All Right."

11. Comments of Bozeman Bulger, reported in "Socker Isn't a Hit," *Buffalo Commercial*, October 24, 1905. The use of the term *socker* in the article suggests that the English contraction of association football was in widespread use when the sport first came to be played in the United States. But *soccer* was used more often than *socker* in American journalistic sources in the early twentieth century, and sometimes "soccer football" was used to distinguish the sport from gridiron football.

12. "'Soccer Man' Is Smoking Some," *Oakland Tribune*, November 29, 1905. Fred Milnes, the "Captain" to which the article referred, had, after writing an account of the Pilgrims' 1905 tour, returned with that club for its 1909 tour. He then declared, in 1912, that he was departing England "for the purpose of locating [in the United States] permanently," and began playing soccer for clubs in New York City and Niagara Falls. In 1915 the newly created United States Football Association suspended Milnes when he was unable to account for the funds of the Northwestern New York State Football Association, with which the Niagara Falls club was affiliated.

After his initial tour with the Pilgrims, Milnes, a steel company executive in Yorkshire who had apparently become wealthy, donated a silver cup to the annual winner of the Intercollegiate Association Football League, composed of six eastern colleges. The cup was known as the Milnes Cup. In 1915, after Milnes's suspension, the Milnes Cup was no longer awarded. Milnes subsequently returned to England, where he died in 1946 at the age of sixty-eight. See David Wangerin, "American Soccer's Forgotten Hero," https://templepress.wordpress.com/20c1/05/09.

13. Stagg, quoted in "The Association Football Game," *Richmond Times-Dispatch*, October 8, 1905.

14. "Soccer Is Disliked by Girl," *Stevens Point Journal*, April 6, 1911.

15. "Soccer Is Dawning in American Sports," *New York Times*, December 8, 1909.

16. Tommy Hall, "Association Football Is Getting a Tighter Hold on American Public," *Washington Post*, December 22, 1907.

17. "One More Sign of Growth of Soccer Football," *Chicago Tribune*, February 21, 1909.

18. "Soccer Football," *Kansas City Star*, September 19, 1912.

19. "Soccer is Popular. Imported Game Fast Gaining Foothold in America," *Portland Morning Oregonian*, December 9, 1907.

20. "Soccer Football Gaining in Favor," *Lexington (MA) Herald*, February 4, 1912.

21. "Ben Levy States Soccer Football Is Coming Sport," *Seattle Morning Olympian*, December 12, 1913.

22. "It's Time for Winter Sports. Why Not Soccer?," *Wilkes-Barre (PA) Times*, December 7,1914.

23. In contrast, most soccer in early twentieth-century St. Louis was played by Italian immigrants or their descendants. Young Italian men had begun emigrating to the St. Louis area in the 1880s to work in brick kilns and mines, and eventually encouraged women to join them, establishing families and some local businesses in a section of St. Louis. Both Lawrence (Yogi) Berra and Joe Garagiola, who eventually became major-league baseball players, had played soccer as youths growing up in St. Louis. For more detail, see Geoffrey Douglas, *The Game of Their Lives: The Untold Story of the World Cup's Biggest Upset* (New York: Henry Holt, 1996), 12–15, 25–31, 79–91.

In Chicago soccer was originally started by English and Scottish immigrants as a recreational pursuit for amateurs. It did not become significantly associated with workplaces, professionalized, or identified with additional ethnic groups until the early twentieth century. See Gabe Logan, *The Early Years of Chicago Soccer, 1887–1939* (Lanham, MD: Lexington, 2019), 31, 51–65.

24. For more detail on Samuel Slater and the formation of the textile industry in America, see Paul T. Rivard, *Samuel Slater: Father of American Manufactures* (Pawtucket, RI: Slater Mill Historic Site, 1974), 17–21.

25. Steve Dunwell, *The Run of the Mill* (Boston: David R. Godine, 1978), 106; Philip Silvia, *Victorian Vistas: Fall River, 1865–1885* (Fall River, MA: R. E. Smith, 1987), 7.

26. "Mills History," www.paisley.org/paisley1/history/mills.php.

27. For more detail, see Zephaniah Pease, *History of New Bedford* (New Bedford, MA: Lewis Historical, 1918); and Seymour L. Wolfbein, *Decline of a Cotton Textile City: A Study of New Bedford* (New York: Columbia University Press, 1944).

28. The category of "gentleman" was not as resonant in nineteenth- and early twentieth-century America as it was in England in the same time period, but there was nonetheless a class of Americans that had inherited wealth and did not work in trades or the professions, and whose lifestyle roughly resembled that of their social counterparts in England.

29. For more detail on the working and living conditions of workers in the nineteenth-century American textile industry, see Dunwell, *Run of the Mill*, 117–18; and John T. Cumbler, *Working-Class Community in Industrial America* (1979), 114–17.

30. Charles K. Murray, "History and Progress of the American Football Association," in *Spalding's Official Soccer Football Guide, 1910–1911* (New York: American Sports, 1910), 27. The Spalding guides, published annually between 1904 and 1924 and edited by Thomas Cahill after 1912, are an excellent source of information about the American Football Association and the United States Football Association in those years. They are available in the Carli digital collections at Southern Illinois University at Edwardsville, http://collections.carli.illinois.edu/cdm/search/collection/sie_soccer.

31. For more detail, see Roger Allaway, *Rangers, Rovers and Spindlers: Soccer, Immigration and Textiles in New England and New Jersey* (Haworth, NJ: St. Johann Press, 2005), 36–40.

32. Allaway, *Rangers, Rovers and Spindlers*, 47–48.

33. Roger Allaway, Colin Jose, and David Litterer, *The Encyclopedia of American Soccer History* (Lanham, MD: Scarecrow, 2001), 6.

34. For more detail on the American League of Professional Football Clubs, see Sam Foulds and Paul Harris, *America's Soccer Heritage: A History of the Game* (Manhattan Beach, California: Soccer for Americans, 1979), 12–16.

35. "Easy for Baltimore," *Washington Post*, October 17, 1894.

36. *Boston Herald*, October 18, 1894, quoted in Foulds and Harris, *America's Soccer Heritage*, 15.

37. *Boston Herald*, October 18, 1894, quoted in Foulds and Harris, *America's Soccer Heritage*, 15.

38. Foulds and Harris, *America's Soccer Heritage*, 15.

39. Foulds and Harris, *America's Soccer Heritage*, 13–14.

40. *Boston Herald*, October 21, 1894, quoted in Foulds and Harris, *America's Soccer Heritage*, 16.

41. Foulds and Harris, *America's Soccer Heritage*, 16.

42. Edward Duffy, *Newark Evening Star*, quoted in Wangerin, *Distant Corners*, 38.

43. *Association Football News*, Harrisburg, Pa., quoted in Wangerin, *Distant Corners*, 39.

44. "True American," *Association Football News*, quoted in Wangerin, *Distant Corners*, 38–39.

45. "Get Together," *Association Football News*, quoted in Wangerin, *Distant Corners*, 39.

46. *Newark Evening News*, quoted in Wangerin, *Distant Corners*, 39.

47. "Get Together," *Association Football News*, quoted in Wangerin, *Distant Corners*, 40.

48. Andrew Beveridge, *Association Football News*, quoted in Wangerin, *Distant Corners*, 40.

49. Duffy, *Newark Evening Star*, quoted in Wangerin, *Distant Corners*, 40.

50. Thomas Bagnall, quoted in Wangerin, *Distant Corners*, 40–41.

51. The representative was Thomas W. Cahill, from St. Louis, who offered to pay his way to attend the meeting if the AAFA would contribute $100 to his expenses. Cahill had joined the sporting goods firm of A. G. Spalding in 1902 and remained with that firm for the next twenty years, although his primary functions, after 1911, were as the honorary secretary of the United States Football Association and the editor of *Spalding's Official Soccer Football Guides*. A. G. Spalding had a particular interest in promoting soccer in the United States because the firm manufactured soccer balls, shoes, and other equipment. In the July 27, 1916, issue of its house organ, *Spalding Store News*, the firm declared that its president, J. W. Spalding, had long believed that "some day 'Soccer' football would take hold in this country," and had "got behind the movement to promote the game in the United States" in order to encourage home-grown players to buy equipment from it instead of "from English concerns." Quoted in Wangerin, *Distant Corners*, 63.

52. For more detail, see Wangerin, *Distant Corners*, 41–42.

53. Thomas Cahill is quoted in Wangerin, *Distant Corners*, 42.

54. Cahill, FIFA minutes, June 30, 1912, quoted in Wangerin, *Distant Corners*, 42.

55. Cahill, quoted in Wangerin, *Distant Corners*, 42.

56. Cahill, quoted in Wangerin, *Distant Corners*, 42–43.

57. Cahill, quoted in Wangerin, *Distant Corners*, 43.

58. Wangerin, *Distant Corners*, 43.

59. Andrew Brown, quoted in Wangerin, *Distant Corners*, 43–44.

60. Wangerin, *Distant Corners*, 44.

61. Wangerin, *Distant Corners*, 44.

62. In contrast, representatives of Chicago soccer supported the USFA after its recognition by FIFA in 1913, with Peter J. Peel, one of the central figures in the early twentieth-century history of soccer in Chicago, being elected president of the USFA in 1917, 1923, and 1924. Chicago clubs consistently played in the National Challenge Cup after 1913. See Logan, *Early Years of Chicago Soccer*, 108–12.

63. "Sporting Comment," *St. Louis Globe-Democrat*, December 27, 1913. With the growth of English soccer, the amount of travel required to participate in the FA Cup or English Football League matches increased, but it was never the equivalent of traveling from the American Midwest to the Northeast, especially at a time when the principal means of long-distance transportation was by railroad.

64. Wangerin, *Distant Corners*, 46.

65. Allaway, *Rangers, Rovers and Spindlers*, 54–56.

66. In 1922, 132 clubs entered the USFA's National Challenge Cup, paying $16,000 in entry fees, and the receipts from the tournament amounted to around $50,000. The final match attracted over 8,500 spectators and grossed $8,400. Wangerin, *Distant Corners*, 72, 157.

67. Matthew Taylor, *The Leaguers: The Making of Professional Football in England, 1900–1939* (Liverpool, England: Liverpool University Press, 2005), 7–8.

68. "Pullmans Down Rovers, 3–0," *Chicago Daily Tribune*, December 8, 1913.

69. Id.

70. E. A. Batchelor, "Packards and Roses in a Draw," *Detroit Free Press*, December 15, 1913.

71. Quoted in Wangerin, *Distant Corners*, 49.

72. "Rangers Take Game Played in Snow," *Detroit Free Press*, February 2, 1914.

73. See Wangerin, *Distant Corners*, 50.

74. Thomas Cahill, quoted in Wangerin, *Distant Corners*, 53.

75. Quoted in Wangerin, *Distant Corners*, 55.

76. Wangerin, *Distant Corners*, 55.

77. Here again Chicago was something of an exception, with several high schools in the Chicago area and Elmhurst College and the University of Chicago fielding soccer teams in the early twentieth century. See Logan, *Early Years of Chicago Soccer*, 72–74, 126–27.

78. For more detail, see Allaway, *Rangers, Rovers and Spindlers*, 55–56, commenting on "a split in the playing styles in American soccer" exhibited in the National Challenge Cup finals between 1916 and 1918, when Bethlehem Steel players, several of whom were imports from England and Scotland, adopted the dribbling and close passing style common to association football in those nations at the time, and Fall River players, "now largely of a generation that had been raised in America," employed "what was becoming the dominant American style of the day, characterized by hard running, long passing and forceful forward movement of the ball."

79. For more detail, see Szymanski and Zimbalist, *National Pastime*, 86–94.

80. For more detail, see G. Edward White, *Creating the National Pastime: Baseball Transforms Itself, 1903–1953* (Princeton, NJ: Princeton University Press, 1996), 10–46, 84–126.

81. For more detail, see White, *Creating the National Pastime*, 84–126.

CHAPTER THREE

1. See, e.g., Ryan Swanson, "The Interwar and Post-World War II Eras, 1920–1960," in *A Companion to American Sport History*, ed. Steven A. Riess (Hoboken, NJ: Wiley, 2014), 61 ("The 1920s has often been called the golden age of sport").

2. Individual sports also experienced a growth in the period, not only in participation but also in spectator appeal, and some such sports began staging competitions designed to attract spectators, for which admission was charged. Illustrations are horse racing, boxing, tennis, golf, track and field, and auto racing. For a review of literature on the growth of those sports in the early and middle years of the twentieth century, see Riess, *Companion*, 271–356.

The relevance of the growth of individual sports in the period covered by this chapter is that they provided alternative attractions and venues for prospective followers and spectators of soccer clubs. None of the sports can be said to have been a direct competitor of soccer in the manner of gridiron football. Their growth nonetheless provides additional evidence of the enhanced interest in spectator sports in the United States in the first five decades of the twentieth century, helping to throw the marginal status of soccer in those decades into sharper relief.

3. Federal Baseball Club of Baltimore, Inc., v. National League of Professional Baseball Clubs, et al., 259 U.S. 200 (1922); Toolson v. New York Yankees, 346 U.S. 356 (1953).

Neither the *Federal Baseball* nor the *Toolson* decision can be explained by established doctrines of antitrust law. In *Federal Baseball* the court mistakenly characterized baseball games as local activities, having no direct effect on interstate commerce, even though teams crossed state lines to participate in them. In *Toolson* the court simply said that Congress could have removed Major League Baseball's exemption from the antitrust laws, but had not acted in the three decades after *Federal Baseball*.

4. In Radovich v. National Football League, 352 U.S. 445 (1957), the Supreme Court held that professional football was subject to antitrust laws. And in Flood v. Kuhn, 407 U.S. 258 (1972), the court noted that both professional basketball and hockey were also subject. Lower-court cases reaching the same conclusion are Washington Prof'l Basketball Corp. v. Nat'l Basketball Ass'n, 147 F. Supp. 154, 155 (S.D.N.Y. 1956); and Bos. Prof'l Hockey Ass'n v. Cheevers, 348 F. Supp. 261, 265 (D. Mass. 1972).

5. *Sixteenth Census of the United States: 1940* (Washington, DC: US Government Printing Office, 1942), vol. 2, pt. 1.

6. *The Canadian Encylopedia*, s.v. "National Hockey League (NHL)," by James H. Marsh, last edited December 12, 2016, https//www.thecanadianencyclopedia.ca/en/article/national-hockey-league. For more detail, see John Chi-Kit Wong, *Lords of the Rinks: The Emergence of the National Hockey League, 1875–1936* (Toronto: University of Toronto Press, 2005).

7. *Encyclopedia Britannica Online*, s.v. "Gridiron Football," by Michael Onard, January 29, 2021, https://www.britannica.com/sports/gridiron-football. For more detail, see Marc S. Maltby, *The Origins and Development of Professional Football* (New York: Garland, 1997); and Craig R. Coenen, *From Sandlots to the Super Bowl: The National Football League, 1920–1967* (Knoxville: University of Tennessee Press, 2005).

8. Leonard Koppett, *24 Seconds to Shoot* (New York: Macmillan, 1968); Robert Peterson, *Cages to Jump Shots: Pro Basketball's Early Years* (New York: Oxford University Press, 1990); and David G. Surdam, *The Rise of the National Basketball Association* (Urbana: University of Illinois Press, 2012).

9. For more detail, see G. Edward White, *Creating the National Pastime: Baseball Transforms Itself, 1903–1953* (Princeton, NJ: Princeton University Press, 1996), 10–46.

10. For more detail, see Raymond Schmidt, *Shaping College Football: The Transformation of a Major Sport, 1919–1930* (Syracuse, NY: Syracuse University Press, 2007). A feature of some of the gridiron football stadiums constructed from the 1920s on was that they were not widely used for other events outside the football season. That type of stadium was designed to house very large numbers of spectators, on the theory that residents of a college community would support the college's football team even though they had no direct connection to the college, so that football games would become large revenue-raising events for the host universities. Although the vast size of these stadiums facilitated very large attendance for games, their size and configuration made them unsuited for multiple uses, and they remained vacant for most of the year.

11. "The Last Days of a Garden Where Memories Grew," *New York Times*, April 16, 1995.

12. On the close relationship between electronic media and college football in the twentieth century, see Ronald Smith, *Play by Play: Radio, Television, and Big-Time College Sport* (Baltimore: Johns Hopkins University Press, 2001).

13. Among the studies providing various explanations for the conspicuous growth of college football in the early twentieth century are Donald Mrozek, *Sport and American Mentality, 1890–1910* (Knoxville: University of Tennessee Press, 1983); Harvey Green, *Fit for America: Health, Fitness, Sport, and American Society* (New York: Pantheon, 1986); Ronald Smith, *Sports and Freedom* (New York: Oxford University Press, 1988); Michael Oriard, *Reading Football* (Chapel Hill: University of North Carolina Press, 1993); Clifford Putney, *Muscular Christianity: Manhood and Sports in Protestant America, 1880–1920* (Cambridge, MA: Harvard University Press, 2001); and Brian Ingrassia, *The Rise of Gridiron University* (Lawrence: University Press of Kansas, 2012). See also John Sayle Watterson, *College Football: History, Spectacle, Controversy* (Baltimore: Johns Hopkins University Press, 2000), 120–76.

14. In addition to the sources cited in note 13, see Benjamin G. Rader, *American Sports: From the Age of Folk Games to the Age of Televised Sports*, 5th ed. (Upper Saddle River, NJ: Prentice Hall, 2004), 103–19; Robert Pruter, *The Rise of American High School Sports and the Search for Control, 1880–1930* (Syracuse, NY: Syracuse University Press, 2013).

15. For more detail on the "capture" of athletics by American colleges and public high schools in the early twentieth century, see Rader, *American Sports*; and Pruter, *Rise of American High School Sports.*

16. See Ingrassia, *Rise of Gridiron University*, 42–70.

17. Steven Riess, *Touching Base: Professional Baseball and American Culture in the Progressive Era* (Westport, CN: Greenwood, 1980), notes that about 25 percent of major-league baseball players in the early twentieth century attended college, although far fewer graduated. For more detail on Mathewson's career, see Philip Seib, *The Player: Christy Mathewson, Baseball, and the American Century* (New York: Four Walls, Eight Windows, 2003).

18. For more detail on the "farm system" by which major-league baseball clubs affiliated themselves with minor-league clubs, see White, *Creating the National Pastime*, 285–92.

19. There was a substantial amount of high-quality amateur basketball played in the 1930s, 1940s, and 1950s, initially centering on athletic clubs in cities and subsequently being dominated by teams associated with corporations, such as Phillips 66 and Caterpillar Industries. Those corporations would hire college basketball stars on their staffs, mainly to play on company teams. For more detail, see Adolph H. Grundman, *The Golden Age of Amateur Basketball* (Lincoln, NE: Bison, 2004).

20. See Gilbert M. Gaul, *Billion-Dollar Ball: A Journey through the Big-Money Culture of College Football* (New York: Viking, 2015).

21. John M. Carroll, *Red Grange and the Rise of Modern Football* (Urbana: University of Illinois Press, 1999), 4–6.

22. Carroll, *Red Grange*, 5.

23. For the details of Grange's four touchdown runs in twelve minutes, see Carroll, *Red Grange*, 6–8.

24. For a summary of that line of criticism, see Carroll, *Red Grange*, 101–3.

25. For evidence of the low esteem in which professional football was held, see commentary in the *New York Times* between December 1, 1925, and January 17, 1926, cited in Carroll, *Red Grange*, 103.

26. Chicago clubs reached the semifinals of the cup in 1916, 1917, and 1918, and Cleveland clubs participated in the cup competition in the latter two years. Gabe Logan, *The Early Years of Chicago Soccer, 1887–1939* (Lanham, MD: Lexington, 2019), 110, 113.

27. A list of the winners and finalists of the National Challenge Cup (also referred to as the US Open Cup) between 1914 and 1999 can be found in Roger Allaway, Colin Jose, and David Litterer, *The Encyclopedia of American Soccer History* (Lanham, MD: Scarecrow, 2001), 376–78.

28. See Allaway, Jose, and Litterer, *Encyclopedia*, 376–77.

29. A list of the American Cup winners and finalists between 1885 and 1929 can be found in Allaway, Jose, and Litterer, *Encyclopedia*, 375–76.

30. Between 1914 and 1921 Bethlehem Steel won the American Cup five times and was the runner-up on one other occasion, and clubs from northern New Jersey (Kearny, West Hudson, Bayonne, and Patterson) won it once and finished second four times. See Allaway, Jose, and Litterer, *Encyclopedia*, 376.

31. In the 1936–37 season, receipts for the Challenge Cup amounted to $36,920; by the 1950–51 season, they had dropped to $1,662. David Wangerin, *Distant Corners: American Soccer's History of Missed Opportunities and Lost Causes* (Philadelphia: Temple University Press, 2011), 77. Information about the 1922–23 Cup competition is from Wangerin, *Distant Corners*, 72–73.

32. See Hallaway, Jose, and Litterer, *Encyclopedia*, 376. For more detail on the St. Louis Soccer League, see Wangerin, *Distant Corners*, 148–62.

33. Geoffey Green, *History of the Football Association* (London: Naldrett, 1953), 285–86.

34. Green, *History*, 307.

35. Green, *History*, 319.

36. Green, *History*, 294.

37. See Gaul, *Billion-Dollar Ball.*

38. Wangerin, *Distant Corners*, 104.

39. A member of the Committee on Association Football wrote in the 1913 *Spalding's Official Soccer Football Guide* that "Club Soccer is coming fast, but collegiate and scholastic soccer is coming to the fore with even greater rapidity." The next year *Spalding's Football Guide* reported that "it would be no exaggeration to state that in the last ten years [soccer] has gone ahead five hundred percent, more than any other game in America." Quoted in *Spalding's Official Soccer Football Guide, 1913–1914* (New York: American Sports, 1913), 104, 106.

40. Wangerin, *Distant Corners*, 124, states that as late as 1939 "college soccer was largely confined to the northeast."

41. In 1941 Harry Brown, in a master's thesis on Penn State soccer in the early twentieth century, interviewed two Penn State professors who had coached the team after 1920. One, William V. Dennis, reported that the players supplied their own equipment, except balls, until 1922. Brown's interview is quoted in Wangerin, *Distant Corners*, 107.

42. Walt Freunsch, "Between the Lions," *Penn State Collegian*, November 22, 1935, characterized the student body as "bovinely indifferent" to soccer, and support for the team as "missing."

43. David Wangerin quotes the *Penn State Collegian* as saying in 1935 that recognition of Penn State's soccer team was adversely affected by the "Penn-dominated" collegiate soccer association in which that team and the University of Pennsylvania's team were grouped. That association, the *Collegian* charged, "has always belittled . . . every effort [on Penn State's part]." Wangerin, *Distant Corners*, 123.

44. From 1926 to 1950 the "national champion" in college soccer was determined by the vote of a committee of the Intercollegiate Soccer Football Association. Wangerin, *Distant Corners*, 110–13.

45. For a summary of rule changes adopted by college soccer between 1925 and the 1950s, see Wangerin, *Distant Corners*, 128–29. More attention is given in the next chapter to the effect of the differences between the rules of college and professional soccer in America on the prospects for college players who aspired to play professionally after graduating.

46. See Wangerin, *Distant Corners*, 109.

47. "Jeffries Selects Varsity Booters," *Penn State Collegian*, October 12, 1926,

48. For more detail on the Penn State team's trip to Scotland, see Wangerin, *Distant Corners*, 117–20.

49. "American Team Defeated," *Inverness Highland News and Football Times*, September 1, 1934.

50. For a list of the clubs in the American Soccer League between 1921 and 1931, see Allaway, Jose, and Litterer, *Encyclopedia*, 359–60. For more detail on the formation and history of the league, see Roger Allaway, *Rangers, Rovers and Spindlers: Soccer, Immigration and Textiles in New England and New Jersey* (Haworth, NJ: St. Johann Press, 2005), 65–90; and David Wangerin, *Soccer in a Football World: The Story of America's Forgotten Game* (Philadelphia: Temple University Press, 2006), 45–80; and Wangerin, *Distant Corners*, 71–83.

51. Allaway, Jose, and Litterer, *Encyclopedia*, 359.

52. For the results of the 1930 US World Cup team and a list of the players on the 1930 World Cup roster and their club affiliations, see Allaway, Jose, and Litterer, *Encyclopedia*, 384 and 398. Eleven of the sixteen players were from ASL clubs, the others being from the Cleveland Slavia, the Philadelphia Cricket Club, the St. Louis Ben Millers, and the Detroit Holley Carburetor, all semiprofessional clubs.

53. See the tabulation of American Soccer League Clubs in Allaway, Jose, and Litterer, *Encyclopedia*, 359–60.

54. Todd Shipyard in Brooklyn, Fall River United, and the Holyoke Falcos withdrew after the 1921–22 season, being replaced, respectively, by the Brooklyn Wanderers, Fall River Marksmen, and Paterson. Allaway, Jose, and Litterer, *Encyclopedia*, 359.

55. The most detailed account of Cahill's life and career is in Wangerin, *Distant Corners*, 58–88.

56. "Cahill Announces He Will Quit as Soccer Secretary," *St. Louis Post-Dispatch*, November 27, 1920.

57. "Soccer Delegates Honor Cahill at Annual Meeting," *St. Louis Post-Dispatch*, May 29, 1921.

58. "New Soccer League Is Formed in the East," *St. Louis Post-Dispatch*, September 18, 1921.

59. For an account of Cahill's involvement, along with Fall River businessman Sam Mark, in the acquisition of an ASL franchise for Mark in 1922, see Frank McGrath, "Sam Mark Brought Big-Time Soccer to FR Area," *Fall River Herald-News*, May 12, 1976.

60. For details of Scholefield's disappearance with $1,200 in USFA funds and subsequent reappearance three years later, see Wangerin, *Distant Corners*, 58–59. When Scholefield was discovered, he had married for a second time, although his first wife was still alive and had not divorced him. After being arrested and sentenced to ten years in a New York state prison for bigamy and embezzlement, Scholefield said that he had "got[ten] into fast company" in New York and needed to absent himself from his office "for a considerable time," then apparently found himself "stranded in Rhode Island." He eventually worked his way south to North Carolina, working as a fundraiser for charitable associations, until starting a new life in Greensboro. See Wangerin, *Distant Corners*, 59, including quotations from Scholefield's testimony at the time of his trial.

61. Wangerin, *Distant Corners*, 73–74.

62. Cahill's and Peel's comments are quoted in Wangerin, *Distant Corners*, 74.

63. Cahill's account of the confrontation with Peel is set forth in Wangerin, *Distant Corners*, 74–75.

64. Cahill's statement that Peel claimed to a "friendly" Chicago newspaper that Cahill had assaulted him with a knife is quoted in Wangerin, *Distant Corners*, 75.

65. Both the USFA's statement about Cahill's "flare of temper" and Peel's subsequent characterization of Cahill as "showing his true colors" in pulling a knife, and generally exhibiting "tyrannical" behavior during his initial tenure as USFA secretary, are quoted in Wangerin, *Distant Corners*, 75.

66. The details of Cahill's reinstatement and eventual reappointment as USFA secretary, including Peel's pledge to appoint a secretary without regard to any "previous history of this organization," are set forth in Wangerin, *Distant Corners*, 80.

67. Wangerin, *Distant Corners*, 77.

68. "Wray's Column," *St. Louis Post-Dispatch*, May 1, 1925.

69. Cahill set forth those goals in an interview with the *St. Louis Post-Dispatch* in 1925. John E. Wray, "Fighting Tom Cahill Now Wins Soccer Battles by Diplomacy, Not with Fists," *St. Louis Post-Dispatch*, July 26, 1925.

70. There is some disagreement among those who have written about Cunningham's appointment as to when it took place. Wangerin, *Distant Corners*, 78, has it in 1926, whereas Andrei S. Markovits and Steven L. Hellerman, *Offside: Soccer and American Exceptionalism* (Princeton, NJ: Princeton University Press, 1991), have it in 1928. The former date seems much more likely, as Wangerin has Cahill essentially being out of work in 1927 and hired by the Victoria, British Columbia hockey team to manage their tour of Europe that year, then being rehired as USFA secretary after he returned. Wangerin (81) quotes from Cahill's 1928 report as USFA secretary, and as we will see, it is extremely unlikely that Cahill would have been affiliated with both the USFA and ASL in 1928, the year they began a "soccer war" against one another.

71. Quoted in Wangerin, *Distant Corners*, 78.

72. "Cahill Promises More Fireworks," *St. Louis Post-Dispatch*, August 3, 1926.

73. Cahill, 1928 Secretary's Report to USFA, quoted in Wangerin, *Distant Corners*, 81.

74. For more detail, see Wangerin, *Distant Corners*, 81.

75. For more detail, see Allaway, Jose, and Litterer, *Encyclopedia*, 268–69.

76. Allaway, Jose, and Litterer, *Encyclopedia*, 268.

77. For more detail on Cahill's involvement in the formation of the Eastern Professional Soccer League in 1928, see Wangerin, *Distant Corners*, 82. For a list of the teams in the league for its only season, 1928–29, see Allaway, Jose, and Litterer, *Encyclopedia*, 4.

78. See Allaway, Jose, and Litterer, *Encyclopedia*, 268.

79. Quoted in Wangerin, *Distant Corners*, 82.

80. Quoted in Wangerin, *Distant Corners*, 83.

81. According to the *Encyclopedia of American Soccer*, Bethlehem Steel disbanded because the vice president of the Bethlehem Steel Company, Horace Edgar Lewis, who had been influential in founding the club in 1909, "decided to give up" on soccer because he was "disillusioned by the Soccer War." Allaway, Jose, and Litterer, *Encyclopedia*, 30.

82. Wangerin, *Distant Corners*, 168.

83. "Wray's Column," *St. Louis Post-Dispatch*, November 7, 1935.

84. For more detail, see Marsh, "National Hockey League"; and Surdam, *National Basketball Association*.

85. Allawy, Jose, and Litterer, *Encyclopedia*, 12.

86. For more detail on the formation and history of the second American Soccer League, see Allaway, Jose, and Litterer, *Encyclopedia*, 11–14. The league had no teams west of the Allegheny mountains until the 1970s; most of its teams were associated with ethnic athletic clubs; and it made no effort to recruit overseas players. As with the first ASL, it relied on matches between its clubs and touring European clubs to boost attendance. In 1947, 43,177 fans attended a match between an ASL club and the touring Hapoel of Palestine at Yankee Stadium in New York. See Allaway, Jose, and Litterer, *Encyclopedia*, 13.

87. In 1917, after returning from a tour of Sweden, Cahill proposed to the *St. Louis Times-Dispatch* that "soccer fields be entirely enclosed in a glass roof of sufficient height

not to interfere with kicks." "Pitchers Lacking for T. Cahill's Tour of Sweden," *St. Louis Times-Dispatch*, January 26, 1917. Nothing ever came of that proposal.

88. For evidence of soccer-specific stadiums outside the United States, see Stuart Fuller, *A Fan's Guide: European Football Grounds* (Shepperton, UK: Ian Allan, 2008).

89.Cahill quoted in Wray, "Fighting Tom Cahill."

CHAPTER FOUR

1. Maarten van Bottenburg, "Why are the European and American Sports Worlds so Different?," in *Sport and the Transformation of Modern Europe: States, Media, and Markets, 1950–2010*, ed. Alan Tomlinson, Christopher Young, and Richard Holt (London: Routledge, 2011), 205–25, stresses the contrast between the European emphasis on locating youth soccer in clubs and associations and the American emphasis on schools and colleges.

2. "History," Premier League, http:/www.premierleague.com/history.

3. Van Bottenburg, "European and American Sports Worlds," 211–12.

4. Works emphasizing the contrasts between European and American education in the late nineteenth and twentieth centuries, with a particular emphasis on sports, include Allen Guttmann, *A Whole New Ball Game: A Reinterpretation of American Sports* (Chapel Hill: University of North Carolina Press, 1988); Andrei S. Markovits and Steven L. Hellerman, *Offside: Soccer and American Exceptionalism* (Princeton, NJ: Princeton University Press, 1991); John Wilson, *Playing by the Rules: Sport, Society, and the State* (Detroit: Wayne State University Press, 1994); James Riordan and Arnd Kruger, eds., *European Cultures in Sport: Examining the Nations and Regions* (Bristol, UK: Intellect, 2003); Benjamin G. Rader, *American Sports: From the Age of Folk Games to the Age of Televised Sports*, 5th ed. (Upper Saddle River, NJ: Prentice Hall, 2004); Stefan Syzmanski, "A Theory of the Evolution of Modern Sport," *Journal of Sport History* 35, no. 1 (2008); and van Bottenburg, "European and American Sports Worlds."

5. For more detail on the topics discussed in the next several paragraphs, see John R. Thelin, *A History of American Higher Education*, 3d ed. (Baltimore: Johns Hopkins University Press, 2019), 43–74.

6. For more detail, see Roger L. Geiger, *The History of American Higher Education* (Princeton, NJ: Princeton University Press, 2015), 76–205.

7. Jurgen Herbst, *The Once and Future School: Three Hundred and Fifty Years of American Secondary Education* (New York: Routledge, 1996).

8. Price V. Fishback, ed., *Government and the American Economy: A New History* (Chicago: University of Chicago Press, 2007), 339.

9. Michael B. Katz, *The Irony of Early School Reform: Educational Innovation in Mid-Nineteenth Century Massachusetts* (New York: Teachers College Press, 2001), 167.

10. Murray Newton Rothbard, *Education: Free and Compulsory* (Auburn, AL: Ludwig von Mises Institute, 1979), 41.

11. See generally Lawrence A. Cremin, *The American Common School: An Historical Conception* (New York: Teachers College, 1951).

12. Joel Turtel, *Public Schools, Public Menace: How Public Schools Lie to Parents and Betray Our Children* (Staten Island, NY: Liberty, 2006), 29.

13. For more detail, see van Bottenburg, "European and American Sports Worlds."

14. Wilson, *Playing by the Rules*, 286.

15. G. Edward White, *Creating the National Pastime: Baseball Transforms Itself, 1903–1953* (Princeton, NJ: Princeton University Press, 1996), 279.

16. For more detail see White, *Creating the National Pastime*, 115–18. In some respects the practice of major-league baseball clubs encouraging gifted young players to forgo college for the minor leagues was comparable to the development of young soccer players in clubs and associations in the UK.

17. White, *Creating the National Pastime*, 349.

18. Oxford and Cambridge began to emphasize some sports, notably rowing, rugby, and cricket, in the nineteenth century, and until the 1960s both universities retained a policy of admitting talented athletes in those sports on the assumption that they would play for university teams.

19. Van Bottenburg, "European and American Sports Worlds," 211–13.

20. Rader, *American Sports*, 116–18; Robert Pruter, *The Rise of American High School Sports and the Search for Control, 1880–1930* (Syracuse, NY: Syracuse University Press, 2013), 45–84.

21. Claudia Goldin and Lawrence F. Katz, *The Race between Education and Technology* (Cambridge, MA: Harvard University Press, 2008), 194–246.

22. Rader, *American Sports*, 116; Pruter, *Rise of American High School Sports*, 45–61.

23. Rader, *American Sports*, 113. For an early twentieth-century illustration of those views, see H. S. Curtis, *The Play Movement and Its Significance* (New York: Macmillan, 1917), 31, 81–83.

24. Rader, *American Sports*, 117; Pruter, *Rise of American High School Sports*, 65–83.

25. The term *varsity* is a corruption of "university," signifying "official" support for an athletic team by an educational institution.

26. Amanda Ripley, "The Case Against High-School Sports," *Atlantic*, October 2013, https://www.theatlantic.com/magazine/archive/2013/10/the-case-against-high-school-sports/309447/.

27. Wilson, *Playing by the Rules*, 70–73.

28. For more detail on the formation of the Intercollegiate Athletic Association in 1905, which became the NCAA in 1910, see Guttmann, *Whole New Ball Game*, 103–5; Arthur A. Fleisher III, Brian L. Goff, and Robert D. Tollison, *The National Collegiate Athletic Association: A Study in Cartel Behavior* (Chicago: University of Chicago Press, 1992), 38–42; Rader, *American Sports*, 185–86; and Joseph N. Crowley, *In the Arena: The NCAA's First Century* (Indianapolis: NCAA, 2006), 37–44, 55–56.

29. For more detail on Walter Camp's career and the rule changes he initiated for the Intercollegiate Football Association between 1880 and 1888, when Camp was directing football at Yale University, see Rader, *American Sports*, 89–93.

On the evolution of gridiron football in early twentieth-century America, see John Sayle Watterson, *College Football: History, Spectacle, Controversy* (Baltimore: Johns Hopkins University Press, 2000), 120–76.

30. Fleisher, Goff, and Tollison, *National Collegiate Athletic Association*, 38–39.

31. Fleisher, Goff, and Tollison, *National Collegiate Athletic Association*, 39.

32. Crowley, *In the Arena*, 44.

33. Rader, *American Sports*, 89.

34. Crowley, *In the Arena*, 44.

35. For more detail on the cartel status of the NCAA, see Fleisher, Goff, and Tollison, *National Collegiate Athletic Association*, 5–10.

36. For more detail, see Fleisher, Goff, and Tollison, *National Collegiate Athletic Association*, 20–25.

37. See, for instance, Allen L. Sack and Ellen J. Staurowsky, *College Athletes for Hire: The Evolution and Legacy of the NCAA's Amateur Myth* (New York: Praeger, 1996).

38. For evidence that those three sports had become established in American high schools by the late nineteenth century, see Pruter, *Rise of American High School Sports*, 3–22, 103–8.

39. See Rader, *American Sports*, 103–23.

40. For more detail on the role of injuries in early gridiron football, see Watterson, *College Football*, 9–142.

41. Watterson, *College Football*, 89–93.

42. Fleisher, Goff, and Tollison, *National Collegiate Athletic Association*, 41–42.

43. For more detail, see Sack and Staurowsky, *College Athletes for Hire*, 21–40.

44. Crowley, *In the Arena*, 57–61.

45. For evidence of the growth of college football in the 1920s, including the construction of large football stadiums, see Fleisher, Goff, and Tollison, *National Collegiate Athletic Association*, 42–44. On the growth of basketball in the same time period, see Guttmann, *Whole New Ball Game*, 71–75.

46. Fleisher, Goff, and Tollison, *National Collegiate Athletic Association*, 42–43.

47. Fleisher, Goff, and Tollison, *National Collegiate Athletic Association*, 4–14.

48. Roger Allaway, Colin Jose, and David Litterer, *The Encyclopedia of American Soccer History* (Lanham, MD: Scarecrow, 2001), 53; "ISFL/ISFA Team Championship Records" and "ISFL/ISFA College Soccer National Champions," https://en.wikipedia.org/wiki/Intercollegiate_Soccer_Football_Association.

49. David Wangerin, *Distant Corners: American Soccer's History of Missed Opportunities and Lost Causes* (Philadelphia: Temple University Press, 2011), 111–13.

50. "ISFL/ISFA College Soccer National Champions."

51. Wangerin, *Distant Corners*, 130.

52. See Wangerin, *Distant Corners*, 112–13; "ISFL/ISFA College Soccer National Champions."

53. Wangerin, *Distant Corners*, 130.

54. https://www.nhfs.org/media/1020206/hs_participation_survey_history_1969–2009.pdf.

55. http://fs.ncaa.org/Docs/stats/m_soccer_champs_records/2012/D1/champs.pdf, 1959 and 1969.

56. Andrew M. Guest, "Individualism vs. Community: The Globally Strange Relationship Between the U.S. Soccer System and the U.S. School System," in *Soccer Culture in America*, ed. Yuya Kiuchi (Jefferson, NC: McFarland, 2014), 27–31.

57. Phil West, *The United States of Soccer: The MLS and the Rise of American Fandom* (New York: Harry N. Abrams, 2016), 68. The emergence of Major League Soccer is the topic of a succeeding chapter.

58. Wangerin, *Distant Corners*, 128.

59. Quoted in Wangerin, *Distant Corners*, 128.

60. Wangerin, *Distant Corners*, 128–29.

61. Markovits and Hellerman, *Offside*, 123.

62. In contrast, the current NCAA substitution rules do not allow substituted players to re-enter a match in the first half and overtime, with one re-entry permitted during the second half. Substituted high school players may re-enter at any time. Don Dennison, *A Comparative Study of Rules and Laws: 2019 Soccer Guide*, Rule 3 ("Players and Substitutes"), http://www.nfhs.org/media/1018270/2019–comparative–study–of–rules–and–laws.pdf.

63. In 1925, we have seen, the ISFL divided matches into four 22-minute quarters, a practice that continued in ISFA and NCAA matches until 1972, when the NCAA adopted two 45-minute halves. Wangerin, *Distant* Corners, 128. Most high schools eventually switched to two 40-minute halves, although some retain 20-minute quarters. See Dennison, *Comparative Study of Rules and Laws*, citing NCAA and National Federation of High Schools, Rule 7 ("Duration of Game").

64. Markovits and Hellerman, *Offside*, 124–25.

65. During my first season as a varsity college player, in 1960, I and one of my sophomore classmates were substitute wing forwards, a position that at the time featured sprinting in the offensive half of the field in pursuit of long passes intended to drop behind defenders, thus freeing wings receiving the passes to run in the direction of the opponent's goal. The coach would typically insert me and my classmate into the game about two-thirds into a quarter with instructions to "go all out," or "turn it up." We were not expected to be conserving energy in order to adapt to the course of continuous play. Nor were the starting wing forwards we replaced.

66. For the rosters of the 1930, 1934, and 1950 US men's World Cup teams, see Allaway, Jose, and Litterer, *Encyclopedia*, 398.

67. Markovits and Hellerman, *Offside*, 172–74.

68. Pruter, *Rise of American High School Sports*, 326–27.

69. Pruter, *Rise of American High School Sports*, 148–51.

70. James M. Pederson, *The Rise of the Millennial Parents* (2014), 13.

71. As of 2019 the 205 colleges and universities offered men's soccer in Division I, with forty-eight teams invited to the NCAA Division I tournament; 214 institutions offered Division II soccer, with forty teams participating in the Division II tournament; and 415 offered Division III, with sixty-two teams participating in the Division III tournament. http://www.ncaa.org/championships/division–1–mens–soccer; http://www.ncaa.org/championships/division–2–mens–soccer; http://www.ncaa.org/championships/division–3–mens–soccer.

CHAPTER FIVE

1. "Soccer-Loved and Ignored," *Inside Sports Magazine*, July 1984, 64, 65.

2. Allaway, Jose, and Letterer, *The Encyclopedia of American Soccer History* (Lanham, MD: Scarecrow, 2001), 13.

3. David Wangerin, *Soccer in a Football World: The Story of America's Forgotten Game* (Philadelphia: Temple University Press, 2006), 123.

4. Arthur Daley, "On a Grandiose Scale," *New York Times*, February 9, 1960. Identifying the "soccer championship in the outer fringes of Brooklyn" that Daley covered is challenging. Only one American Cup championship was held after 1925, a two-match series in which the Providence Gold Bugs defeated the New York Nationals. Neither of those clubs was based in Brooklyn. Nor were any of the finalists in National Challenge Cup matches between 1926 and 1937 from Brooklyn. And although the Brooklyn St. Mary's club participated in two-match National Challenge Cup finals in 1938 and 1939, none of those matches featured three-overtime scoreless ties. There was a scoreless tie between Baltimore SC and Chicago Sparta in the first match of a two-match final in 1940, but those matches were not held in Brooklyn. See Allaway, Jose, and Litterer, *Encyclopedia*, 376–77.

5. Arthur Daley, "Start of a Long Climb," *New York Times*, April 18, 1967.

6. For more detail see Wangerin, *Soccer in a Football World*, 129.

7. Jack Gould, "TV: Soccer Makes Its Network Debut," *New York Times*, April 17, 1967.

8. Allaway, Jose, and Litterer, *Encyclopedia*, provides a list of the rosters of US World Cup players in 1930 and 1934, together with their clubs (398), as well as the names of clubs in the two versions of the American Soccer League (360, 385).

9. Allaway, Jose, and Litterer, *Encyclopedia*, 328.

10. Allaway, Jose, and Litterer, 326–27.

11. Allaway, Jose, and Litterer, 329.

12. For a list of the 1950 men's World Cup roster, with club affiliations, see Allaway, Jose, and Litterer, 398.

13. For more detail on tryouts for the team in 1949 and 1950, and a list of the eventual starting players on the roster, see Geoffrey Douglas, *The Game of Their Lives: The Untold Story of the World Cup's Biggest Upset* (New York: Henry Holt, 1996), 8–9.

14. Joe Gaetjens, from Haiti, washed dishes; Joe Maca, from Belgium, stripped wallpaper; and Ed McIlenny was a full-time professional player for the Philadelphia Nationals in the ASL. Douglas, *Game of Their Lives*, 9.

15. Forwards Frank Wallace and Gino Pariani, center halfback Charley Columbo, and goalkeeper Frank Borghi. For this, and more detail on the ancestry of the players, see Douglas, *Game of Their Lives*, 8–9.

16. As citizens of Haiti, Belgium, and Scotland, Gaetjens, Maca, and McIlenny were ineligible to play on the US team. They mispresented their citizenship status, which was apparently not investigated by the USSF. Douglas, *Game of Their Lives*, 9.

17. That was Dent McSkimming, a sportswriter for the *St. Louis Post-Dispatch* who took a "vacation" to attend the 1950 World Cup in Brazil, paying his own way. Douglas, *Game of Their Lives*, 4.

18. Douglas, *Game of Their Lives*, 6.

19. Douglas, *Game of Their Lives*, 6.

20. Douglas, *Game of Their Lives*, 5.

21. Douglas, *Game of Their Lives*, 6, 17.

22. Douglas, *Game of Their Lives*, 17, 116–17.

23. Douglas, *Game of Their Lives*, 17.

24. Douglas, *Game of Their Lives*, 1–2.

25. Walter Winterbottom, interview by John Sugden and Alan Tomlinson, November 24, 1996, in *FIFA and the Contest for World Football: Who Rules the Peoples' Game?*, ed. John Sugden and Alan Tomlinson (Cambridge, UK: Polity, 1998), 206.

26. Douglas, *Game of Their Lives*, 25.

27. Douglas, *Game of Their Lives*, 44–45.

28. Douglas, *Game of Their Lives*, 131–33.

29. Douglas, *Game of Their Lives*, 134.

30. *London Times*, June 30, 1950.

31. Douglas, *Game of Their Lives*, 140.

32. Douglas, *Game of Their Lives*, 140–41.

33. Douglas, *Game of Their Lives*, 142–44.

34. "Television," *American Memory*, Library of Congress, http://www.memory.loc.gov/ammem/awhhtml/awmi10/television.html.

35. Steve Wiegand, "The Impact of the Television in 1950s America," http://www.dummies.com/education/history/american-history/the-impact-of-the-television-in-1950s-america/; "Classic Car Models and Prices for Cars from the Fifties," www.thepeoplehistory.com/50scars.html.

36. "American TV Prices," www.tvhistory.tv/tv-prices.html.

37. "Television in the U.S: History and Production," www.northern.edu/wild/th100/tv.html.

38. The information about American television networks and professional sports in the 1960s comes from Wangerin, *Soccer in a Football World*, 121–22.

39. The match was a specially arranged one between the Arsenal club and its reserves on September 16, 1937. See "Happened on This Day—16 September," *BBC Sport*, September 16, 2002.

40. "Cup Final to Be Televised," *Manchester Guardian*, March 19, 1938; "A Rousing Cup Final," *Observer*, May 1, 1938.

41. For floodlights, competition between ITV and BBC to gain viewers through televised football, and introduction of *Sports Special*, see Richard Haynes, "A Pageant of Sound and Vision: Football's Relationship with Television, 1936–60," *International Journal of the History of Sport* 15, no. 1 (1998): 221–23. For ITV's £150,000 contract in 1960 to broadcast twenty live Football League games, see "Campaign to Boost Football Gates, League's Use of ITV Money," the *Guardian*, August 17, 1960. For Blackpool and Wanderers on television, see Eric Todd, "League Match by Floodlight: An Experiment Begins," *Guardian*, September 10, 1960. For Arsenal opposing televised match due to threat to attendance, see "More Clubs Attack Soccer TV Plan: 'Glorious Method of Suicide,' " *Guardian*, August 23, 1960. For Tottenham refusing to allow ITV to broadcast its match, see "Tottenham Hotspur Reject ITV Plan," *Guardian*, September 10, 1960. For ITV's decision to withdraw its television offer, see "League Players Angered by Pay Rebuff," *Guardian*, November 9, 1960.

42. For joint ITV-BBC contract for £5.2 million over two years, see Charles Burgess, "More Live Football in New Television Deal," *Guardian*, July 16, 1983. For Match of the Day moving to BBC1, see "Again No Choice on Saturday Afternoon," *Television Today* (London), July 28, 1966.

43. Winston Burdett, "TV Commercials Come to Britain," *Quarterly of Film Radio and Television* 10, no. 2 (Winter 1955): 180–85.

44. For creation of the Premier League, see "First Division Clubs Sign up for the Premier League," *Guardian*, July 18, 1991; and David Hoppe, "Green Light for New League," *Guardian*, February 21, 1992. For bidding over television contract, see Russell Thomas, "ITV Plan a Unique Premier Monopoly," *Guardian*, February 26, 1992; and "BSkyB Joins Race for TV Coverage," *Guardian*, February 27, 1992. For BSkyB's 1992 contract, see "BSkyB Corners Live Coverage," *Guardian*, May 19, 1992; and, confirming £191.5 million contract amount, Chris Barrie, "TV Teams Up to Cut Soccer Bills," *Guardian*, December 1, 1997. For BSkyB's 1996 contract, see John Duncan and Andrew Culf, "Sky Wins Football Rights for £670m," *Guardian*, June 7, 1996.

45. For more detail on the International Soccer League, see Allaway, Jose, and Litterer, *Encyclopedia*, 129–30.

46. For more detail, see Wangerin, *Soccer in a Football World*, 123–24.

47. Wangerin, *Soccer in a Football World*, 124.

48. Wangerin, *Soccer in a Football World*, 124–25.

49. Wangerin, *Soccer in a Football World*, 125–26.

50. For more detail, see Wangerin, *Soccer in a Football World*, 136–42.

51. Wangerin, *Soccer in a Football World*, 135.

52. Wangerin, *Soccer in a Football World*, 129.

53. From a peak of over 16,000 spectators per game in 1960, attendance at major-league baseball games irregularly declined for the next sixteen years, only returning to 1960 levels in 1978 and reaching a low of 13,000 fans per game in 1963. Scott Lindholm, "Major League Attendance Trends Past, Present, and Future," *SB Nation*, http://www.beyondtheboxscore.com/2014/2/10/5390172/major-league-attendance-trends-1950-2013.

54. See Allaway, Jose, and Litterer, *Encyclopedia*, 3, 60.

55. See Allaway, Jose, and Litterer, *Encyclopedia*, id., 360–361.

56. See Wangerin, *Soccer in a Football World*, 168–69.

57. Wangerin, *Soccer in a Football World*, 169.

58. Wangerin, *Soccer in a Football World*, 167.

59. For more detail on Chinaglia's signing, see Wangerin, *Soccer in a Football World*, 174–75.

60. See Allaway, Jose, and Litterer, *Encyclopedia*, 361.

61. For more detail, see Wangerin, *Soccer in a Football World*, 180–84.

62. The NASL's average attendance went from 10,960 in 1976 to 14,406 in 1978. Allaway, Jose, and Litterer, *Encyclopedia*, 201–2.

63. Wangerin, *Soccer in a Football World*, 193, 202.

64. For more detail on the NASL's rule changes and FIFA's reaction, see Wangerin, *Soccer in a Football World*, 196, 206–7.

65. For more detail, see Wangerin, *Soccer in a Football World*, 209–11.

66. Wangerin, *Soccer in a Football World*, 190.

67. Wangerin, *Soccer in a Football World*, 141, 143, 181.

68. Wangerin, *Soccer in a Football World*, 160, 186.

69. See Fraser John Boyd, "Failure to Launch: A Study of the North American Soccer League and the Women's United Soccer Association," Tennessee Research and Creative Exchange, University of Tennessee, https://trace.tennessee.edu/utk_gradthes/3668/.

70. For more detail on the rise and fall of the Philadelphia Atoms, see Wangerin, *Soccer in a Football World*, 158–59, 172–73.

71. Lists of clubs in the NASL in particular years can be found in Allaway, Jose, and Litterer, *Encyclopedia*, 360–63.

72. Boyd, "Failure to Launch."

73. Allaway, Jose, and Litterer, *Encyclopedia*, 154.

74. Details on outdoor and indoor professional soccer leagues in the United States between 1984 and 1966 can be found in Allaway, Jose, and Litterer, *Encyclopedia*, 220–22.

75. Allaway, Jose, and Litterer, *Encyclopedia*, 220–21.

76. For more detail, see Allaway, Jose, and Litterer, *Encyclopedia*, 220–22.

77. For more detail, see Allaway, Jose, and Litterer, *Encyclopedia*, 214–15.

78. Michael Janofsky, "U.S. Awarded '94 World Cup Tourney in Soccer," *New York Times*, July 5, 1988.

CHAPTER SIX

1. FIFA Statutes, General Provisions, section 1, https://digitalhub.fifa.com/m/7e791c0890282277/original/FIFA-Statutes-2021.pdf.

2. FIFA Statutes, General Provisions, section 2.

3. Swiss Civil Code of 10 December 1907, ch. 2, art. 60, https://www.fedlex.admin.ch/eli/cc/24/233_245_233/en.

4. Alan Tomlinson, *FIFA: The Men, the Myths, and the Money* (New York: Routledge, 2014), 29.

5. Tomlinson, *FIFA*, 29.

6. Tomlinson, *FIFA*, 30, 32.

7. Tomlinson, *FIFA*, 32–34.

8. Tomlinson, *FIFA*, 34.

9. Tomlinson, *FIFA*, 34–35.

10. Tomlinson, *FIFA*, 36–37.

11. Tomlinson, *FIFA*, 35.

12. For more detail, see John Sugden and Alan Tomlinson, eds., *FIFA and the Contest for World Football: Who Rules the Peoples' Game?* (Cambridge, UK: Polity, 1998), 212–18.

13. Quoted in Christiane Eisenberg, Pierre Lanfranchi, Tony Mason, and Alfred Wahl, *100 Years of Football: The FIFA Centennial Book* (London: Weidenfeld and Nicholson, 2004), 119.

14. See Eisenberg, Lanfranchi, Mason, and Wahl, *100 Years of Football*, 248–50.

15. Eisenberg, Lanfranchi, Mason, and Wahl, *100 Years of Football*, 119.

16. For more detail on the partnership between FIFA and ISL, and its effect on broadcasting, advertising, and merchandising rights to World Cup tournaments, see Sugden and Tomlinson, *FIFA and the Contest for World Football*, 90–94.

17. Sepp Blatter, quoted in Keir Radnege, "Cashing In," *World Soccer* 36 (1996): 25.

18. Guido Tognoni, interview by John Sugden and Alan Tomlinson, May 21, 1996, in Sugden and Tomlinson, *FIFA and the Contest for World Football*, 82.

19. Eisenberg, Lanfranchi, Mason, and Wahl, *100 Years of Football*, 102–8.

20. Sugden and Tomlinson, *FIFA and the Contest for World Football*, 6, 203.

21. Sugden and Tomlinson, *FIFA and the Contest for World Football*, 204.

22. Sugden and Tomlinson, *FIFA and the Contest for World Football*, 106–7.

23. For more detail, see Sugden and Tomlinson, *FIFA and the Contest for World Football*, 207–8.

24. Carlos Torres, captain of the Brazil World Cup team in 1970, interview by John Sugden and Alan Tomlison, January 23, 1996, in Sugden and Tomlinson, *FIFA and the Contest for World Football*, 207.

25. Eisenberg, Lanfranchi, Mason, and Wahl, *100 Years of Football*, 133.

26. Eisenberg, Lanfranchi, Mason, and Wahl, *100 Years of Football*, 132.

27. Eisenberg, Lanfranchi, Mason, and Wahl, *100 Years of Football*, 133–34.

28. Eisenberg, Lanfranchi, Mason, and Wahl, *100 Years of Football*, 127–28.

29. Eisenberg, Lanfranchi, Mason, and Wahl, *100 Years of Football*, 233.

30. Eisenberg, Lanfranchi, Mason, and Wahl, *100 Years of Football*, 134–35.

31. Eisenberg, Lanfranchi, Mason, and Wahl, *100 Years of Football*, 134.

32. Tom Weir, *USA Today*, December 17, 1993. A 1988 article on the reaction of American audiences and media to this staging of the 1986 World Cup in Mexico concluded that the event "failed to capture the imagination of the American public" and that although international media considered the cup "the world's most important media event," the American media's interest was "strikingly minute in comparison to that exhibited by virtually every [other] country in the world," despite the fact that the cup was held in close proximity to the United States. Andrei Markovits, "The Other 'American Exceptionalism': Why Is There No Soccer in the United States?" *International Journal of the History of Sport* 7, no 2 (1990): 230.

33. Rous, *Football Worlds*, 162.

34. Jim Trecker, interview by John Sugden and Alan Tomlinson, February 3, 1996, in Sugden and Tomlinson, *FIFA and the Contest for World Football*, 207.

35. Phil West, *The United States of Soccer: The MLS and the Rise of American Fandom* (New York: Harry N. Abrams, 2016), 4–5.

36. Sugden and Tomlinson, *FIFA and the Contest for World Football*, 213. For more detail on the somewhat inept efforts on the part of the USSF to promote the 1994 World Cup, see 211–13 in Sugden and Tomlinson's book.

37. Sugden and Tomlinson, *FIFA and the Contest for World Football*, 213.

38. Sugden and Tomlinson, *FIFA and the Contest for World Football*, 213.

39. Sugden and Tomlinson, *FIFA and the Contest for World Football*, 213.

40. Alex Fynn and Lynton Guest, *Out of Time—Why Football Isn't Working* (London: Simon and Schuster, 1994), 381.

41. Hank Steinbrecher, interview by John Sugden and Alan Tomlinson, November 12, 1996, in Sugden and Tomlinson, *FIFA and the Contest for World Football*, 221.

42. João Havelange in *Report—FIFA World Cup '94*, quoted in Sugden and Tomlinson, *FIFA and the Contest for World Football*, 220.

43. For more detail, see Eisenberg, Lanfranchi, Mason, and Wahl, *100 Years of Football*, 188–92.

CHAPTER SEVEN

1. Christiane Eisenberg, Pierre Lanfranchi, Tony Mason, and Alfred Wahl, *100 Years of Football: The FIFA Centennial Book* (London: Weidenfeld and Nicholson, 2004), 192.

2. Eisenberg, Lanfranchi, Mason, and Wahl, *100 Years of Football*, 188–92.

3. And even earlier, in Scotland and England in the 1880s and 1890s; but the exhibitions in which women soccer players participated in those decades were commercial ventures, designed to attract male audiences as a form of satiric entertainment. The belief that soccer was an "unsuitable" pursuit for women would endure in England deep into the twentieth century. For more detail on late nineteenth-century exhibitions, see Tony Collins, *How Football Began: A Global History of How the World's Football Codes Were Born* (New York: Routledge, 2018), 65–69.

4. For more detail on the Dick, Kerr Ladies Football Club, see Gail J. Newsham, *In a League of Their Own: The Dick, Kerr Ladies, 1917–1965* (Chorley, UK: Pride of Place, 1994). Information about the Dick, Kerr club in the next several paragraphs is taken from Newsham, 18–36.

5. See Newsham, *In a League of Their Own*, 19–20.

6. Newsham, *In a League of Their Own*, 48–51.

7. Newsham, *In a League of Their Own*, 52–69.

8. The FA Resolution was quoted, among other places, in the *Hull Daily Mail*, December 6, 1921.

9. Newsham, *In a League of Their Own*, 77–102.

10. For more detail on the 1922 Dick, Kerr tour of the United States, see Alathea Melling, "'Charging Amazons and Fair Invaders': The 1922 Dick, Kerr Ladies' Soccer Tour of North America," *European Sports History Review* 3 (2001): 155.

11. Timothy F. Gainey, *Beyond Bend It Like Beckham: The Global Phenomenon of Women's Soccer* (Lincoln: University of Nebraska Press, 2012), 215–22. The coverage of the 1922 Dick, Kerr Ladies' tour was sparse: see Melling, "Charging Amazons and Fair Invaders."

12. The date the United States Field Hockey Association was founded is listed in "Constance Mary Katherine Applebee," obituary, *New York Times*, January 28, 1981. Applebee was the cofounder of the USFA.

13. "Constance Mary Katherine Applebee." Applebee died at the age of 107.

14. For more detail, see "USA Field Hockey," http://www.teamusa.org/usa-field-hockey/about.

15. Illustrations of this gender bias are discussed in Dominick Cavallo, *Muscles and Morals: Organized Playgrounds and Urban Reform, 1880–1920* (Philadelphia: University of Pennsylvania Press, 1981); Mabel Lee, *A History of Physical Education and Sports in the U.S.A.* (New York: Wiley, 1983); Sheila Fletcher, *Women First: The Female*

Tradition in English Physical Education (Dover, NH: Athlone, 1984); Eric Dunning, "Sports as a Male Preserve: Notes on the Social Sources of Masculine Identity and Its Transformation," in *Quest for Excitement: Sport and Leisure in the Civilizing Process*, ed. Eric Dunning and Norbert Elias (Oxford, UK: Basil Blackwell, 1986), 267–83; Helen Lenskyj, *Out of Bounds: Women, Sport, and Sexuality* (Toronto: Women's Press, 1986); R. W. Connell, *Gender and Power* (Stanford, CA: Stanford University Press, 1987); J. A. Mangan and Roberta J. Park, eds., *From "Fair Sex" to Feminism* (London: Frank Cass, 1987); Cynthia Eagle Russett, *Sexual Science: The Victorian Construction of Womenhood* (Cambridge, MA: Harvard University Press, 1989); Patricia Vertinsky, *The Eternally Wounded Woman: Women, Doctors, and Exercise in the Late Nineteenth Century* (Manchester, UK: Manchester University Press, 1990); and Allen Guttmann, *Women's Sport: A History* (New York: Columbia University Press, 1991). Some of those sources discuss the legacy of stereotyped perceptions about women's "frailty" and the purported risks to women of vigorous exercise; others discuss the idea of sports as a "male preserve."

Jennifer Hargreaves, *Sporting Females: Critical Issues in the History and Sociology of Women's Sports* (New York: Routledge, 1994), discusses the evolution of attitudes toward exercise for women between the last two decades of the nineteenth century and the first two of the twentieth from a variety of perspectives, and traces the emergence of gymnastics and subsequently competitive sports for women; see 42–103 for a survey of changing attitudes toward those issues, including a variety of citations for additional works on the topics discussed.

These explanations have continued to be advanced in more recent studies. See, for example, James Schultz, *Qualifying Times: Points of Change in U.S. Women's Sport* (Urbana: University of Illinois Press, 2014); Susan K. Cahn, *Coming on Strong: Gender and Sexuality in Women's Sport*, 2d ed. (Urbana: University of Illinois Press, 2015); Brenda Elsey, *Futbolera* (Austin: University of Texas Press, 2019); and Julie DiCaro, *Sidelined: Sports, Culture, and Being a Woman in America* (New York: Dutton, 2021).

16. Welch Suggs, *A Place on the Team: The Triumph and Tragedy of Title IX* (Princeton, NJ: Princeton University Press, 2005), 20.

17. For more detail see Hargreaves, *Sporting Females*, 42–64.

18. See Clifford Putney, *Muscular Christianity: Manhood and Sports in Protestant America, 1880–1920* (Cambridge, MA: Harvard University Press, 2001); and Benjamin G. Rader, *American Sports: From the Age of Folk Games to the Age of Televised Sports*, 5th ed. (Upper Saddle River, NJ: Prentice Hall, 2004), 103–6.

19. See, e.g., Suggs, *A Place on the Team*, 13–23.

20. See Cahn, *Coming on Strong*, 31–54.

21. For more detail, see Newsham, *In a League of Their Own*, 103–25.

22. The height of the net for men's volleyball is approximately eight feet, and that for women slightly over seven feet four inches. "Improve Your Volleyball," http://www.improveyourvolley.com/volleyball-net-height.html. For the originally different rules of women's basketball, see Cahn, *Coming on Strong*, 84–88.

23. With the exception of a few women's soccer clubs in New York and Chicago in the second and third decades of the twentieth century, to subsequently be discussed.

24. See Robert Pruter, *The Rise of American High School Sports and the Search for Control, 1880–1930* (Syracuse, NY: Syracuse University Press, 2013), 8–21, indicating that the principal sports offered by public high schools in the late nineteenth and early twentieth centuries were baseball and gridiron football, followed by track and tennis. Pruter also notes that although girls in public high schools were introduced to track and field, tennis, and golf in the 1920s, most public high schools discouraged interscholastic competition, adopting positions similar to those of many early twentieth-century physical educators, who believed that women's sports should be undertaken at "play days" rather than through the sorts of competitions engaged in by young men at high schools and colleges (244–72).

25. Andrei S. Markovits and Steven L. Hellerman, *Offside: Soccer and American Exceptionalism* (Princeton, NJ: Princeton University Press, 1991), 126, indicate that the absence of qualified coaches extended to colleges and universities as well.

26. On hooliganism among the fans of European soccer clubs, see Bill Buford, *Among the Thugs* (Pomfret, VT: Trafalgar Square, 1990).

27. Major League Soccer is the subject of the next chapter.

28. As we have seen, all of the NASL's predecessor leagues tended to cater to male ethnic audiences.

29. For evidence of the ethnic orientation of Chicago soccer leagues in the early twentieth century, see Gabe Logan, *The Early Years of Chicago Soccer, 1887–1939* (Lanham, MD: Lexington, 2019), 106–23.

30. For evidence of the appeal of soccer in southern New England to spectators in the 1920s, see Roger Allaway, *Rangers, Rovers and Spindlers: Soccer, Immigration and Textiles in New England and New Jersey* (Haworth, NJ: St. Johann Press, 2005), 66–70. David Wangerin, *Distant Corners: American Soccer's History of Missed Opportunities and Lost Causes* (Philadelphia: Temple University Press, 2011), 52–58, notes the sizable attendance at National Challenge Cup semifinal and final matches in New England in the 1910s and 1920s.

31. *New York Times*, "Women Play Soccer," December 26, 1913; *Chicago Tribune*, "Women to Play Soccer Game," December 24, 1913.

32. *Chicago Tribune*, December 26, 1913.

33. Logan, *Early History of Chicago Soccer*, 158–59. The Dick, Kerr club's 1922 tour of the United States initially included a match in Chicago, but the promoters canceled the match after Dick, Kerr demanded a $1,000 fee. See "Women's Soccer Team to Visit Chicago," *Chicago Tribune*, September 24, 1922; "English Girls' Soccer Team Game Here Is Called Off," *Chicago Tribune*, November 10, 1922.

34. For more detail on the introduction of soccer as an intramural sport for women at Smith in the 1920s, see Shawn Ladda, "The Early Beginnings of Intercollegiate Women's Soccer in the United States," *Physical Educator* 57 (2000): 106, 110–12.

35. See Marion Knighton, "Development of Soccer for Girls," *American Physical Education Review* 34 (1929): 372.

36. Ethel Penin, introduction to Helen Frost and Hazel Cubberley, *Field Hockey and Soccer for Women* (New York: Scribner's, 1923), xvii.

37. Hazel Cubberley, "Soccer for Girls," in *Spalding's Athletic Library—Soccer for Women* 7 (1932).

38. *Smith Sports Book—Soccer*, 1924, quoted in Ladda, "Early Beginnings," 111.

39. Ladda, "Early Beginnings," 111.

40. Ladda, "Early Beginnings," 111.

41. Why some Canadian universities decided to adopt women's soccer in the 1950s is itself a puzzle and offers a prospect for research. It is interesting to note that two of the features retarding the development of women's soccer in the United States—the overshadowing of association football by an indigenous version, in this instance the Canadian form of gridiron football, and the virtual absence of women's soccer from high schools and universities in the early and middle years of the twentieth century—were both present in Canada. See M. Ann Hall, "The Game of Choice: Girls' and Women's Soccer in Canada," *Soccer & Society* 4 (2003): 30–46.

The only source of information about the Lyndon State women's soccer team's early history is Ladda, "Early Beginnings," 114–15. In 1995 Shawn Ladda interviewed Dudley Bell, who had been hired by Lyndon State as athletic director and men's soccer coach in 1959. Bell recalled hiring a women's soccer coach, Dominic Marabella, in 1959, but could not recall whether the women's team engaged in any intercollegiate competition. Ladda, "Early Beginnings," 114.

The distances between Johnson, Vermont and the Canadian colleges were no more than 117 miles. In 2016 Johnson State and Lyndon State Colleges merged to become Northern Vermont University.

42. Ladda, "Early Beginnings," 112–14.

43. Ladda, "Early Beginnings," 112.

44. Roland Hess, quoted in Ladda, "Early Beginnings," 112, 113–15.

45. When Title IX of the Educational Amendments Act was initially proposed, its general purpose, that of preventing sex discrimination in all programs receiving federal funding, was widely recognized and not widely opposed, so long as explicit quotas based on gender were disclaimed. The details of Title IX's application, especially to college and high school athletics, were not focused upon in hearings on the legislation. For more detail see Suzanne Sangree, "Title IX and the Contact Sports Exemption," *Connecticut Law Review* 32 (2000): 381, 410–14; and Jessica Gavora, *Tilting the Playing Field: School, Sports, Sex and Title IX* (San Francisco: Encounter, 2002), 21–22.

Eventually an amendment proposed by Senator Jacob Javits of New York was adopted, requiring the Department of Health, Education, and Welfare, when publishing its regulations implementing Title IX, to "include with respect to intercollegiate athletic activities reasonable provisions considering the nature of particular sports." Education Amendments of 1974, section 844, 88 Stat. 484 (1974). For more detail, see Jamal Greene, "Hands Off Policy: Equal Protection and the Contact Sports Exemption of Title IX," *Michigan Journal of Gender and Law* 11 (2005): 133, 137–39. For an overview of Title IX and its recent application to women's athletics, see Charles L. Kennedy, "A New Frontier for Women's Sports (Beyond Title IX)," *Gender Issues* 27 (2010): 78–90.

46. Title IX of the Education Amendments of 1972; A Policy Interpretation: Title IX and Intercollegiate Athletics, 44 FR 71413, 71419 (December 11, 1979), 45 CFR pt. 86.

47. That was the basis of Brown University's defense that it violated Title IX when it reduced its women gymnastics and volleyball teams from varsity to club status in an effort to reduce costs without making comparable reductions in the men's gymnastics and volleyball programs. In Cohen v. Brown University, 991 F.2d 888 (1993), the US Court of Appeals for the First Circuit held that although there was a substantial discrepancy in the numbers of male and female students at Brown, and an even more substantial discrepancy in the number of male and female students participating in varsity athletic programs, Brown, in reducing the women's gymnastics and volleyball teams from varsity to club status without taking comparable measures for the men's teams, failed to meet Title IX's requirement of "fully and effectively" accommodating the interests of a historically disadvantaged sex.

48. For a brief interval in the 1980s Title IX was held by the Supreme Court of the United States not to apply to private schools unless that school's athletic programs, as distinguished from the institution at large, received direct federal funding. Grove City Coll. v. Bell, 465 U.S. 555 (1984). In 1987 Congress overturned that decision in the Civil Right Restoration Act of that year, which applied Title IX to any educational entity receiving federal funding, regardless of whether its athletic programs did. 102 Stat. 28 (1988).

49. The HEW explanatory notes accompanying the provision did not discuss a rationale for the contract sport exemption. See Nondiscrimination on the Basis of Sex, 40 FR 24, 128–145 (June 4, 1975).

50. The combat sport exemption justified Duke University's dismissing Heather Sue Mercer, who had been a place kicker for her high school football team in Yorktown Heights, New York, from its football team after initially inviting her to join after she had kicked a field goal in the team's spring scrimmage game. Mercer v. Duke Univ., 190 F.3d 643 (4th Cir. 1999).

51. All of the lawsuits involving volleyball and field hockey involved efforts on the part of boys to play on high school girls' teams. On volleyball see Attorney General v. Mass. Interscholastic Athletic Ass'n, Inc., 393 N.E. 2d 284 (Mass. 1979), (holding that the Title IX, or an equal rights amendment to the Massachusetts Constitution, required boys to be allowed to try out for girls' teams); Gomes v. Rhode Island Interscholastic League, 469 F. Supp. 659 (D.R.I. 1979); Petrie v. Illinois High Sch. Ass'n, 394 N.E. 2d 855 (Ill. App. Ct. 1979); Forte v. Bd. of Ed., N. Babylon Union Free Sch. Dist. 105 Misc. 2d 36 (N.Y. Sup. Ct. 1980); Muradellis v. Haldane Cent. Sch. Bd., 427 N.Y.S. 2d 458 (N.Y. App. Div. 1980); and Clark v. Arizona Interscholastic Ass'n, 995 F. 2d 1126 (9th Cir. 1982) (holding that boys may be excluded from girls' teams).

On field hockey, see B.C. v. Board of Educ., Cumberland Regional Sch. Dist. 531 A.2d 1059 (N.J. Sup. Ct. App. Div. 1987); Williams v. Sch. Dist. of Bethlehem, 998 F.2d 168 (3d Cir. 1993). The first of those declined to allow a boy to try out for a girls' field hockey team; the second concluded that whether field hockey was a "contact" sport, exempting a school district from requiring separate teams for males and females in field hockey, was a question of fact.

On baseball, see Carnes v. Tenn. Secondary Sch. Athletic Ass'n, 415 F. Supp. 569 (E.D. Tenn. 1976), an effort on the part of a girl to play on a boy's high school baseball team, questioning whether baseball was a contact sport under the rules of a high school athletic association.

52. Regulations of 1975 enforcing Title IX gave high schools until July 21, 1978, to comply with the legislation, and subsequent efforts to delay Title IX's impact on high schools succeeded in postponing its legal effect until 1988. See 34 C.F.R. 106.41 (d) (1991).

53. Colorado High School Activities Association, rule XXI, section 3, quoted in Hoover v. Meiklejohn, 430 F.Supp. 164 (D. Colo. 1977), 166.

54. Colorado Activities Association, 166.

55. Colorado Activities Association, 166.

56. Colorado Activities Association, 166–67.

57. Colorado Activities Association, 166–67.

58. Colorado Activities Association, 170–72.

59. See Greene, "Hands Off Policy," 9.

60. See Greene, "Hands Off Policy," 171.

61. The Department of Education's Office of Civil Rights defines a contact sport under Title IX as including "boxing, wrestling, rugby, ice hockey, football, basketball, and other sports in which the purpose or major activity involves bodily contact." Under this definition sports that regularly involve incidental bodily contact, such as volleyball, baseball, field hockey and soccer, would only seem included if a word such as "some" were read to modify "bodily contact." U.S. Department of Education, Office of Civil Rights, "Requirements Under Title IX of the Educational Amendments of 1972," http://www2.ed.gov/about/offices/list/ocr/docs/interath.html. Since the acknowledged purpose of the contact sport exemption, when it was first promulgated, was to protect women from the risks of sports where continual, violent bodily contact was an essential feature of the sport, treating the exemption as governing any sport where some bodily contact occurred would seem inconsistent with that purpose, especially since one of the goals of Title IX was to increase the opportunities of women to participate in athletics.

62. See Title IX and Athletics, 12, citing National Women's Law Center, *The Battle for Gender Equity in Athletics in Colleges and Universities* (Washington, DC: National Women's Law Center, 2011).

63. Moira Donegan, "USA's Formidable Women Soccer Team Is No Accident," *Manchester Guardian*, July 6, 2019, http://www.theguardian.com/commentisfree/2019/jul/06/usa-womens-world-cup-netherlands-title-xi.

64. "[The UNC women play] an aggressive style of soccer, always pressing forward while also having to double back to help on defense. Coach Anson Dorrance frequently turns to his bench and makes substitutions." "UNC Women's Soccer Combines Depth and Experience to Defeat Duke, 2–0," *Daily Tarheel*, http://www.dailytarheel.com/article/2019/08/womens-soccer-uses-depth-in-duke-win#.

65. Eisenberg, Lanfranchi, Mason, and Wahl, *100 Years of Football*, 188–92.

66. Eisenberg, Lanfranchi, Mason, and Wahl, *100 Years of Football*, 192.

67. Eisenberg, Lanfranchi, Mason, and Wahl, *100 Years of Football*, 191–92.

68. Nakul Karnik, "1991 Women's World Cup in China," Soccer Politics, http://www.sites.duke.edu/wcwp/tournament-guides/world-cup-2015-guide/history-of-the-womens-world-cup/1991-womens-world-cup-in-china/.

69. Quoted in Alexander Abnos, "Goal 4: Start of Something Big," *Sports Illustrated*, http://www.si.com/longform/soccer-goals/goal4.html.

70. Karnik, "1991 Women's World Cup."

71. Scores and other details of the 1991 matches in China can be found in Karnik, "1991 Women's World Cup."

72. Quoted in Abnos, "Goal 4."

73. Quoted in Abnos, "Goal 4."

74. FIFA had initially awarded the 1995 women's World Cup to Bulgaria. See Anthony Russo, "1995 Women's World Cup," Soccer Politics, http://www.sites.duke.edu/wcwp/tournament-guides/world-cup-2015-guide/history-of-the-womens-world-cup/1995.

75. Linda Medalen, quoted in Jere Longman, "Norway's Rivalry with the U.S. Is Intense," *New York Times*, June 13, 1995.

76. Russo, "1995 Women's World Cup."

77. Medalen, "Norway's Rivalry."

78. Wangerin, *Soccer in a Football World*, 297.

79. See Roger Allaway, Colin Jose, and David Litterer, *The Encyclopedia of American Soccer History* (Lanham, MD: Scarecrow, 2001), 393–94.

80. Allaway, Jose, and Litterer, *Encyclopedia*, 393–94.

81. Quoted in Wangerin, *Soccer in a Football World: The Story of America's Forgotten Game* (Philadelphia: Temple University Press, 2006), 297.

82. "Anson Dorrance," GoHeels.com, http://www.goheels.com/sports/womens-soccer/roster/coaches/anson-dorrance/2119.

83. One magazine named the North Carolina women's team from 1982 to 2000 the sixth most successful "sports dynasty" in the twentieth century, trailing the 1957–1969 Boston Celtics, the 1947–1962 New York Yankees, the 1963–1975 UCLA men's basketball team, the 1991–1998 Chicago Bulls, and the 1953–1960 Montreal Canadiens. "Anson Dorrance."

84. Between 1989 and 1992 I was the coach of the Charlottesville High School girls' soccer team, the first one instituted at the high school. At that time Lauren Gregg, who had played under Dorrance at North Carolina, was the coach of the University of Virginia women's soccer team. Lauren would "loan" me one of her graduating senior players, since they were ineligible to practice with their team in the spring semester of their senior year (soccer being a fall sport in college, but a spring sport in Virginia high schools), to help me with the girls' team's practices. In the course of seeking advice from Lauren and other persons about conducting soccer practices (a great deal had changed in that area since I had played in college in the early 1960s), Lauren introduced me to Anson Dorrance, who on one occasion invited me to watch

the North Carolina women's team practice a day before they were playing a game against Virginia in Charlottesville. Every moment of the practice was choreographed by Dorrance and his assistants, with the players moving from one drill to another. Among the drills included some half-field scrimmages in which the defensive players practiced double-teaming and the offensive players practiced responses to it.

85. On more than one occasion I have heard Dorrance tell the following story about coaching both men's and women's soccer. He put a hypothetical situation in which his team was trailing at half-time and had "come out flat," with little collective energy or purpose, in the first half.

At half-time, when the men's team gathered, Dorrance would sometimes bring a wastebasket or some other disposable item in front of the team, pick it up, and slam it to the floor, announce that the team "had sucked" or the equivalent, and stalk out of the gathering. His intent was to "fire up" the team by shaming the players.

In a comparable situation with the women's team, Dorrance would say that if he repeated that gesture, the players would only attempt to comfort him. Instead he would bring the players together, encourage them to sit down, and tell them that they were all good players but could play better in the second half and needed to help each other out. "They're already feeling guilty that they let their teammates and me down," he would say. He would encourage the players to "talk about" their first half performance, and many would often blame themselves for the team's poor play.

For more detail on Dorrance's views on the difference between coaching men and women players, see Dorrance, interview by Welch Suggs, December 2003, in Suggs, *A Place on the Team*, 101–3.

86. For a list of the rosters of the 1991, 1995, and 1999 women's World Cup teams, see Allaway, Jose, and Litterer, *Encyclopedia*, 399.

87. "Soccer Soars," *Time*, May 24, 1976, p. 39.

88. Sarah K. Fields, *Female Gladiators: Gender, Law, and Contact Sport in America* (Urbana: University of Illinois Press, 85–86). For more detail on hooliganism among European soccer fans, see Bill Buford, *Among the Thugs* (1992).

89. Fields, *Female Gladiators*, 86.

90. "Soccer Soars," 39.

91. Allaway, Jose, and Litterer, *Encyclopedia*, 201.

92. Allaway, Jose, and Litterer, *Encyclopedia*, 202.

93. "Soccer Soars," 39.

94. David Anable, "Soccer's U.S. Success Story," *Christian Science Monitor*, August 8, 1977.

95. Lowell Miller, "The Selling of Soccer Mania," *New York Times Magazine*, August 28, 1977, p. 12.

96. Charles Osgood, "Rising Popularity of Soccer," *CBS Evening News with Walter Cronkite*, July 22, 1977.

97. Jeanne Clare Feron, "Connecticut Reverberates to the Soccer Boom," *New York Times*, October 9, 1977.

98. Gramaine L. Jones, "Soccer Hits Stride as U.S. Sport," *Los Angeles Times*, October 8, 1977; and "From Kids to Pros . . . Soccer Is Making It Big in U.S.," *U.S. News & World Report*, October 17, 1977, 100.

99. Tony Kornheiser, "Americans Have Adopted Soccer, No Longer an 'Immigrant' Sport," *New York Times*, July 9, 1977.

100. Paul Garner, "Making Soccer an American Sport," *Horizon*, November 1977, 78.

101. Miller, "Selling of Soccer Mania," 12.

102. Steve Bogira, "Resolving an Identity Crisis in Chicago," *Chicago Tribune*, June 1, 1977.

103. Steve Bogira, "Women Step into Soccer," *Chicago Tribune*, June 1, 1977.

104. "Records Crash as USA Rejoice," https:/www.fifa.com/womensworldcup/news/fifa-women-world-cup-usa-1999-502003.

105. For more detail on the WUSA, see Wangerin, *Soccer in a Football World*, 310–13.

106. "WPS Lives On, Looks toward Future," *Marietta Daily Journal*, November 16, 2010.

107. Julie Fowdy, "WPS Suspension a Setback for Women's Soccer," January 31, 2012, ESPN, www.espn.com/espnw/news-commentary/story/_/id/7522499/wps-suspension-setback-women-soccer.

108. Dan Lauletta, "Eight Teams to Start New Women's Pro Soccer League in 2013," *Equalizer*, November 21, 2012.

109. Hagey Keach, "A&E Networks Buys Stake in National Women's Soccer League," *Wall Street Journal*, February 2, 2017.

110. "NWSL Inks Multi-Year Deal With CBS Sports, Twitch," Sports Video Group, March 13, 2020, https://www.sportsvideo.org/2020/03/12/nwsl-inks-multi-year-deal-with-cbs-sports-twitch/.

111. All of the players on the 2019 US women's World Cup roster were from NWSL franchises. Jonathan Tannewald, "All 23 USNWT World Cup Champions Play in the NWSL," *Philadelphia Inquirer*, July 19, 2019.

112. "FIFA Women's World Cup 2019 Watched by More Than 1 Billion," ifa.com/tournaments/womens/womensworldcup/france2019/news/fifa-women-s-world-cup-2019tm-watched-by-more-than-1-billion.

CHAPTER EIGHT

1. Quoted in Michael Janofsky, "U.S. Awarded '94 World Cup Tournament in Soccer," *New York Times*, July 5, 1988.

2. David Wangerin, *Soccer in a Football World: The Story of America's Forgotten Game* (Philadelphia: Temple University Press, 2006), 241.

3. Wangerin, *Soccer in a Football World.*

4. Alan Rothenberg, interview by Phil West, October 15, 2015, in West, *The United States of Soccer: The MLS and the Rise of American Fandom* (New York: Harry N. Abrams, 2016), 4. West's book is the fullest account of the emergence of the Major League Soccer league in the United States.

5. CONCACAF—identified in chapter 6 as the Confederation of North, Central American, and Caribbean Association Football—was established in 1961, with founding members Canada, Costa Rica, Cuba, El Salvador, Guatemala, Haiti, Honduras, Mexico, the Netherlands Antilles (now Curaçao), Panama, Suriname, and the United States. It now has forty-one members.

6. Roger Allaway, Colin Jose, and David Litterer, *The Encyclopedia of American Soccer History* (Lanham, MD: Scarecrow, 2001), 395–97.

7. Wangerin, *Soccer in a Football World*, 250.

8. Allaway, Jose, and Litterer, *Encyclopedia*, 387.

9. Wangerin, *Soccer in a Football World*, 258–63.

10. Alexander Wolff, "On the Rise," *Sports Illustrated*, June 21, 1993.

11. Jake Vest, "World Tour Includes a Touch of Country," *Orlando Sentinel*, June 22, 1994.

12. Allaway, Jose, and Litterer, *Encyclopedia*, 392–93.

13. The USSF allegedly earned about $50 million from staging the 1994 World Cup, and Rothenberg, in his capacity as president, was awarded $7 million. Wangerin, *Soccer in a Football World*, 267.

14. For more detail on the bidding process that resulted in Rothenberg's group being awarded the league, see West, *United States of Soccer*, 8–9.

15. Michael Lewis, "Looking Back at the 1994 FIFA World Cup Draw," on official website for US Soccer, December 3, 2013, http://www.ussoccer.com/stories/2014/03/17/13/44/131203-mnt-1994-we-draw (this story had been removed from the US Soccer website by September 2021).

16. Rothenberg interview, 6.

17. Mark Abbott, interview by Phil West, September 17, 2015, in West, *United States of Soccer*, 7.

18. Abbott interview, 7.

19. That rule was eventually changed, not only in MLS but throughout soccer. Goalkeepers now may only pick up balls from their teammates that are headed back to them by players on their own team. Any other passes from teammates must be played by goalkeepers with their feet. Goalkeepers are, of course, free to pick up shots or passes from their opponents within the goal area by their hands.

The rule change means that defenders are much more likely to attempt to clear balls from the goal area than to pass them back to goalkeepers, which prevents the action in a soccer match from repeatedly slowing down while a goalkeeper picks up a ball within the goal area and decides what to do with it.

20. Wangerin, *Soccer in a Football World*, 253–57.

21. Abbott interview, 90.

22. Kevin Payne, interview by Phil West, October 13, 2015, in West, *United States of Soccer*, 30.

23. Rick Lawes, interview by Phil West, September 2, 2015, in West, *United States of Soccer*, 30–31.

24. Lawes interview, 30–32, 45–48.

25. See Lawes interview, 30–33, 45–49, for the efforts of DC United and the Chicago Fire to create supporters' groups.

26. Wangerin, *Soccer in a Football World*, 262–63.

27. Gary Peterson, "Kick of an Opener, but Will League Fly," *Contra Costa Times*, April 7, 1996.

28. The details of MLS's single-entity structure are taken from Fraser v. Major League Soccer, 7 F. Supp. 2d 73 (D. Mass. 1998) and Fraser v. Major League Soccer, 97 F. Supp. 2d 130, 132–34 (D. Mass. 2000). The former of those cases was, a decision in favor of Major League Soccer, was subsequently appealed to a three-judge panel of the US Court of Appeals for the First Circuit, which affirmed the decision. Fraser v. Major League Soccer, LLC. 284 F.3d 47 (1st Cir. 2002).

29. *Fraser*, 97 F. Supp. 2d at 132–33.

30. *Fraser*, 97 F. Supp. 2d at 133.

31. *Fraser*, 97 F. Supp. 2d at 133.

32. *Fraser*, 97 F. Supp. 2d at 133.

33. After the 1997 season MLS expanded, awarding franchises to Miami and Chicago, each with an operator/investor management structure. The operator/investors of those franchises were added as defendants as the lawsuit progressed through the federal courts. When the lawsuit reached the US Court of Appeals for the First Circuit, there were nine operator/investor defendants because Kraft Soccer, L.P., owned and operator by Robert Kraft, was running both the New England Revolution and San Jose Earthquakes franchises.

34. *Fraser*, 7 F. Supp. 2d 73.

35. Two claims, a challenge to FIFA's fee transfer policies and a state contract law claim, were severed by the district court and stayed pending the final resolution of the case on appeal. See *Fraser*, 284 F.3d at 55.

36. 15 U.S.C., sections 1–15 (1890).

37. 15 U.S., sections 12–27 (1914).

38. *Fraser*, 97 F. Supp. 2d. at 131.

39. *Fraser*, 97 F. Supp. 2d at 131–32.

40. *Fraser*, 97 F. Supp. 2d at 131.

41. *Fraser*, 7 F. Supp. 2d at 76.

42. *Fraser*, 7 F. Supp. 2d at 78,

43. *Fraser*, 7 F. Supp. 2d at 75.

44. *Fraser*, 7 F. Supp. 2d at 75–76.

45. *Fraser*, 97 F. Supp. 2d at 135–36.

46. Initially the operator/investors named as defendants in the suit were included as participants in this purported conspiracy to monopolize the market for Division I player services in the United States. After evidence had been submitted, the trial judge dismissed Section 2 claims against the operator/investors, leaving only MLS and the USSF as defendants on those claims. That ruling was not appealed. See *Fraser*, 284 F.3d at 55.

47. *Fraser*, 284 F.3d at 55.

48. *Fraser*, 284 F.3d at 56–61.

49. *Fraser*, 284 F.3d at 57.

50. *Fraser*, 284 F.3d at 58.

51. *Fraser*, 284 F.3d at 61.

52. West, *United States of Soccer*, 66.

53. See Jere Longman, "Questions Are More Plentiful for MLS." *New York Times*, July 9, 1997, referencing Logan's comment and his subsequent retraction at the 1997 MLS All-Star Game, when the average attendance was announced as 15,500.

54. Payne interview, 37–38.

55. Lawes interview, 38.

56. For more detail on the rollout of the Chicago Fire in 1998, see Lawes interview, 44–49.

57. Barry Jackson and Karen French, "Will Fusion Play at OB?" *Miami Herald*, August 30, 1997.

58. Jeff Rusniak, "Fusion's Lockhart Stadium Stint Paved Way for New MLS Ventures," *Miami Sun-Sentinel*, October 12, 2008.

59. West, *United States of Soccer*, 50.

60. See the sources interviewed in Peter Golenbock, *Go Gators: An Oral History of Florida's Pursuit of Gridiron Glory* (St. Petersburg, FL: Legends, 2002).

61. West, *United States of Soccer*, 51.

62. Michele Kaufman, "MLS: It's Time to Kick It into High Gear," *Miami Herald*, March 21, 1999.

63. Michele Kaufman, "Future Not Looking So Bright for Fusion," *Miami Herald*, December 31, 2000.

64. West, *United States of Soccer*, 83.

65. Gabe Gabor, interview by Phil West, October 16, 2015, in West, *United States of Soccer*, 84.

66. Ken Horowitz, interview by Phil West, October 7, 2015, in West, *United States of Soccer*, 84.

67. Payne interview, 88–89.

68. Anschutz was already the operator/investor of the Chicago Fire, Colorado Rapids, Los Angeles Galaxy, and New York Metrostars. He agreed to take over the San Jose Earthquakes and become the sole investor/operator of DC United.

69. Payne interview, 90.

70. For more detail see Payne interview, 90–92.

71. Allaway, Jose, and Litterer, *Encyclopedia*, 388.

72. "ABC/ESPN Announce World Cup 2002 Broadcast Schedule," May 1, 2002, http://www.ussoccer.com/stories/2014/03/17/12/12abcespn-announce-world-cup-2002-broadcast-schedule.

73. West, *United States of Soccer*, 97–99.

74. West, *United States of Soccer*, 99–100.

75. West, *United States of Soccer*, 64.

76. West, *United States of Soccer*, 64.

77. Steve Sirk to Phil West, email, October 19, 2015, quoted in West, *United States of Soccer*, 63.

78. "Columbus Crew Set for May 15 Opener," *Soccer America*, May 11, 1999, http://www.socceramerica.com/article/8891/mls-columbus-crew-stadium-set-for-may-15-opener.html.

79. Sirk to West, 64–65.

80. For more detail, see West, *United States of Soccer*, 106–8.

81. Don Garber, interview by Phil West, September 15, 2015, in West, *United States of Soccer*, 107–8.

82. West, *United States of Soccer*, 172.

83. Atlanta United FC, a member of MLS since 2017, plays its home game in Mercedes-Benz Stadium, a multipurpose facility it shares with the Atlanta Falcons professional gridiron football team. The stadium seats 71,000.

The Chicago Fire, after moving from Soldier Field, a stadium built for gridiron football in downtown Chicago, to a soccer-specific facility in Bridgeview, Illinois, about twelve miles southwest of the center of Chicago, moved back to Soldier Field beginning in the 2020 season. Dan Garber, the current MLS commissioner, characterized the move back to Soldier Field as consistent with the "evolution of [MLS's] fan base, which is very young, very millennial, and very focused downtown." "Does Chicago Have a MLS Soccer Team?" QuestionerLab, https://questionerlab.com/does-chicago-have-an-mls-team. It will be interesting to see whether the move, once limits on spectators at MLS games are lifted, will result in consistently good attendance for the Fire's matches.

84. In 2005 Philip Anschutz announced that the San Jose Earthquakes franchise, which had been in MLS since 1998, would be moved to Houston. Anschutz's management group had repeatedly attempted to get public funding for a new soccer-specific stadium to replace the existing one, an inadequate high school facility. Thus the Houston Dynamo joined MLS in 2005, with a soccer-specific stadium to follow in 2011. In 2006 an investment group announced that it would seek to revive the Earthquakes in San Jose, and did so in 2008. A soccer-specific stadium would follow in 2015.

85. West, *United States of Soccer*, 68, 73.

86. Eric Wynalda, interview by Phil West, November 3, 2015, in West, *United States of Soccer*, 26.

87. Garber interview, 135. Garber added, "A research study . . . told us the fans are looking for more players that they recognize. We then met as a league, utilizing the value of our single entity, and met to come up with a strategy that would allow us to do that and provide the opportunity to sign a player outside the budget" (136).

88. Jack Bell, "David Beckham Is Coming to America," *New York Times*, January 12, 2007.

89. Alexi Lalas, interviews by Phil West, November 24 and 25, 2015, in West, *United States of Soccer*, 136.

90. For more detail on Beckham's career and his signing with MLS's Los Angeles Galaxy, see Grant Wahl, *The Beckham Experiment* (New York: Crown, 2009).

91. Bell, "David Beckham."

92. Jen Chang, "Debunking the Myths Behind Beckham's Contract," ESPN, January 12, 2007, http://www.espnfc.us/story/399597/debunking-the-myths-behind-beck

hams-contract (this story had been removed from the ESPN website by September 2021).

93. West, *United States of Soccer*, 144.

94. For more detail on the latter years of Beckham's career, see Tracey Savell Reavis, *The Life and Career of David Beckham: Football Legend, Cultural Icon* (Lanham, MD: Rowman & Littlefield, 2014).

95. West, *United States of Soccer*, 205–10.

96. "MLS Announces Additional Investment in Club Rosters with Introduction of Target Allocation Money," MLS, July 8, 2015, http://www.mlssoccer.com/post/2015/07/08/mls-announces-additional-investment-club-rosters-introduction-targeted-allocatio.

97. Kevin Brown maintained that "the only relevant detail from a fan perspective is it means better (or at least more famous) players have another pathway to join MLS. . . . For . . . the fan who invests time and energy in search of entertainment, this is a win." "The L.A. Galaxy Signed Giovani dos Santos Because Rules Are for Chumps," *Fusion*, July 15, 2015, http://fusion.net/story/167406/giovani-dos-santos-signs-with-la-galaxy-mls.

98. Laura Greene, "The 15 Worst Transfer Moves on the Back of World Cup Performances," *Bleacher Report*, June 11, 2014.

99. An illustration of the latter is the Premier League club Chelsea dispatching one of its best known players, Frank Lampard, to NYCFC in MLS in 2015. Lampard played two seasons for NYCFC before retiring and returning to England as the manager of lower-tier club Darby County in 2018 and Chelsea in 2019.

100. Steven Goff, "MLS Is Turning 25 This Season," *Washington Post*, February 28, 2020.

101. West, *United States of Soccer*, 216.

102. West, *United States of Soccer*, 216.

103. For more detail on MLS's efforts to expand its "digital space," see West, *United States of Soccer*, 219–24.

104. For more detail on the incident, see West, *United States of Soccer*, 211–12.

105. Jonathan Tannewald, quoted in West, *United States of Soccer*, 212.

106. "Gabriel Brener Acquires AEG's Interests in Houston Dynamo, BBVA Compass Stadium and Houston Dash," December 15, 2015, http:/www.houstondynamo.com/post/2015/12/15/gabriel-brener-acquires-aeg-interests-in-houston-dynamo-bbva-compass-stadium-and-houston-dash.

107. With the possible exception of the minor leagues in baseball, which are arranged in a hierarchy, including AAA, AA, and A leagues, ostensibly based on the levels of play. But minor-league baseball teams are affiliated with the major-league clubs and serve as vehicles for moving players up and down the hierarchy, based in part of performance. Nothing like promotion and relegation exists in American professional baseball.

108. For more detail on the multiple professional soccer leagues in the United States in place in 2016, the twentieth anniversary of MLS's founding, see West, *United Sates of Soccer*, 227–28.

109. See West, *United States of Soccer*, 224–26.

110. Ted Westervelt, interview by Phil West, August 28, 2015, in West, *United States of Soccer*, 225. Westervelt is a longtime advocate of promotion and relegation for American professional soccer leagues.

111. Westervelt interview, 225–26.

112. Garber interview, 226–27.

113. It is not precisely clear what Garber meant by saying that "all the playoffs" in American professional sports leagues "rate anywhere from two times to five times their regular season," but since he followed that comment by saying, "Their championship events are some of the biggest events on television that year," it seems probable that he was referring to television ratings.

114. On closed leagues, see John Jasina and Kurt Rothoff, "A Model of Promotion and Relegation in League Sports," *Journal of Economics and Finance* 36 (2009): 303.

115. See Allaway, Jose, and Litterer, *Encyclopedia*, 302.

116. The affluence of many English Premier League clubs and some clubs in Division I European leagues, however, allows a form of bidding to take place through "transfer windows" in league seasons in which clubs can transfer players from one elite team to another, often at very high transfer fees. Clubs can compete with one another in offering transfer payments to other clubs. Transfer fees, however, initially benefit clubs, not players, although players coveted through a transfer fee are typically able to renegotiate contracts to their advantage. European clubs are not permitted to negotiate directly with players about salaries without having them on club rosters or obtaining transfer rights to them.

CHAPTER NINE

1. All comments are from Ronald Blum, "Owners Predict MLS Will Surpass MLB, Premier League, La Liga," Fox Sports, February 26, 2020, https://www.foxsports.com/midwest/story/owners-predict-major-league-soccer-will-surpass-major-league-baseball-premier-league-la-liga-022620.

2. "Most Popular High School Sports in America," Stadium Talk, March 12, 2020, https://www.stadiumtalk.com/s/most-popular-high-school-sports-america-a68e565ca65541f7.

3. Michael Lore, "Soccer's Growth in US has International Legends Buzzing," *Forbes*, April 26, 2019.

4. The Most Popular Sports in the World," http://www.worldatlas.com/articles/what-are-the-most-popular-sports-in-the-world.html

5. Steven Goff, "MLS Is Turning 25 This Season," *Washington Post*, February 28, 2020.

6. Goff, "MLS Is Turning 25."

7. In 2020 MLS matches were scheduled to appear on national networks forty-six times, the majority on ESPN and Fox Sports 1, with ABC and Fox carrying some matches. Spanish-speaking networks Univision and UniMas were expected to carry an additional thirty-two matches. Goff, "MLS Is Turning 25." That coverage has been adversely affected by the coronavirus pandemic.

8. "DI Men's 1959 Soccer Championship," http:/www.ncaa.com/history/soccer-men/d1.

9. By "foreign" players in the National Hockey League, I do not, of course, mean Canadians, that league initially being formed with a majority of teams from Canada and overwhelmingly including Canadian-born players on team rosters. I mean, rather, the influx of players in the NHL, over the last three decades, from Russia and eastern Europe.

Index

Page numbers in *italics* indicate illustrations.

About the Author

Photo: Jesús Pino

G. Edward White is David and Mary Harrison Distinguished Professor of Law at the University of Virginia Law School. He was law clerk to Chief Justice Earl Warren of the Supreme Court of the United States during the 1971 term. White's twenty published books have won numerous honors and awards, and his 1996 book, *Creating the National Pastime: Baseball Transforms Itself, 1903–1953*, reflects his life-long participation and interest in athletics.